Praise for *Shadows Over Baku*

Karina Y. Khachatorian tells a personal and devastatingly powerful tale of the ethnic cleansing (i.e. genocide) of Armenians during the last years of the Soviet Union. Because Armenians have a rich, inspired and courageous history, they were, ever since the early days of the Soviet Union, natural dissidents of Stalin's Communist regime.

Accounts such as this cannot be more to-the-heart than one told by someone who lived through it. Shadows Over Baku *is such an account.*

Kudos to Karina for having the courage to shine the light of truth.

—Foster Kinn, author of award-winning
Freedom's Rush: Tales from the Biker and His Beast

Karina Y. Khachatorian is a survivor of the dreadful persecution of Christian Armenians that took place in Azerbaijan during 1988 through 1991. As a resident in its capitol city Baku, along with her family members, she struggled to keep her family alive and find a way to flee the country. She eventually migrated to America, settling in Providence, Rhode Island in 1991

Shadows Over Baku *highlights the ethnic violence brought on by Azerbaijan's within the on-going context of hostilities, when the majority of Nagorno-Karabakh Armenians in southwest Azerbaijan declared secession from Azerbaijan to unify with Armenia.*

Karina is able to relate her story of surviving violence and ethnic hatred against her family (most notably her two small children) with both drama and humanitarian interest. The story is full of intrigue as Karina is able to get her family out of Azerbaijan into Armenia but then is devastated by the great Armenian earthquake. She then has to make several trips to Moscow to the American embassy.

Caught in this quagmire of ethnic emotions, her life becomes exaggerated and unreal. Karina reels through succeeding episodes, each deeper than the previous, yet lives with hope and the fortitude that her life can only improve. It was these crises and associated politics combined with institutional constraints of ancient hatreds, which clouded Karina's life and of thousands of others. She lost everything—her property, her sense of place, and perhaps saddest of all, good neighbors who turned from her in hate; this story relates her determination and success.

—Varoujan Karentz, retired corporate executive, Rhode Island Historian, and board member to numerous historical organizations including Heritage Harbor Corporation, Beavertail Lighthouse Museum, and the Armenian Historical Association of Rhode Island.

This is the author's personal journey fleeing her beloved city of Baku and emigrating to Rhode Island in order to literally save her family from the pogroms of the Azeri population instigated by their government in retaliation for the Karabakh conflict. For this Armenian author and her fellow Azeris of Armenian descent, it was a grim reminder of the 1915 Armenian genocide inflicted by the Turkish Ottoman Empire on its Armenian Christian population.

The author describes her shock and fear of how her Azeri neighbors turned against Armenians in her beloved city of Baku, a city she cherished as one where people of different religious and ethnic backgrounds lived in harmony. But as the Karabakh conflict escalated, the Azeri government spread rumors that Armenians had killed numbers of Azeris in cold blood. This incited hordes of militia-type groups to hunt down Armenians of all ages to torture, rape and kill. For Karina—as with any Armenian of the 20th or 21st century—the memories of her ancestors who were brutally killed and driven from their ancestral homes in Western Armenia began to haunt her. Was history repeating itself now in Azerbaijan?

Karina's work is written in a journal entry style bringing the reader close to her thinking and feeling. We track her difficult decision to leave her life in Baku and emigrate to Rhode Island for her and her family's new life. The reader feels the trauma the author and family are experiencing as well as the mixed emotions they encounter when they finally get their visas to emigrate to America.

A superb personal account of the not widely known incidents that happened as the great USSR began to crumble in the late 1980s.

—Martha Jamgochian,
Vice Chairman of the Armenian Historical Association of Rhode Island

SHADOWS OVER BAKU

The Armenian Massacre in Azerbaijan

Karina Yesayeva Khachatorian

HUGO HOUSE PUBLISHERS, LTD.

ISBN: 978-1-948261-17-3

Library of Congress Control Number:2019911064

Cover Design & Interior Layout:
Ronda Taylor, www.HeartWorkPublishing.com

Hugo House Publishers
Denver, Colorado
Austin, Texas
www.HugoHousePublishers.com

Dedication

To my lovely mom
and to my children,
With love.

Contents

Shadows Over Baku is the first—perhaps the only—authentic, eye-witness account of the Armenian massacre in Baku, Azerbaijan, 1988–1990.

Foreword

SHADOWS OVER BAKU IS THE STORY OF A WOMAN WHO LOVED HER birthplace, the multi-ethnic, multi-religious city of Baku, capital of Azerbaijan. She loved her city, her family, her neighbors, her Armenian ethnicity.

It is a love story that went sour and turned violent when segments of the majority Muslim-Azeri population lost its civility and attacked, maimed, killed, and otherwise deported those who shared her Armenian heritage. Karina and her family were among those deported.

This happened as the very solid looking Soviet Union underwent its rapid descent into dismemberment, caused by the ideological, moral, and financial bankruptcy of the Communist system. That multiple bankruptcy provided an opportunity to many of the constituent republics of the Soviet federal government and autonomous regions to claim increasing powers for themselves. The Communist party and central authorities of the USSR were unable to stem the tide of dissolution, since the experiment to create *Homo Sovieticus*, the (new) Soviet Man, had apparently failed. Identity markers other than class, as imagined by the Bolsheviks and their ideological children, had failed to neutralize the strength and importance of ethnic and religious identity and belonging.

The author is not a scholar; nor is she trained in the social sciences. But she is a keen observer of the mores and interpersonal relations of the variety of peoples living in the capital of Azerbaijan. She knows her neighbors and relatives and how human geography functioned in her city, how the city with its historically diverse groups was held together. Throughout her ordeal and the ordeal of her family and friends, Karina never loses her humanity and never denies the humanity of others; she remains magnanimous.

Karina describes the disintegration of social norms as she had known them and as so many average citizens saw them. She uses language and terminology that reflect the views, perspectives, the everyday world of these citizens as national identity and nationalist rhetoric takes over political processes, as violence replaces civility, as neighbor goes against neighbor and, sometimes, conversely, saves him or her.

This is a personal saga of how a woman and her family happen to escape the real danger of potential murder during the violent pogroms in Azerbaijan in the late 1980s and early 1990s. We read about fear, persecution; we also read about coping and survival mechanisms which betray the horrendous coexistence of danger, death and violence with hope, and precarious optimism, where one sees the best and the worst in ordinary human beings.

The author's remarkable memory and her natural talent to tell a story— in fact many intertwined stories told as one—are compelling on another, more general level.

In this small but significant story we see how differences—differences in ethnicity, religion, language—are transformed into categories of discrimination. We see how the order of regulated, even balanced, identity markers are replaced by a hierarchy of markers. We see how people use differences and how power plays lead to brutalization and to violent behavior; how words matter and why rhetoric matters; and how seemingly innocuous policies end up destroying culture in its most basic sense. We see the lives of hundreds of thousands upended—both of victims and of victimizers. We see how a state in transition and in search of a new legitimization can sit by, but also sanction, maybe even participate and direct that destruction.

Sometimes it is inaction in the face of evil that dominates; sometimes it is an active promotion of racist and hateful views that dominate discourse and lead to the violence by the commoner against the commoner. How is it that a citizen's good neighbor will be transformed, in the eyes of that citizen, into an enemy whose neighborliness and existence constitutes an existential threat to that citizen's existence? When is it and how is it that a neighbor ceases to be defined as a neighbor and is now identified solely by his/her ethnic origin or religion, ascribed aggressive, evil essence and intent?

We see how large political conflicts are translated into personalized hatred toward a fellow citizen who happens to belong to a different ethnic or religious group. How differences are vested with symbolic meanings, how the sense of anger is stoked by rumors and a sense of danger dawns on a neighbor who very quickly becomes the "other."

These are questions that might seem rhetorical, or worse, only relevant to societies too far away to be of concern to us American readers. But perhaps the reader will find in these questions raised by this small, yet valuable book echoes of questions we are faced with today in our society. We may want to think about the values that are being shattered slowly but steadily and the dangers posed by such dangerous erosion of civility and shared humanity. There is no simpler way to phrase it.

Gerard J. Libaridian
Cambridge, Massachusetts
April 2019

Prologue: Attack

MY HUSBAND, ANATOLIY, AND I ARE IN BED, BUT WE DARE NOT SLEEP. We are both on our backs, looking at the ceiling. I try to close my eyes for a moment. These dangerous days, sleep comes only in short intervals and only when I am so tired that I lose focus temporarily. The respite never lasts long. The threat of violence keeps us on a razor's edge so thin we can feel it cutting our skin.

There are never any dreams, only nightmares. We are prepared to jump to our feet at the slightest sound. We do not bother changing for bed, lying down in the same clothes that we were wearing when we came in earlier that night. We have our passports in our pockets, which we know could be a danger themselves because they specify our nationality as Armenians. The secure wrought-iron gate that surrounds our property and the two hundred feet that separates our home from the street do not make us feel safe. Not with what was going on around Baku.

Close at hand, we have several rudimentary weapons. A ten-inch carving knife is under a pillow between us and a small hatchet leans against the bed. Anatoliy keeps a heavy screwdriver by his side at all times. If all else fails, just behind the door is a long, sturdy piece of wood, like a Karate fighting stick.

On December 5, 1988, the city was paralyzed with the news that trainloads of Muslims arrived in Baku Railroad Station from Armenia and every one of them with an injury. The hysterical news was that some of them lost an arm or two; some had injuries in the head with open wounds and some with no legs and on and on. Later we learned that all this was a provocation and did not have any evidence of true facts. It did not take too much effort or time to be spread around the Azeri (the regional name for Azerbaijanis) population.

The city was wrapped in rabid anger. The air smelled bloody.

On this day we were in a rush to decide to take my kids and my mother to my aunt's, my mother's sister. She used to live in an area called Musabekovo named after an Azeri historical revolutionary. It was in a heavily populated Azeri area, even though there were many mixed Armenian/Azeri marriages and different nationalities.

For several days prior, there had been fabrications circulating around Baku that an "echelon" of Azeris arriving in the city from Armenia was under constant assault by the Christian Armenian population in the city. The reports claimed that the Azeris were being victimized, injured and in some cases gruesomely maimed, some losing limbs in these alleged unprovoked attacks. While none of this is true, this lie does exactly what it is designed to do: incite Azeri rage against Armenians living among the majority Azeri population.

It is truly unbelievable for me and my family because we still had trust in the Soviet Union. Even with this obvious campaign against Armenians by the local government, I still find it difficult to accept that we are in grave mortal danger living in such a powerful, prosperous and benevolent country. That belief is so strong in my mind, and in the minds of my family and neighbors, it is practically hardwired into us from the moment of birth.

As the bogus news of violence against Azeris by Armenians quickly spreads, the Azeri population becomes rabid with anger and hungry for vengeance. The smell of blood is in the air, even though no blood had been shed in Baku.

Yet.

This is why we are so ill at ease, whether awake or asleep. And it is not just my husband and I who are on edge, but all Armenians living in Baku. With the constant threat of physical harm becoming so much a part of daily life in recent days, there is no choice but to factor it into everything you do as a citizen and every personal decision you make. It is something that you had to not only think about but plan for.

In the United States, citizens are reminded and encouraged to make preparations for various unforeseen disasters, from the complicated formulation of evacuation plans to more elementary provisions of just being sure to have flashlights, clean drinking water, and non-perishable foods on hand in case of a power outage. This is not the Soviet mindset. Few people I know even had insurance. The prevailing mentality is that government would take good care of you. That is what we have been taught from an early age, and part of me still did believe it.

Now, under our bedroom rug we have a secret trapdoor that leads down eight steps into a small dusty cellar where we keep jams and preserves. "If ever you have to hide," Anatoliy would tell me, "You take the kids and go down there."

These constant threats and fears are responsible for our recent decision to have my mother take our children to stay with my Aunt Lyalya at her apartment in Musabekovo, an area the city named after an Azeri revolutionary hero. Musabekovo is a relatively new development in Baku, and even though it has seen rapid growth, becoming a large residential area, it is not fully developed economically and culturally. It is a heavily Azeri area, but there are many mixed marriages and different nationalities in the community.

While it might initially appear to be a rather risky and illogical step to bring my Armenian family into such a heavily Azeri region during this violent time, there are a number of reasons for this decision. To begin with, my aunt has several neighbors to whom she is close and trusts implicitly. Across the small hall at the entrance of her building lives another Armenian family with three small children. It also makes sense to me because it would be easier to remain unknown and concealed here as opposed to our own home, which is conspicuously Armenian in its design and location. This would be the first place Azeri revenge-seekers would look, rather than in their own backyard.

I also know that my mother's house is out of the question. It is located downtown where my brother and I grew up. My children have spent time there as well, particularly when they were in pre-school, so we are all known by sight. Because of all the violent rallies taking place downtown, it would be exceedingly dangerous for any of us to be there. My aunt's house is the only real option.

Two days earlier, on Friday, December 4, when Anatoliy and I drove my mother, our ten-year-old daughter Ani, and our eight-year-old son Arthur to my aunt's apartment in Musabekovo, I thought it would be only a temporary arrangement. They could hide in plain sight until things calm down while my husband and I try to come up with a solid, actionable plan for the future. Life in Baku is changing, and definitely not for the better.

Also taking refuge in Aunt Lyalya's apartment is my Uncle Ramses and my cousin, Alec. My uncle is a pleasant man despite a life of labor as a metal worker and supporting a family with three children. He is short, almost bald, with a prominent nose and is famously known to snooze wherever he is sitting. Alec is his oldest son, full grown and married with a son of his own. He is a younger version of his father and works as a professional youth athletic coach.

The apartment is on the ground floor of a three-story gray stone and mortar building. Like the other two- and three-bedroom units, it has its own entrance, a small kitchen and a bathroom. Each apartment also has its own balcony with metal grates all around for safety and security, a feature not part of the original architectural model, but ordered and paid for by the always security-conscious residents.

The two previous nights that the children and my mother had spent at my aunt's apartment were without incident, so with the fortifications to the apartment and plenty of family around, I believe that I made the right decision.

Upon visiting them the previous evening, I could see that Ani and Arthur are clearly miserable. They hate being stuck inside the house all day and not being able to play with their friends. Here, they are not allowed to go outside and do not have any toys to occupy themselves. It is heartbreaking for me as well, but I believe that being there is for their own good, and absolutely essential to keeping them safe.

Anatoliy and I stay as long as we can, but we must leave early to be sure we are home before the nine o'clock emergency curfew. We do not want to get stopped on the road again by an MVD unit like the night before, when we had been detained briefly and interrogated while our car was searched. It was an experience we did not want to repeat. You never know how these things will end up. The previous week in Baku, mass meetings of Azeri crowds were held in Central Square in defiance of an ultimatum from military authorities with the outcome of mass arrests.

The Internal Troops of the Ministry of Internal Affairs (MVD) was a military Soviet force designed to deal with large-scale crowd control, internal armed conflicts, prison security and safeguarding of highly important facilities, somewhat similar to the gendarmerie of nineteenth century Europe. Just hearing the initials MVD was enough to strike terror in the heart of any Soviet citizen, regardless of ethnicity.

Immediately after getting home later that evening, I try calling my aunt. I want to speak with the kids and say goodnight, but there is a constant worrying busy signal. This is another reason why I am unable to sleep this night. Suddenly the red phone on the black grand piano in the living room begins to ring and I instantly rise from my shallow slumber to answer it. Apprehensively, I look down the open vestibule from the bedroom and through the window that looks out into the garden. I see the plants moving outside, gently nudged by the midnight breeze, but there is no one there.

I feel a chill, so I put on my slippers before I walk out of the bedroom, taking a quick glance at the clock on the bedside table. It is a few minutes before midnight. I intentionally do not switch any lights on, and I nearly trip and fall over something on the floor. We are in the middle of a construction project, building an add-on room for the kids in our "country house."

I reach the red phone on the piano in the darkness on the third ring. "Hello," I say, sensing something bad from any phone call at this hour of the night.

"We were attacked!" I recognize Aunt Lyalya's frantic voice even though it is barely above a whisper. "We were attacked!"

"What?" I ask. "What happened?"

"We are okay now," she says in a more reassuring tone, which makes me feel a little better. "They cut the wires to the telephone in my apartment," she adds, and then her voice disappears.

"Who attacked you?" I ask, screaming frantically, "Aunt! Hello? Hello?"

"What's wrong?" I hear the voice of my husband, who is standing behind me.

"There's been an attack," I wail without turning around. I continue to scream at the telephone, asking more questions, but I get no answer.

"Oh my God!" I cried.

I call her back immediately, but all I hear is a busy signal: *beep-beep-beep-beep.* I keep trying anyway.

Nothing.

My heart virtually stops; I am stunned, dazed and angry. This is a living nightmare.

I curse the violence and hatred that has taken a stranglehold on my beautiful city.

I finally put the phone down, not knowing what else to do. I just want to confirm that everyone is safe and unharmed. My aunt had definitely said, "We are okay now," but that doesn't mean that someone hadn't gotten hurt.

I turn to my husband. "Anatoliy, what are we going to do? No one's picking up."

He has the hatchet in his hand, clenching it tightly. "Did you hear any sounds or voices in the background?" he asks. "How bad was it?"

"I don't know. She just said they were attacked and that they were okay. We have to go there."

"We can't," Anatoliy says in an irritated tone. "You're forgetting the curfew."

I stared at him, asking him without words if we should just go anyway. He knows what I want to do by the look in my eyes reflected from the yard lamppost and I know his answer before he gives me a slow disapproving shake of his head.

I say, "We can explain to the MVD that we're worried about our kids."

"You want to tell them that you are worried about your Armenian children? They are going to say, 'So what, who cares?'"

I want to get in the car right then and there and drive to Musabekovo, but Anatoliy is right. I realize that we would not get far. Any attempt to travel that night would only make things worse because we would be detained immediately. We have no choice but to wait until the official military curfew is lifted in the morning at 7:00 a. m. before we can leave.

The government had declared a state of emergency and we have to obey the law.

The sense of living a normal life is slowly disappearing. There is no regular December holiday routine. Usually people make a big effort preparing for the holiday and New Year: cleaning and preparing good food, shopping for presents for everyone. But now, there is no cleaning or planning. It is a time of "deficit" or shortages, and shopping is not easy. It's actually almost impossible to find things for your family and kids.

We have a limited time to be with our children. No Christmas tree, no gifts, no plans, no wishes and no dreams. We can hope only to keep our family safe and sound.

Our son Arthur had just turned eight on December 1, and although we had done our best to give him a party, it is not a time to celebrate. We live from moment to moment, day to day, and cannot be certain of what the future might bring, unable to plan or have any real expectations.

While Christmas was not recognized in USSR/Russia, the New Year has always been an important event to the Soviet people, much as Christmas is to the British, or Thanksgiving is to Americans. Schools are closed for around two weeks to give people a chance to celebrate and spend time with their families.

Even this, however, matters no longer.

How do you explain to your young children that we are going through different times, when violence and hatred against them dominates everything else—and their only "crime" is that they are Armenian?

You can't.

While unable to get through to my aunt, I feel that I should call *somebody*. But there is no one else. My family is effectively cut off from me. They are only a twenty-minute drive away, but they may as well have been on the other side of the world. The curfew that protects us also makes us prisoners in our own home. You may think that having a cluster of tanks roaming the streets and a military curfew in place would make you feel safe, but that is not always the case. If I had known the phone numbers of Aunt Lyalya's neighbors, I would be dialing them already. Beyond that, there is nothing more I could do besides worry.

In between failed attempts to get through to my aunt, I begin to pace nervously around the living room while the most terrible images force their way into my mind unbidden. Through the years I have heard many horror stories from family members and other Armenians who know survivors of the 1915 genocide. I am aware of the death marches, the killing squads, the raping and enslavement of young girls. Now, I can't help imagining Azeri men breaking in my aunt's apartment, their filthy hands reaching for my daughter, trying to touch her, take her with them, overpowering my son and battling with the men for possessions in the house. Aunt Lyalya's words, "We are okay now," quickly begin to evaporate, pushed out by these uncontrollable and disturbing thoughts.

I feel like a caged tiger, walking from room to room. When Anatoliy makes tea, I drink some without tasting it. We try not to make any noise and refrain from putting on any lights we don't need. I turn on the television to pass the time, but the local channels air nothing but inflammatory Azeri programming that spouted anti-Armenian tirades from the mouths of obtuse "journalists" and pseudo- news analysts.

National news is even worse, providing no useful information whatsoever. Reports are heavily edited, short, and incomplete. *Vremya* (meaning *Time*), the main evening newscast in Russia, clearly has a pro-government bias, promoting socialism, negatively portraying the capitalist West, and never reporting anything that could potentially fuel anti-government sentiment.

Every day, however, we watch, always waiting and hoping to hear news of something positive coming from the capital of Russia, anxious to hear something that "they"—the all-powerful politburo in Moscow—are going to do about the developing conflict. Instead, we are losing hope and growing more fearful. "They" do not divulge the nature of the danger and tragic reality that is threatening the Armenian people in Baku and elsewhere. "They" pretend that there is no ongoing genocide.

The news is little more than a propaganda show, controlled by the local Azerbaijani Communist Party. One after another, Azeris, calling themselves poets, artists, leaders, politicians, would appear on TV for the sole purpose of rabble-rousing and inciting hatemongering against Armenians. We all know that something bad, very bad, is going happen. We just don't know when.

We learn more about what was going on in the part of the world where we were living by listening to the BBC and Voice of America, which gives us only sporadic updates on the situation in Baku. Even in the early hours of the morning, you can't always tune in to these programs because the government would jam the frequency to try to prevent the public from knowing what was happening. Social media won't be invented for another five years, and no one had a smart phone. In other words, we are kept pretty much in the dark. The only real news we can rely on is what comes through the grapevine, the telephone, and word of mouth from family and friends.

Time, I have come to realize, goes by very slowly when you're scared, but it's even worse when you're terrified for the lives of your children and dark thoughts consume your mind. It is absolute torture. The night seems endless. I cannot even pray because I am so nervous.

There is a lot of time to think, however, and I do, mostly about Baku and what is happening there. It is probably the first time that I honestly confront the full gravity of the situation in Baku and how dangerous it has become. I finally grasp the reality that it is not going to get any better, and that it is likely only to get worse. If I don't get my family out of the city, I will not have a family. It is a frightening realization, especially after everything I had been witnessing lately and what was happening now.

How could I not have seen it this way before?

I recall an incident that took place right here in our home only a few days before which served to intensify my feeling of insecurity and should have prompted us to do something more decisive than to split the family up and temporarily separate our children from us. The episode begins innocently enough with the bell at the gate ringing. We used to have an open house, a home full of friends and relatives coming to visit us, especially in the summer, gathering in the cool garden under a canopy of trees: walnut, black and white berries, apples, cherries, apricots, pears, dates and grape vines on shady trellises. These are dangerous days, however, and we are resolute in keeping the gate closed.

Outside, there are three young Azeri men, waiting for my husband.

As Anatoliy approaches them, he realizes immediately that this encounter could mean trouble.

"Someone told us," one of the men tells Anatoliy in the Azeri language, "that there are Armenians living in this house. A fuckin' guy called *Tolik*." (*Tolik* is the Russian nickname for Anatoliy.)

I am inside the house with the children and quite concerned, and although my husband is tense in this confrontation, he keeps his composure. Thinking defensively, he attempts to bluff them by opening the gate for them. It is a gesture that they would never have expected from an Armenian. Anatoliy plays along with them, pretending to be Azeri and speaking their language perfectly, something he is able to do from his days playing with Azeri children growing up.

"No," Anatoliy tells them, "I don't know this goddamned Armenian. I never met him. That *oghrash!* (pejorative Azeri word for "cuckold.") He left a long time ago."

The three men soon leave, still angry, but satisfied that there are no Armenians living in the house. This could very easily have become a deadly altercation. We breathe easy. But we know it isn't an isolated incident

―――――

At 7:00 a. m. when the curfew is lifted, we are finally able to escape the prison walls that our own home has become. My husband and I jump into the car and drive straight to my aunt's. After calling the apartment all morning and getting only a busy signal, I am even more uneasy.

If I could just hear my aunt's voice, or the voices of my children, it would make me feel so much better. The uncertainty makes the short trip to my aunt's house absolutely terrifying. We don't know what we're going to walk into. I try to think the best, but I can't help envisioning the worst. I think about the recent slaughter of Armenians in Sumgait and Kirovabad, and all the lives that have been exterminated and ruined. I feel all the anguish and the torment of the Armenian mothers whose children were lost or killed in the pogroms.

The Encarta dictionary defines *pogrom* as a planned campaign of persecution or extermination sanctioned by a government and directed against an ethnic group, especially against the Jews in tsarist Russia. Thus it is still closely associated with Jews in the public's mind. Unfortunately, the term has not fallen out of use with the end of the Tsars and their violent persecutions of the Jews. For example, in the twentieth century U.S. Yiddish language newspapers reported the lynching of blacks in the South as "pogroms," much too close to their experience or their ancestors' experience in Europe.

The same government-sponsored terror displayed nowadays all over the world tightly fits the term pogrom, wherever it is: Europe, Asia, Africa or Latin America. It was happening—almost unbelievably—here in my home and the hate and violence was directed against me and my family.

We drive in near silence and I stare out the window. No one is on the road. People are afraid to leave their homes. Looking at the city, I realize that I do not recognize it. It looks different, changed somehow. Even the buildings and landmarks I know so well do not seem familiar to me anymore. It is eerily quiet, almost surreal. Everything looks dark and seedy, as if a shadow has been cast over Baku, even though the sky is clear, and the sun is just beginning to rise.

How long has it been like this, I wonder, a*nd why haven't I noticed it before?*

Ten months prior, the Azeri violence against Armenians started in the nearby town of Sumgait. One hundred people were brutally tortured and murdered, and dozens injured. But even after learning of those horrendous atrocities, I was still in a deep state of denial. I remember not taking it seriously as I should have, showing more concern about finding someone to paint the veranda that we shared with a Russian neighbor.

"Are you crazy?" I recall my Aunt Julieta screaming at me. "We're packing to leave. Are you going to abandon your place nice and freshly painted for *them*?!"

"Oh, no, nothing will happen," I start to tell her. "It will never happen in Baku. They won't allow it." While I want to believe this more than anything, something inside me suddenly snaps, like a thread you bite while you are sewing. My aunt's reaction is like a slap in the face, awakening me to reality, and I know she is right.

Driving through the unfamiliar city now, I realize that it is I who have changed, or at least shifted my perception of Baku. Either way, it no longer feels like home, and that makes me sad because I had grown up on these streets and raised my own family here. I didn't think I would ever leave. Not this way.

We get to Musabekovo in less than twenty minutes, but it still feels like it took forever. Fresh tears are flowing uncontrollably from my eyes by the time we arrive at my aunt's apartment complex. The sight that strikes me first is the balcony in complete shambles with shattered glass everywhere. I gasp, swooning, and Anatoliy reaches out to support me and keeps me from falling to the ground.

My husband begins calling the names of our children, "Ani! Arthur!"

As we make our way through the courtyard to my Aunt's unit, we find her apartment door wide open. Now I am sure that something is really wrong, and I scream, imagining a grisly tableau of carnage just beyond the threshold. But the apartment is empty, and as we walk out into the lobby, a neighbor and longtime friend of my aunt's family suddenly appears, startling me. With a nicotine-stained finger poised on his lips, he beckons us with his other hand, and we follow him upstairs. Although he is an Azeri, I am not worried or scared. He is the one who is taking a big chance just being seen with us, particularly as an official in the Azerbaijan government.

Finally, when I see my family waiting for me in the doorway at the top of the stairs I start to cry with joy. I hug my mother, my two children, Aunt Lyalya, Uncle Ramses and my cousin Alec. Ani and Arthur look scared and tired like they hadn't slept much, but they are clearly unharmed and safe, and that is all that matters. I hug them both a second time, shedding fresh tears of happiness as we all embrace.

"Is everyone all right?" my husband asks anxiously, as if what he is seeing is too good to be true.

"They are well," murmurs Aunt Lyalya dully.

"Thank God," I say.

Arthur is sobbing and will not stop.

"Everything is okay," I reassure him.

"I promised Arthur you would come just as soon as you could," my mother interjects loudly.

"We must continue to be silent," our righteous Azeri friend and neighbor, Ismail, interrupts.

Stowing away in a heavily Azeri neighborhood is like being in an unfortified bunker. By giving our family of six Armenians shelter in his apartment, this Azeri man has put himself, his wife, and their three daughters in grave risk. Such a kind or merciful gesture may not have been at all uncommon in this otherwise ruthless and hostile social setting, but it is nonetheless dangerous.

It is a long while before Arthur could be sufficiently consoled, but he eventually calms down and actually falls into a shallow, exhausted sleep. It has all been such a thoroughly terrifying event for him, as well as for Ani, I suspect that it will be something that will stay with both children for a long time afterward. In fact, we would become further concerned that these experiences would have a detrimental impact on their psychological well-being and, indeed, the earmarks of post-traumatic stress disorder (PTSD) would become immediately apparent.

For years afterward, their anxiety would surface whenever they become startled by any unsuspected noise, no matter how innocuous it might be. This is something that would continue to occur even after our later arrival in America and we were living in Rhode Island. To help them, their great-grandmother would suggest an old folklore remedy of sleeping with a knife and a piece of bread placed under their pillows. Maybe it worked; maybe it didn't. I know that they would often wake up crying in the middle of the night from nightmares. My grandmother also contacted a Russian spiritualist who she believes had the capability of wrenching the fear out of their little bodies with prayer, laying on of hands and a piece of bread.

"Where are we going now?" Arthur suddenly wakes, sobbing.

It is a poignant question for a young boy, and while I could not fully grasp all the details of what happened to them that night because I was not there, I try to calm Arthur and Ani down as best I can by continually telling them that they are safe and that we will never leave them again. My husband and I both know that we may not be able to keep the first promise as long as we remain in Baku. I know that leaving not only the city, but this part of the world will be a massive undertaking, but it had to be done. I've become completely convinced of that now.

Over the course of time, as I learn all about the terrifying encounter my family had with a blood-thirsty Azeri mob, I feel tremendous guilt for putting them in harm's way. The details are bone-chilling, and I had a difficult time thinking about it.

About two hours after my husband and I had left my aunt's apartment the evening of December 6, her doorbell rang. Of course, bells ringing at this hour are now considered dangerous. Knowing this, my Aunt Lyalya approached the door with caution and peered through the peephole. She saw a young man, mostly enveloped in shadow, standing outside the front door.

"Who is it?" she asks in a broken Azeri tongue, trying her best to disguise her Armenian nationality. She knows her limited language skills would give her away if the young man outside was Azeri.

"Aunty, can you help me, please? I cannot go home because of the military curfew. I need to make a call for somebody to come and pick me up. Can I use your phone?"

This reply is not in Azeri, but in Armenian, and although the young man outlined in the tiny peephole articulates the language very well, Aunt Lyalya hesitates. She realizes that it could be a ploy to get her to open the door so he can get inside. She knows as well as anyone that Azeris running away as "refugees" from Armenia did speak the Armenian language as perfectly as some Armenians in Baku spoke perfect Azeri.

"I need to make a call," the stranger repeats. "Please, let me use your phone."

"We don't have a phone," Aunt Lyalya lies.

Everyone in the apartment is listening tensely to both sides of this confrontation from less than a meter away.

He pleads, "You must have a son or daughter. Just think of me. I am like them, who needs your help. I am Armenian and I am in the same situation as you. I'm stuck here and I am so afraid. Please! Please!"

My aunt, who has as big a heart as anyone, starts to feel bad for the young man who speaks Armenian so well and is in need of help.

What if he is telling the truth, she wonders?

She opens the door but keeps the chain on. She is trusting, but she is not a fool. As soon as she spots four more men lurking in the shadows behind the Armenian-speaking stranger rushing forward, she quickly tries to slam the door shut against the weight of their bodies. She catches glimpses of them through the widening crack as she pushes her shoulder up against the metal door to keep it closed. My aunt is a very large woman, but she is no match for the five young men.

As they fight to keep it open and gain entry, my uncle Ramses and cousin Alec quickly rush over to help. They fling themselves against the wooden surface of the door, which is heavily fortified with a sturdy interior metal frame. They are able to overpower the attackers, and once the door is closed and locked they begin dragging over furniture and other heavy objects to reinforce the only barrier between them and the savage attackers, who continue to throw themselves against the door like wild animals, swearing and yelling in a coarse Azeri dialect, blaming one another for failing to gain entry into the apartment. This cacophony accompanies the noise of my family yelling, crying, screaming, and pleading for their lives.

Inside, Aunt Lyalya begs the men in Russian, "Leave us alone," as the panicked children cling to their grandmother for protection. Ani and Arthur do not understand what is happening. My daughter Ani presses her face with her curly dark hair and big tear-filled eyes in her grandmother's bosom and cries, "What do they want from us?"

My little boy, Arthur, terrified and screaming, his dark eyes wide and wet with tears, clambers up on top of his grandmother's shoulders. Despite her diminutive size, my mother is a strong woman, having worked her whole life in the foodstuff industry, which requires a lot of lifting and carrying. She manages to keep a firm, protective grip on both the children. It is a struggle keeping Ani on her back and she inadvertently digs her nails into Ani's arm so that she does not fall off. Ani winds up with scars on her skin as a physical reminder for many years.

The adults don't really understand what is happening either. These young thugs don't even know the names of the people they are attacking, but they still want to kill everyone in my family, not because their blood is not as red, and not because their God is not as righteous, but because they are Armenian. They also did it because they could, and with the full support of the Azerbaijani State and the local Azeri police, with an assist by the local Azeri news media which downplayed or altogether disregarded the acts of violence in their news coverage.

Suddenly, the riot of noise and commotion outside my aunt's apartment stops. It is tempting for my family to believe that the attackers have given up and left. Any feelings of security, however, are short-lived when the mob moves over to the balcony in the back. Fortunately, the metal grate around the structure is spaced too closely together for a person of any size to squeeze through, but this does not deter them.

My mother guides Arthur and Ani to a back bedroom, pushing them against the far wall and standing in front of them. She shields the kids behind her and holds high a small open bottle which is filled with an acrid smelling acid. Ramses is a metal worker and stores various tools and chemicals in the house, including different acids which he keeps on hand for use as a weapon to protect his family against an attack such as this one.

The faces of the five young men are clearly visible through the windows that look out onto the small porch and railed balcony. They are all wearing dark clothes, jihadist black. Four of them have mustaches and all of them have angry faces, their eyes blood-red.

As the men fight amongst themselves, frustrated to the point of fury that they cannot get their hands on the Armenians inside the apartment, they pick up rocks and large branches and begin to throw them toward the porch. Some of the stones find their way through the metal bars, fracturing the windows. Shards of glass fall on the carpet inside.

A couple of the hooligans discover another part of the porch on the other side of the house. They split into two groups and continue their attack from both sides of the apartment at the same time, throwing anything they can get their hands on. The porch along the side of the bedroom quickly becomes damaged and then one of the men, the shortest and smallest, scrambles up and attempts to squeeze through the loose metal railing. He fails, but as he holds onto the bar with one hand, a co-conspirator passes larger rocks to him which he then tosses against the already cracked and shattered windowpanes. When he is handed a long stick, he uses it to poke through the broken glass into the apartment.

For my family, they are all alone. Despite the ruckus, none of the neighbors intervene or offer to help. No police come. Many local residents, too afraid to get involved, turn a blind eye. Some "mixed families" are even more likely to embody the proverbial principle, *see no evil, hear no evil, and speak no evil* out of fear of reprisals if they are discovered because of their children, in whose veins flow mixed bloodlines, two opposing lineages which boiled against each other. This behavior of silence and apathy does no good, only provoking further abuse and violence against Armenians.

My family knows that the terrorists would never relent, and this night of hell will only end with the destruction of the apartment and when their Azeri lust for Armenian blood is satiated. It seems just a matter of time.

Outside Aunt Lyalya's apartment, the Azeri rioters continue their angry dance. Inside, another loyal member of the family fears for life and limb. The pet parrot, Mimi, is going berserk, throwing its large and multicolored body, dominated by a metallic sky blue, against the bars of its cage. It, too, seems to know it is going to die as it mimics the sounds that the human captors are making in their own cage. The bird screams and cries, "Help!" in a sharp, metallic Russian timbre, *"Pomogite! Pomogite!"* But nobody pays attention. Nobody is listening. The bird cannot fly to safety. There is no escape for any of them, human or avian.

Heightening their fear, armed men suddenly appear in the near distance outside. Their voices can be heard screaming incoherently.

"Move! Move!" my cousin Alec shouts. "Get down! They're going to shoot. Get down!"

My family all drops to the floor, thinking this is the end.

A harsh voice outside is yelling out military orders in Russian. The voice grows louder as the individual gets closer. Then, through the broken window, several armed soldiers can be seen following alongside an advancing military tank in the street. The soldiers surround the Azeri attackers, who obey the shouted commands, putting their hands behind their heads and moving away from the balcony. The Azeri criminals then drop to their knees as the advancing soldiers point their weapons at them.

After nearly completely surrendering to their worst fears, it is hard for anyone in the apartment to believe that the danger is over, even after the tanks and troops leave, marching the attackers away with them.

During this entire episode, not a single neighbor, Azeri or mixed family, have come to their aid, even though some have been living together for twenty to thirty years. It is only when the imminent danger has passed that my aunt's Azeri neighbor comes downstairs ever so stealthily in black-stockinged feet. Nobody even hears him until he reaches the final three steps above the landing. *Gardash* (brother) Ismail twists his body around, sneaking a quick look around first, before inviting my family up to his third-floor apartment with him. This is from where my aunt phoned me and curtly told me about the attack.

While I know the terrible risk Ismail took coming to the aid of my family, sheltering, feeding and caring for them the rest of the early morning until my husband and I were able to get there after the curfew, I still harbor a strong sense of distaste against this man for his serial womanizing. I put that aside temporarily, realizing how lucky my family is to have made it through the night. I could not bet that things would work out the same way if any of us were to find ourselves in a similar plight once more. This lesson is not lost on me. It is time to move on and leave Baku and everything we know and love behind.

So who is this Ismail, my aunt's neighbor and my husband's friend, who took such a chance to help us?

As a mother, as a wife, as a woman, I mostly feel sorry for Ismail's wife, a simple village Azeri woman who raised their children and put up with Ismail's lifetime of cheating. On the other hand, I do not feel complete sympathy for her because it is part of what I have seen too often in Azeri society. I do not know her, nor has she ever come to my house. If she could put up with her husband's peccadilloes, who am I to judge?

Ismail would visit our house on occasion and share evening meals with us. He was accompanied by his mistress, whom he referred to as "my real wife." She was much younger than he was, and I am sure she was mistaken by many as his oldest daughter. Their visits made me extremely uncomfortable and I found their relationship personally offensive. Once, when Ismail was asked what he would do if his adult children found out about his mistress or if his wife confronted him on the matter, he just shrugged and said, "If my wife complains, I will send her back where she came from."

Ismail had a high government position and felt he should not parade his mistress and bastard son around in public, though this was not for ethical considerations but because he feared he might lose his job. A political enemy could take advantage of this bit of scandal, especially while the government of Azerbaijan was in such turmoil.

It took me several years to realize that Ismail always took the same seat in the garden when we ate dinner there. He would sit with his back to the gate and ask if we expected any visitors, and if an unannounced visitor rang the bell, Ismail would continue to sit facing away. When I brought up this observation to Anatoliy, he explained to me, "Ismail will always be careful."

Yet, here he is taking an awful risk with so much chaos and turbulence all around. An Azeri protecting hated Armenians flies directly in the face of the false official propaganda that was used stir up the basest instincts of his brethren, who were being urged *en masse* to plunder, rape, and kill us.

I judged him. After December 6, 1988, however, I had a much different opinion of him.

Every day in the news we still see that human kindness and friendship *can* overcome the pressures of ethnic violence. Yet, when I recently watched a Fox News American television story featuring a man being interviewed in some godforsaken country engaged in a civil war, it stirred a dark remembrance of Baku in my breast.

"How could you kill a neighbor and his children when you lived together in peace for so many years, went to his weddings and baptisms, shared his holidays?" the reporter asked.

The man's chilling, if simple, response was, "I ... don't ... know."

It makes one wonder if things will ever change and if people will ever learn from our mistakes.

Albert Einstein said that insanity is doing the same thing over and over again and expecting different results. He also said that only a life lived for others is a life worthwhile.

CHAPTER 1

Stroke of a Pen

WHAT DOES IT TAKE FOR ONE GROUP OF PEOPLE TO INDISCRIMINATELY slaughter another? "Ethnic cleansing" doesn't even begin to describe the terror, the horror, the abject refusal of all semblance of anything human.

This particular breed of inhumanity does not spring spontaneously.

The massive rift that existed between Armenia and Azerbaijan did not happen by accident.

The seeds of violence and hate were planted in the very nascent stages of what would become the colossal USSR—the Union of Soviet Socialist Republics. It was a sad but too-typical rift between one of the oldest Christian civilizations in Europe—Armenia—and Azerbaijan, a newly formed country after World War I peopled by an ancient tribe of Muslim Turks who lived primarily in Iran

In 1921, Joseph Stalin took pen in hand and with his signature ordered the borders to be moved. We, as an Armenian family, a minority in the Azerbaijani capital of Baku, were to feel the painful thrust of Stalin's pen directly into our hearts when the Armenians of Nagorno-Karabakh revolted against being thrown under a Turkic Moslem umbrella. Conversely, the Azeri population was outraged by this direct affront to their power, reputation, and *amour-propre*.

When Stalin moved the border, all those people in Nagorno-Karabakh, a little enclave of 90 percent Armenians near the frontier with Armenia, were now thrust into a larger province of Azerbaijan which straddles Armenia

1

and Persia. This group of Armenians was well-established. Nagorno-Kara-bakh was the territory to where my family and other Armenians had been forced to flee a century prior to the genocide in World War I. This group of Armenians had established this enclave to escape being brutally attacked and murdered by the Ottoman Turks in 1915 in Constantinople a scant six years prior to Stalin sealing our eventual fate in Baku.

In 1915, the Ottoman Turkish empire systematically exterminated any-where from 800,000 to 1.8 million Armenians in what has been rightfully called the "Armenian Holocaust," in and around current-day Istanbul, Turkey.

As a side note, this was the first of the "modern genocides," and the mass massacre of the Armenians during this time is the second-most studied case of genocide after the Jewish Holocaust in World War II.[1] This began the great Armenian diaspora through Europe, the Middle East, and the United States-the diaspora that led to my family settling in the Nagorno-Karabakh region on the border. This small enclave of Armenians that sat on the border of Azerbaijan was well established by the time I was born. We Armenians had our own Churches, newspapers, and theater, and Baku was our capital.

This arbitrary shifting of borders relocated an area of mostly Christian Armenians into the authority of a large republic dominated by Azeris, speaking a Turkic, language, following the Shi'a sect of Islam, but still a socialist republic of the Soviet Union.

Stalin's purpose when he remade the border between Armenia and Azerbaijan was obvious: to "divide and conquer." It was a means to stir up the Azerbaijanis, also known as "Azeris" who were afraid of losing what they claimed was their own territory against Armenians. It also stirred up the Armenians in that corner who wanted to join their cousins next door as part of Armenia. Overnight, we became an Armenian minority in the province we had been in for centuries because of this act of an absolute dictator for whatever were his own reasons.

Maybe Stalin moved the border because Armenia is neighbors with Stalin's native Georgia, a fact that did not leave us in good standing with the dictator. Maybe it was because this area is the Caucasus Mountains. When people call white people "Caucasians," it originates from old ideas of the history of mankind. Even Noah's Ark is supposed to be stranded on the top of one of the mountains there. Maybe it was because Armenia was (and still is) a long-standing Christian nation and served as a reminder to Stalin of his former self. He was a former seminary student. Much to his mother's great disappointment, this absolute dictator of a sixth of the world never became a priest.

Whatever the reason, the borders were moved, and Stalin, I'm sure, looked down over his massive moustache with satisfaction onto the proclamation perhaps for no other reason than *he could*. But it was as absolute and unchangeable as the *ukase* of the Tsars or the Imperial *rescript* of the Emperor of Japan. Armenia was reluctantly co-opted into the colossal USSR. But my brethren were determined to retain their religion—a major part of our nationalism—even though Russian Communism preached an atheistic form of "brotherhood of nations."

The Armenians at that point were determined never to be a victim to Stalin's whim—or to anyone else's for that matter. Armenians are proud of our ancient heritage. Ours was the first nation in the world to adopt Christianity, mentioned by name as a unique people in the documents of the Near East, in Babylonian clay tablets. Our culture is heralded in Near Eastern monuments carved in stone and on ancient Greek and Egyptian papyrus fragments. We may have had our hands tied by Stalin, but our hearts, minds, and souls remained fully Armenian.

***

The USSR was more multinational than almost any other empire in the history of man. But it was also an empire that wanted everyone to live, think, even feel the same. The Union of Soviet Socialist Republics (the USSR), emphasizing the Russian language and values, frowned upon individual nations asserting their religion and sense of national pride as a form of superstition.

It was all a recipe for sheer disaster. Stalin's edict held for almost seven decades. But it wasn't a question of "if" but of "when."

When the Azeris attacked the Armenians in Sumgait (February 1988), it was the first chink in the mighty "Iron Curtain" of communist Russia. Armenia had already petitioned the USSR to seek its independence. Thus, it's not surprising that the Sumgait massacre was allowed to happen by Russian officials. They may have wanted to use the Azeri uprising as a way to squash the Armenian desire for autonomy. The exact opposite actually occurred: the events in Sumgait marked the first time mighty Communist Russia saw a fundamental schism of its "great experiment," that ultimately brought down the whole structure of the Soviet Union. To put this into perspective, the Berlin Wall fell November 9, 1989.

The politics, however, can never mitigate or even begin to justify the suffering we Armenians endured at the hands of the Azeris. It was brutal, and it mirrors the brutality that Stalin meted out upon his people. Stalin may have wanted to ensure his great USSR would continue, but the stroke of his pen that appeared to "ensure peace" in the region by "conquering" both the Azeris and the Armenians only served to divide these two nationalities even more.

In hindsight, the unmitigated violence of "ethnic cleansing," or "genocide" was inevitable. Massacre of one group by another always follows the same foundation, no matter where it happens in the world: one minority becomes a majority. The new "majority" now lords it over the underlings, and the new "minority" demands its rights in fairness against an oppressive majority.

There are those who want to deny that what happened in 1991 in Baku wasn't genocide or "ethnic cleansing" because it didn't happen on a large scale. These "deniers" mirror the Turks who refuse *to this day* to admit to the holocaust of the Armenians in 1915. But the "Baku pogrom" did happen. But by definition a "pogrom" is a "violent riot aimed at the massacre or persecution of an ethnic or religious group." The Wikipedia description still sends chills down my spine: "According to the Human Rights Watch reporter, Robert Kushen, 'the action was not entirely (or perhaps not at all) spontaneous, as the attackers had lists of Armenians and their addresses."[2] That list included my address and my aunt's where our children were so brutally traumatized. I don't know if you can ever get completely over the fact that your home—your children—were targets for no other reason than you weren't the "right" nationality.

Ironically, Leon Trotsky, the leader of the Bolshevik revolution in Russia that paved the way for Stalin's communist regime to conquer the entire region, was the one who first, and notably, said in the Twentieth century that there was a "trash bin of history."[3] So that my story does not get swept into that same trash bin and forgotten, the story of the Azerbaijani massacre of Armenians in that small USSR country must be told. It reverberates into the present moment, even in my adopted and very beloved United States of America.

PART ONE

Shades of Unrest.
Exposing the Great Lie

A ZERI HATRED OF ARMENIANS DIDN'T JUST HAPPEN BECAUSE STALIN drew new borders on his own whim seventy years prior. The people in Azerbaijan were no dummies. They were scrutinizing segments of the Soviet Union in the Baltic countries who were attempting to secede to establish their own independent nations. The Berlin Wall was down. Eastern bloc countries were seceding. "Why not us, too?" the Azeris asked. Openness or "glasnost" was the refrain of President Gorbachev, but openness in a dictatorial society is letting the genie out of the bottle.

That genie needed a scapegoat, and Armenians were the easy target. Nothing unifies people against the other than the suppression of kinfolk and exaggerated stories of atrocities spread and encouraged by the locals in power.

We saw the predictable reaction among the Azeris of our city Baku. "*The Armenians cut off the hands of our precious young men,*" was the common cry. Young Azeris arrived in Baku in droves as professed "victims" and enflamed the native population even more against us Armenians in Baku. Armenians are good business people and constituted a sizable—even a majority—of the middle class in Baku. That enflamed the refugees even more as they turned their envious eyes on Armenian money and our property.

The government, comprised chiefly of Azeris, used this unifying antagonism to support their dream of forming an Independent Nation of Azerbaijan, stirring up hatred and violence against us Armenians, encouraging mobs to seize our homes, our properties, our bodies and sometimes annihilate our lives, forcing us to flee.

This was the impetus for the Sumgait massacre and the ethnic cleansing of Baku.

There were signs, however, of what was to come—long before the first whispers of hate were slung from Azeri lips, far longer, even, than the first overt acts of torture were perpetrated on the Armenian victims in Sumgait.

CHAPTER 2

Sad Harmony

WAS IT NOT ENOUGH THAT GOD MADE HER UNATTRACTIVE? OR WAS it not enough to be rejected by her family for marrying a hated Armenian who was much older than she was? Or still not enough being unable to have her own child when she was middle-aged?

She was a beautiful soul who made music come alive for so many. Perhaps that's why she was the focus of jealousy and hatred from colleagues at work and parents of students for her high ideals and her ability to resist corruption.

Her name was Leila Xanum, and she was the Professor of Harmony and then became director of the music college where I took my music lessons.

Her story is tragic on many levels, for it is a microcosm of the unholy intersection of cultures pitted against each other, a war that pays no heed to the deep abiding beauty that music, culture, and the arts can imbue into any situation, no matter how adverse the circumstance.

I had been a music student of hers, Leila Xanum, at the Music College for many years and over the course of time we grew quite fond of one another. We became so close that when she fell ill, I made a promise to her that I would take care of her adopted daughter in her absence. What makes my personal pledge to this teacher so notable is that Leila Xanum was an Azeri woman.

"Xanum" is an Azeri title of respect for a woman, similar to the word Madam, but initially I was not pleased to have her as my new teacher, despite her reputation and obvious talent and ability. My original music teacher, Rachela Shein, a Jewish woman, spoke to me one day after class to deliver the unwelcome news.

"I think I told you that sometime I am moving to Leningrad (now St. Petersburg) where my daughter lives and the time has come for me to go," she informed us. "I am sorry. I enjoyed you as my students so much, but, unfortunately, that's life. Oh, don't make faces. You will be all right! I am transferring my students to other teachers"

"Enough sad faces! Let's talk about whom I signed you up with."

She turned to me.

"Karina, you are being moved to Leila Xanum, my friend and colleague." She said this with proud distinction, as if I should be so honored. "She is a very talented teacher and a talented musician."

Still, I was not happy about the transfer. In the Soviet Union sudden changes of any kind were rarer than in other countries.

After first talking to Leila Xanum on the phone, however, I was instantly impressed by her very cultured and pleasant voice. I felt even more respect and admiration for her when she invited me to her home to get acquainted. I remember walking up to her third-floor apartment and ringing the bell.

"Are you expecting someone?" I heard a man's distant voice ask behind the door.

"Yes. It's for me, a new student," the now-familiar pleasant voice declared.

When the door opened, I was shocked. Leila Xanum did not look the way I had expected after hearing her elegant voice on the phone. She was of medium build, very dark, and she did not dress the part of a music director of a big institution. She looked like a village Azeri teacher. Her hair was short. Her blouse was silk, and she had thrown a wool jacket loosely over her shoulders just like librarians here used to wear in drafty rooms. Her skirt was hiked up too high above her waistline the way old men tended to wear their belts.

Rachela Shein, my former teacher, was a marked contrast. Rachela was tall, blond, flamboyant, and outgoing. Her hair was always carefully coiffed; she wore big rings with precious stones on her hands and dressed in fashionable bright colors. She would take breaks from lessons so she could smoke, but would sternly warn her voice students, "Puff, puff. This is very bad for your voice." Though outspoken and direct, she was very feminine.

Leila Xanum was altogether different. She had large pores in her dark complexion and made no attempt to utilize available makeup to cover them. Her heavy, mannish eyebrows overpowered the dark frames of her thick glasses. Her conspicuous ears, protruding out a little further than average under the unfashionable short black coiffure added to her unexpected and uncharacteristic appearance.

Her hands were quite hairy, particularly on the tops of her fingers near the knuckle. Her fingernails were cut short, though appropriate for a pianist, but were natural in color, not even toned with colorless nail polish. She only wore costume jewelry, displaying clip-on earrings with tiny stones of no particular design or value.

I observed all these things very quickly and thought to myself, "What am I getting into?"

However, as soon as Leila Xanum opened her mouth to speak, all the misgivings I had about my new teacher dissolved instantly. In the most beautiful Russian, she told me about herself in a humble, tactful way.

"Well, you must be disappointed," she told me.

I shrugged my shoulders and gave her a weak denial which she did not believe for a second.

After her introduction, she, as Professor of Harmony, provided me with a list of the expectations that she had for her serious students. She displayed a charisma of culture and education in the soft way she spoke and in the way she patiently listened. It put me instantly at ease.

Our meeting primarily concerned the scheduling of our days and times, but as she spoke of her acquaintance with art, music history, literature, and music theory, I couldn't help but think of the incredible contrast between her outward appearance and her resplendent inner soul. The ambiance of her apartment perfectly reflected her affinity for high culture, a taste of cultivated milieu that featured an array of books, periodicals and artwork.

I was deeply impressed, and she noticed I was browsing with my eyes.

"Do you like to read?" she asked me.

"Yes," I answered.

"I'd like to introduce you to my husband," she said. "Please look around. I'll be right back. Excuse me." She walked out and left me alone in the room for only a moment.

"Avetik, darling," I heard her say.

"Please come here. I want you to meet my new student."

She returned accompanied by a well-dressed man in a long-sleeved shirt, suit pants, and shoes. He was not tall, a little chubby, about twenty years her senior. And he is Armenian.

"Avetik, this is Karina," she announced.

"Karina, my husband Avet Semeonovich. He is also a musician—cello and violin."

I was impressed by the very affectionate nickname, "Avetik," that she had used for his Armenian first name, Avet.

"You have the best teacher you could ever have," he boasted proudly as he gently stroked his wife's hair.

This man, I learned, had two advanced graduate degrees in two disciplines, one from the Music Conservatory in Armenia and another in history from Moscow University. He had published journal articles in both disciplines and carried the highly esteemed category of a professorship, called "*zasluzhennyi* professor" in the USSR.

He also had two grown sons from a previous marriage. While his boys initially were not happy about their father's marriage to an Azeri Muslim woman, they eventually came around and developed a relationship with their stepmother. Leila Xanum's sister, however, never accepted an Armenian brother-in-law. Sadly, no close connection ever existed between the families, except in extreme necessity. All through the years, her sister remained antagonistic toward the Armenian husband.

Victims are hated most by the same ones who have wronged them, as goes the Roman adage.

I quickly got to know him as well as I did Leila Xanum, and the two of them seemed perfect together, doting on each other and using warm pet names. One day, he showed me a black-and-white photograph of him with his wife leaning her head on his shoulder, their hands enfolded in a typical formal photographic studio portrait of those days. There he was, a strikingly handsome younger man with a slight mustache, dark hair and chiseled features. As young as Leila Xanum was, she still looked the same. I know that he saw in her the same thing that I did upon meeting and getting to know her. It was the same thing that other fortunate people like us so cherished about her: charm, culture and kindness. That was her beauty; you could see it as well as feel it.

Theirs was a rare example of a very happy inter-ethnic marriage, despite their representative families' opposition to the union. However, although the relationship on the Azeri side never fully blossomed, the couple was forever united in the dimension of music. The two-decade gap between their birthdays was even less withstanding, with musicians' histories showing many such age differences in marriages, including the conductor Stokowski and Gloria Vanderbilt, and composers like the Hungarian Kodály, and the Austrian Gustav and Alma Mahler who married a man nineteen years her senior.

Soon after becoming Leila Xanum's pupil, I found out that my friend Marina, who was also studying at the Music College, had a very different opinion of my esteemed teacher.

Marina's divorced mother, who worked as an accountant in a museum, had money, enough to be able to provide her daughter with a free ticket with bribes all along her educational path. I was aware that Marina did not have any real commitment to music. As near as I could tell, her vocation was boys. With Leila Xanum in charge now, reorganizing the Music College and raising its standards, Marina did not have a chance of advancing to the next level.

When I mentioned the name of the new music director to Marina and her mother, they both exclaimed, "That witch!" and "that snake!"

Later, I learned that when her mother tried to bribe Leila Xanum, she was thrown out of the Music Director's office posthaste. Such a thing was unheard of in Baku at this time, and Marina's mother was infuriated that she could not influence the music director with money the way she had so many others previously. I am sure she made an immediate attempt to go over Leila Xanum's head and reach out to higher authorities through her network of "connections," but as far as I know her efforts were in vain.

One day after class, while chatting with Leila Xanum, I said, "One of my friends is your student."

"Oh, really? Who?"

"Marina Arakelova."

"Well, unfortunately, she's lazy," Leila Xanum exclaimed bluntly. "But I hope she will improve."

Her simple comment, without being judgmental, was something to be admired, and I respected her even more because of it. Such honesty was so untypical of that country and society. Teachers were known to humiliate their students in front of the entire class with sarcastic comments and jokes. Leila Xanum was always so simple, so classy, and so professional.

Through the years, as Leila Xanum became more than a teacher, but a mentor and a trusted friend, I realize that this was also something that was very unusual in the Soviet Union. The social, cultural and economic gap between student and teacher is typically very wide. It was not like that with Leila Xanum, who would often hold classes in her home with her own quality grand piano. Both she and her husband would often give lessons at their home, despite how busy they were with other professional activities, she as director of the Musical Institute and he as a performer in the Baku Symphony Orchestra.

Each time I visited their home, I would be captivated by something new. The walls of their apartment were lined with photographs of famous musicians, with Avet appearing in some of them. It was not unusual in Baku homes to find a lot of books; we were all Europeanized devoted readers. But, here, the tables, chairs and sofas were covered with books and periodicals which were placed down, opened to the last page which was being perused. The shelves were filled with colorful books, not selected for their interior decoration, but for their content. Everything spelled an environment of high culture in art, literature, history, and music.

The books and magazines were from USSR and abroad. The bookshelves also held items that I did not know existed, indicative of the family's high level of culture, which added to my admiration of Leila Xanum and her husband, Avet.

This remarkable woman, friend and mentor, would offer me and my family scarce tickets to cultural events as Director of the major Cultural Center in Baku. My daughter enjoyed these events, so I frequently took her. I also got to share in many personal happenings in Leila Xanum's life, such as the adoption of her five-year-old daughter, whom she treated so wonderfully as a mother and teacher.

One day after a class, Leila Xanum confided in me that she was very worried about the health of her husband. I had grown very fond of him—he would sometimes accompany us on the cello, and those were moments of pure pleasure.

He suffered a mild stroke and was on leave from his duties as a cellist in the Symphony Orchestra and professor of history. While taking care of him, Leila Xanum continued to teach her classes at home. I would see her husband shuffling around in small steps when he walked. Later, after he had a second stroke, he'd wobble while leaning on a cane.

One day he saw me and came over.

"Honey," he said, and with difficulty raised his hand to cup my chin. An outside observer might have assumed he was a dirty old man touching a young woman's face, but his illness could not erase his refinement or kindness.

"Avetik, enough!" Leila Xanum said gently. She tactfully moved his hand to her own chin as his hazel eyes stared vacantly into the air.

"Okay, okay, let's go. That's not nice." With a gentle push, she guided him to where he had to go.

Around this time, it came to my attention that her husband was in need of a very rare medicine, which Leila Xanum, even in her position, could not find. Ordinarily, people in such high standing in Baku would have sufficient money and the connections to get whatever they wanted. The favors she could bestow on children of important people in all the music schools under her administration should have given her power to achieve virtually any goal. Fortunately or unfortunately, she was scrupulously honest and could not compromise her standards, even in the sick and corrupt atmosphere of Baku where everything was for sale.

There, I think, in a notorious center of shadiness like Shakespeare's *The Merchant of Venice,* Leila Xanum glowed brightly.

"How far that little candle throws his beams! So shines a good deed in a weary world."

Of course, I offered Leila Xanum any help I could provide, but she just shook her head and smiled; a silent refusal.

"Let me try," I insisted. "I have an idea. Let me try."

She finally copied the name of the medicine onto a slip of paper. My plan was based upon a friend who had a boyfriend in the merchant marine who often traveled to foreign ports. I would ask her to prevail upon her boyfriend, Petya, to try to get the scarce drug in Odessa. The Ukrainian seaport city was famous for its international black market. Any item that could be purchased in a capitalistic city could be obtained in Odessa if you put in your order in advance.

About a month later, I called my teacher and friend at her home. While she continued teaching her students at home, she announced, "Karina, It is not your scheduled class day."

"I have to visit you," I insisted. "It's very important."

"I'm sorry, Karina, it's not a good day. Avetik is very sick, and I do have a few students coming."

"Please, Leila Xanum, I will make it a very short visit." I did not divulge the reason for my visit, wanting to surprise her with the medication in person.

She reluctantly agreed. When I arrived, I held the box behind my back, enjoying the moment of anticipation until I revealed what I have been concealing and presented it to her.

"What is this?"

"This is the medication."

"What medication?"

"The one your husband needs."

She puts on her glasses with bottle thick lenses and examined the box, scrupulously compared it with the name she pulled out of a desk drawer. After a pause, with look of shock and amazement she exclaimed,

"They match exactly!" Then she started to cry.

This is not a reaction I expect, so unusual for a woman who is always in control of her emotions.

She hugged me.

"How did you manage it? The doctor said there is no hope of obtaining the medicine!"

I told her, feeling such pride and joy that I was able to help someone I respected so much.

I was initially given a quoted price of a dollar each for a thousand pills, but I managed to bargain down to seventy cents. Even so, it was big money. It was almost the monthly paycheck of an office cleaner. The pills, however, quickly brought noticeable improvement in Avet's health, which was all that really mattered. The drug must have been very powerful, because the dosage had to be slowly increased every day until it reached a peak, then the dosage had to be slowly decreased until the thousand tablets were gone.

Leila Xanum was ecstatically grateful to me for helping her husband, whom she so observably loved. Usually laconic, she opened up to me, revealing that she and her husband had to live a solitary life together because his family and her family shunned them. Her sister was angry with her not only because she was married to an Armenian, but because Leila Xanum would not bestow favors on her which she could milk from her high position and connections in Baku society.

They had no children but adopted a little girl, Rena, from the orphanage. When they offered the child the advantages of music and ballet classes they could afford and had access to, Rena showed surprising natural talent, almost a prodigy. Leila Xanum was so proud of her, but her ability was both a blessing and a curse.

"Why did God send me this talented child?" she would ask me. "Why does she have to be so musical?"

Under Leila Xanum's administration, students lacking talent and good grades would no longer be promoted in spite of the pleadings and offers of bribes from the influential parents of students. That would be her downfall. One day, she confessed to me,

"I can't take it anymore. I can't take that pressure. They have complaints against me. I'm going to resign."

I could have shared with her that I knew exactly which mother was infuriated that her child could not advance in the Music School with all her connections and money. I remembered my mother's friend's exact words:

"What is wrong with that woman? Does she want more? I offered more money. My Marina is so talented! Everyone says so but that bitch!"

She talked of revenge against the "witch" for rejecting her bribe. She said these things in front of me because I would defend Leila Xanum. Being an accountant, the infuriated mother fantasized about dropping a roll of bills onto her desk after having copied all the serial numbers as proof.

"Then, let her say she does not accept bribes!"

While Leila Xanum's life with her husband was a very private one, it was not without depth and significance. They surrounded themselves with art, music, journals and intellectual values and love, and friends who shared their world. I can vividly recall hearing her playing a sweet song on the piano for Avet while he was sick.

"Very often," she once told me, "we play recitals for each other, he on the cello and I on the piano." They would frequently play duets, for me, he on the cello or violin, she on the piano. It was beautiful. It was as if they were using the instruments to talk to one another. It always made me feel a little embarrassed, as if I were eavesdropping on an intimate romantic moment.

Only in Baku could there be such a couple, an Armenian husband, an Azeri wife, both highly cultivated and sophisticated. This, indeed, was a representative couple of the city that was supposed to be the model for the "New Soviet Man." Like this dream that could not be sustained, individual lives were on the verge of change.

One unhappy day, I kept calling and calling Leila Xanum without an answer. I was extremely worried until she finally called me back.

"Leila Xanum, how are you?"

"Well, there was an accident," she said in a steady, nonchalant tone. "Rena and I got hit by a drunk driver while we were crossing the street. Rena is okay, but I am in the hospital."

I immediately rushed to the hospital to see her. I found her seated in the hallway, her belly huge, distended like a pregnant woman's about to give birth. Her legs and ankles were swollen.

"I look terrible because the kidney is not working," she said matter-of-factly, speaking in her familiar calm voice, and avoiding telling me any details.

After I got over my initial shock, I insisted on knowing what the hospital was doing for her.

She waved her arm disparagingly.

"Aah! They don't have the medication."

Even in the face of her own malady, she still managed to keep her professionalism, refusing to pull strings for her own benefit.

"What medication?" I asked, ready to get my much-loved teacher the medicine she needed the way I did for her husband previously.

"I am concerned what is going to happen to Rena and my husband," she told me. "You know my life story. Sometimes, at this time now, I think it is over and maybe I am not living in the right way. Maybe all this was a mistake. I should have lived like everyone else."

"Why are you talking like that?" I asked. "You will be okay!"

She touched my hand impatiently. Her face was placid, eyes dull. She looked defeated, sad. It was the first time I saw her like this, and it frightened me.

"Let me continue," she said. "I made a will. I don't have much. I want to leave everything to my daughter. It will come to her when she reaches eighteen years old. She will be put back in the orphanage after I die. My sister has no interest or feeling at all. My husband is too sick. Will you promise me that you will keep an eye on my Rena?"

"Leila Xanum, maybe you should talk to your sister?"

"No," she said, and that was the end of that. I knew that there would be no reconciliation until her sister accepted Avet.

One evening, months earlier, I had been attending a children's ballet show where Rena was participating. When she attempted a difficult piano piece that her teacher thought was too hard for her, the little girl insisted on trying, and explaining, "My mother showed me how to play the hard parts."

"Does your mother play piano?" the teacher asked.

"My mother is professor of piano," Rena proudly stated.

Until that moment, no one knew, not the music teacher, not the parents of the other students, none of them were aware that Rena's mother was such a jewel in the crown of musicians in Baku.

I could not help thinking how truly astonishing it was that such a woman, who could open any door for herself and for other people, most of whom were scheming to get favors from her, could remain so modest and selfless. Equally amazing to me was how Leila Xanum, while occupying such a high position as an Azeri living in the Azerbaijan Republic dominated by a nationality averse to its Armenian minority, would select me, an Armenian and a student, for such an important responsibility as looking after her daughter.

I remember one of the last times I was with Leila Xanum. She unexpectedly took off a very thin ring from one of her fingers. It looked strikingly yellow against her dark skin.

"I want you to have this," she said to me.

I refused to take the ring, though I don't exactly know why. Something about it just didn't seem right. Maybe deep down I thought this symbolic gesture would hasten the initiation of my responsibilities for her death. Whatever the case, Leila Xanum continued to insist that I have the ring despite my protests. Finally, I acquiesced.

"You can give it to me tomorrow," I told her, "Tomorrow, Leila Xanum."

Reluctantly, she replaced the ring on her finger as I ran out to seek help from various drugstore connections. I had no luck at first. It was not uncommon that a hospital would not have a particular medication, especially when it was expensive or scarce.

It only takes one pharmacist to make a difference, and I finally found that one.

"This medication is very hard to get," the pharmacist told me. "I can give you just one pack. Come back tomorrow."

I waited two days. The medication came in a small, long package like a toothpaste box, and I immediately went to deliver it to Leila Xanum. The hospital is in walking distance, twenty minutes away, and I took it with me, clutching it close and full of joy.

I arrived but learned that I was too late. "She died two days ago," the attendant at front desk stated coldly.

It didn't hit me until I saw her empty bed, and of all the overriding emotions I felt at that moment, guilt was probably the most pervasive. I had not visited her the day before I found the medication, selfishly anticipating the joy of placing the medicine in her hands. I cried for days.

My mother could not stand to see me like this and reprimanded me.

"You can't go on like this, Karina," she said, standing over me as I lay sobbing on the sofa. "It's almost like you're crying like I am dead. She was nobody to you. Are you going to cry as much when I die? And remember, you have a husband and children!"

Of course, she was right. I had been so distraught I lost track of the days. I knew that Muslims bury the same day before sunset, and I assumed that Leila Xanum's sister took care of the funeral. I had never been to a Muslim funeral. I had seen them passing on the street, heard the wailing in the neighborhood, but in this case, if I had known the place and location, I would have gone to pay my final respects to this amazing woman.

Still, I needed to know the details of what happened and made for her apartment house and inquired from their Armenian neighbor of many years who told me in her big voice what she knew.

"The family vanished," I was told. "The sister had the apartment emptied. I think they came to take the child to the orphanage. I don't know what happened to Avet Semeonovich. Such a nice man."

I do not know either, except to add that I heard that he died shortly after. I do not even know whether or not he knew of the loss of his beloved Leila Xanum. Both families, Armenian and Azeri, like the Capulets and Montagues, saw the end of their conflicts in death.

I pounded on the door just as a way of saying goodbye and heard the thumps echoing through the empty apartment. I imagined through my tears that I heard the strum of a cello accompanied by chords of a piano.

My only thought was bleak: what chance did that piece of paper have in corrupt Baku, that last will and testament, to help that little orphaned Azeri girl?

I have often wondered what became of Rena. Who knows if the daughter ever received anything of her legacy? I did not know if the child bore her adoptive mother's name or her adoptive father's name.

I have the daydream of someday seeing a ballet on television from Baku with a young woman with the first name Rena. Her last name is unknown to me. I hope the seeds of love and support of those two artists will have flowered in the ballet slippers of that little girl.

In music, "A dissonance has its resolution when it moves to a consonance." The ideal theory of harmony of Bach, Handel and Mozart was not resolved in this sad harmony of Baku.

CHAPTER 3

The "Accident"

ETHNIC CLEANSING CAN'T HAPPEN IN THE LATE PART OF THE TWENTIETH century. At least that's what most people want to believe. That happened "back then," in World War II, in the holocaust and Stalin's pogroms.

Ethnic hatred runs deep, and it pushes people to commit acts of violence upon one another that are by all accounts insane—even though those who commit them would swear upon their holy text that what they are doing is completely in the realm of their sanity.

I had heard of the acts of inhumanity that the Azeris had perpetrated upon my fellow Armenians. They were almost too evil to confront—both at the time they were happening and years later when I decided I had to write about what occurred. It is a truism that it is easier to turn the other way, pretend that nothing out of the ordinary is happening than face up to what is really going on.

When I decided to write down what happened to my family and to the Armenians living in Baku at the time of the massacre, I knew that others had compelling stories. But no one wanted to share them. They brought back too many painful memories.

In the course of my travels, I finally met one woman, Maya, who was willing to talk. She had found a way to get out of the bad situation for Armenians in Baku. She had moved to Moscow, biding her time there like many Armenians outside their native country, waiting for the government to release them for travel. Her parents, however, remained in Baku essentially because they were stubborn, old, and refused to understand the situation until something struck them right between the eyes. This was very common behavior for people who lived their entire life there, particularly the old, the handicapped, and the ill.

When Maya received a distressing phone call from Baku from her mother, Margo, informing her that her father had fallen and was badly hurt, Maya made immediate arrangements to travel to Baku from Moscow.

She was told that her father had an accident while working at his job in the landscaping department of the city.

"Come quickly. He is very sick."

His job involved climbing high up into the canopies of Caspian locusts, chestnut oaks, elder pines, and the argans, all unique to Azerbaijan and cherished as local botanical treasures, to cut off the top of the trees to encourage new growth as well as saw off extra branches.

They did not have cherry-picker machines like we have here in America to hoist him safely off the ground in a bucket. Instead, the men held themselves in place on a ladder with hands and legs or sometimes with a belt.

It was less than forty-eight hours after her arrival that her mother, Margo, told her the real story. The fall was no accident.

Aram, her father, had become gloomy and depressed and was not going through his normal daily routines. He wouldn't answer Margo when she kept asking him, "What is the matter?"

Finally, she got the truth out of him.

"I don't want to go to work," Aram told her.

"They are killing us, and every single day there is something."

"Then don't go, Aram," Margo replied, knowing full well that it was not in Aram's nature to skip work. He went, and later that same morning Lida, a woman who lived in the neighborhood ran up to Margo, screaming,

"He fell. He fell. He fell! Go! Go!" Lida kept holding her hands tight over her ears, as if she didn't want to hear what she was saying.

Margo knew that this Armenian woman was employed as the cleaning lady in the building where her husband worked.

The only person it could be whom she was bemoaning was Aram, her husband. He was found in walking distance from the City Tree Services Department, about ten minutes away.

When Margo arrived at the scene he was still breathing, lying face down under a Persian silk tree. She seized Aram by his broad shoulders and with difficulty turned him over and talked to him. Gasping, he looked up at her with his red face twisted in pain, gazing at her worried face and dark hair haloed by the pink brush-like blossoms among the leaves of the mimosa tree, and managed only three words.

"They pushed me," he groaned.

Any clever detective in a mystery novel would have noticed the out-of-place heavy oak branch lying between him and the bottom of the ladder. He landed face down, yet he was profusely bleeding from the back of his head; clear evidence of being struck on the head from behind.

After many calls and much waiting, an ambulance finally arrived to take Aram away after lying there for who knew how long bleeding from his wound. No one reported any irregularity. No police report was made. No complaint filed. It was simply regarded as an unfortunate work-related accident.

The weeping daughter found her father unconscious in a hospital room with three other seriously ill patients. She never had an opportunity to talk to him. Margo pleaded with the Azeri doctor to do something for her husband, but no one in the hospital paid any attention. This happened in the era just after the Sumgait massacre when an Armenian life was not deemed important by official Azerbaijanis. We saw the change in behavior at official places like the hospital and on TV and radio that demonstrated hatred towards Armenians.

Within twenty-four hours Aram was dead.

"I begged you to get out of this god damned place when you had the chance," the daughter told her brother and mother.

"But, no, you all stayed put. You all said, 'The Sumgait pogrom is an aberration. Gorbachev will not allow anything bad to happen to us.' Now, see where we are."

"I can't wait to get out of here!" Maya cried.

The daughter went by herself in person to the police, the *militsia*. They were Azeris, and they just laughed.

"Always, you Armenians want to blame us for every dead dog in the road," they scoffed to the daughter. The Soviet military, when she paid a visit to their headquarters, reacted in much the same manner.

"What evidence do you have?" the soldiers sneered.

"Do you have any witnesses or any photographs?"

Only Lida commiserated and understood.

"The Azeris have one less Armenian in their labor pool. I must work among those *Chooskis*, and who knows when *I'll* be next? If they could, they would cut down a tree and have it fall on me. How sad when all the trees are beautifully in flower. If I didn't need this job, I would quit."

She used the term *Chooskis,* a pejorative term for country bumpkin Azeris. Not used only by non-Azeris, but also by urbanized Azeris against their "redneck" kinfolk.

"I know what that poor man was going through working with those animals," she told Margo at the funeral, and again at the Armenian traditional ceremony meal forty days later. Still, the daughter could not persuade her mother to leave before the forty days.

By that time, the daughter was back in Moscow, while Margo and her son and her grandchildren remained in the city where the stares of hatred and mutterings of Azeris grew worse. The media's indifference to the attacks on Armenians reached a whole new level, with coverage in the newspapers and on the radio and television not only condoning the savagery but instilling anti-Armenian rage and inciting further violent tirades.

It had been such hard work for Maya to persuade her old parents to leave. Even after all this, Margo refused to leave Baku because she wanted to be able to visit her murdered husband's grave in the Armenian cemetery.

Her father, too, could not imagine changing his daily routine of going to the park and playing backgammon with his old cronies. Soon, thereafter, there would be no chance for Margo to visit the tomb of her husband, as the Azeris went and destroyed the Christian cemetery sometime after the later Baku pogrom, selling the marble tombstones and developing the land. Nor was there any chance of lighting a candle in their Armenian church. It, too, was savaged.

Following his father's tradition, Aram's son would find work in the Los Angeles Tree Management Department; only, he climbed palm trees in a cherry picker. His Spanish-speaking fellow workers translated his Armenian name, Aram, into Spanish and called him, Armando. The beards of palm trees are heavier than they look and can be dangerous, but the perils of his job are not reflective of any ethnic conflict and the chance of falling is slim. Probably the only legitimate threat comes when a surprised and infuriated squirrel chatters and lunges to bite the intruder who disturbs her nest beneath a shady palm leaf on a sunny Los Angeles afternoon. Even an animal cherishes its own home.

We all lost ours. It felt like we could not fight back.

CHAPTER 4

Massacre

I N HINDSIGHT, MASSACRE WAS PRACTICALLY INEVITABLE.
The present Azeri-Armenian conflict has been evolving in large part over the control of the region of Nagorno-Karabakh, the region that Stalin so cavalierly gave to Azerbaijan in 1921.

In 1988, this region was still part of the Soviet Republic—meaning it was supposed to be a peaceful part of the brotherhood of Communist Russia.

The enclave housed a majority of Armenians surrounded by an Azeri republic. Interethnic fighting broke out in earnest shortly after the parliament of the Nagorno-Karabakh Autonomous Oblast (NKAO) precariously located in Azerbaijan, voted to pull out of Azerbaijan and unify the region with Armenia on February 20, 1988. Azerbaijan, in turn, wanted to curb this secessionist movement, and in a subsequent referendum, the Azerbaijani population fiercely rejected the unification of Nagorno-Karabakh with Armenia.

Armenian rallies were countered by strong anti-Armenian sentiments that were voiced by Azeri citizens and officials alike, including one leader of the Communist Party of Azerbaijan who warned Armenians in Sumgait, "If you do not stop campaigning for the unification of Nagorno Karabakh with Armenia, if you don't sober up, 100,000 Azeris from neighboring districts will break into your houses, torch your apartments, rape your women, and kill your children."

These were by no means idle threats.

On February 26, 1988, there were rallies at Lenin Square in the small industrial seaside town of Sumgait, which is located only twenty miles outside Baku. There were explicit calls for violence against Armenians. This sentiment was agitated by the fallacious reports that Azerbaijani refugees fleeing Armenia from the towns Kafan and Masis were being brutalized and murdered by Armenians.

The following day, violence exploded, becoming what would be known as the *Sumgait Pogrom*. A pogrom, as I have noted earlier, is a violent riot aimed at massacre or persecution of an ethnic or religious group. Most people outside of the Russian spheres of influence are familiar only with the word "pogrom" in relation to the history of anti-Jewish attacks by Cossacks. It was a frightening picture, soldiers on horses brandishing sabers and whips; it was official terrorism organized by the pre-revolutionary Tsarist government both to subdue the Jews and to feed the prejudices of the non-Jewish population as a well-practiced scapegoat plan. The target of the Sumgait pogrom was Christian, not Jewish: the Armenian population

On February 27, 1988, mobs made up largely of ethnic Azeris formed into groups that waged an orchestrated attack on Armenians. Sumgait residents were brutally beaten, mutilated, raped, and killed both on the public streets of Sumgait and inside their homes during three days of unchecked violence. The official count of those murdered is thirty-two. Unofficial numbers have been reported at around two hundred.[4] No one knows how many were tortured and mutilated. The manners in which the victims were killed reverberated among Armenians, recalling bitter memories of the Armenian Holocaust of the First World War.

Still, the violence in Sumgait came as a shock to many, including me. It was unprecedented in scope in the Soviet Union and received heavy coverage in the Western media. A number of international and Soviet sources described the events in Sumgait as genocide of the Armenian population. There was no initial intervention from the police or the local governmental bodies and most of Sumgait's Armenian population left the city in the aftermath of the pogrom amid widespread looting of their homes.

On February 28, a small contingent of military Russian troops (MVD) entered the city and unsuccessfully attempted to quell the rioting. The situation was not fully defused until more professional military units entered with tanks and other armored vehicles a day later. The forces sent by the government imposed a state of martial law in Sumgait and established a strict curfew, which finally helped bring the crisis under control. However, it all came a little too late for many Armenians, who expressed strong objections to President Gorbachev for the delay in response in putting a stop to these murderous actions by Azeris against the Armenian people in Sumgait

The violence continued sporadically for four more days. President Gorbachev's official public response is that he was *only* four hours tardy in responding to the crisis. It was the same old misinformation and lies.

In the past, people would rely on Moscow, expect fairness and believe that they would be defended, especially at a time when there was much chaos in the Republic. One thing was becoming abundantly clear to me at the time: people were losing hope and felt that they had been abandoned. The powerful Soviet Union suddenly did not look as powerful as we had been led to believe.

Through the summer of '88, mass demonstrations continued, and inter-ethnic fighting spread to other cities in Azerbaijan. Then, in November 1988, an Azeri-led pogrom targeting Armenians living in the city of Kirovabad, what is today Ganja, was responsible for the massacre of at least 130 Armenians and injuries to hundreds more. This led to a massive refugee problem. Emergency measures were imposed, and Azerbaijan instituted a blockade of enemy Armenia with a trade and travel embargo.

This is what my family and I were facing ten months later in Baku. Yet, even after all this, in my heart of hearts I still did not think it would happen in our beloved city. I don't know why I continued to cling to this delusion. But I did, and I was not alone. Many Armenians still held out hope.

If there was any logic to it all, it would have to be attributable to the general ethos of Soviet society, where change comes slowly, if at all. People there did not jump from locality to locality, from job to job like they do in America. People form strong ties to neighbors, to their teachers, to communities and even to their belongings. This collective inertia, for lack of a better term, was now something I started to recognize as being dangerous for my family, even potentially deadly. It was the same for all Armenians living in Azerbaijan.

CHAPTER 5

The Courtyard

IT IS NATURAL FOR A PERSON IN A STRESSFUL SITUATION TO LOOK BACK on a simpler time. Life in Baku certainly wasn't always so unpleasant and perilous as it became in the late 1980's. When Anatoliy and I got married, we first lived with my mother in her Mediterranean Courtyard apartment in the center of the city. I had grown up with my brother and family in the same apartment, and it was also where both my children had been born. The unique and wonderful experiences there shaped my life and the destination of my family in many ways, and a lot of it had to do with the simple architectural design of the city dwelling where my family resided for so long.

The Mediterranean courtyard apartment complex has long been a favorite structure throughout the world and only became popular in the United States starting in Los Angeles in the 1920's. The ancient basic features include the entrances and windows of apartments around a central grassy courtyard of flowers, trees and shrubs that is open to the sky. In Western civilization, courtyard buildings were an invention dating to the Roman Empire.

Having a series of rooms around a court, they could build city dwellings and not have to worry about light and air. In ancient Roman cities, the courtyard or closely related atrium buildings were constructed as residences, both single- and multifamily, and as government forums and markets. The courtyard design has endured from that period to the present day. The most frequent use in medieval times and the Renaissance was in the monastery, in which the monks' rooms opened onto a courtyard. The courtyard design was used for some European castles for purposes of security.

The Soviet model of the Mediterranean courtyard apartment complex that I was familiar with had its own intrinsic minor variations. They were usually two stories in height and there could be a public toilet in the middle because in the older complexes there were no indoor bathrooms. This left very little space for children to play. Near the entrance were three or four trash containers for the entire building. No concierge. No security. The design was made for convenience rather than comfort.

When my brother was to return from the army with plans to get married, it became clear to Anatoliy and me that we should find a separate home. Anatoliy's parents had a piece of property in a district of Baku, just beyond an area called "Armenikent," twenty minutes away from the center of the city by car with some undeveloped land attached to their house. We saw this as an opportunity to build our own home and move out of the city.

This was ideal for a number of reasons. With our new home, we would have our privacy and room to grow, yet we were still in close enough proximity to enjoy one another's company anytime.

Even after we moved out, our children would spend their days at my mother's apartment and attend preschool in the center of the city. Many nights they stayed over at my mother's.

One of the clear advantages of living in such a courtyard environment is the sense of community it fosters. The entrance through the main gate leads into the central yard where people can congregate, gossip or quarrel. Because everyone can see who comes and goes, it always provides a topic of hot discussion. Everybody knows who is visiting, whether they are friends, relatives, even unwanted guests. You could leave your keys with a neighbor and drop your children off there without worry. I would take a day off from work to help a neighbor, and they would do the same for me.

The definition of "neighbor" is one that seems to be largely dependent on geographical considerations. In many modern countries in the West, neighbors do not even know each other's names, and are unlikely to offer one another anything more than a wave from the car as they pull in and out of their driveways. In Baku, neighbors are not just people who live next door; they are close friends whom you turn to in an emergency.

You know you can turn to your neighbors, and they know that they can rely on you, such as when a family member dies, for example. With no funeral homes, the deceased relation is laid out in the home or apartment, as once was the tradition in the United States many decades ago. Neighbors in Baku would come to visit and bring food and drink, showing respect to the family.

If anyone had a money problem, whether it was with the legal system and you needed money to buy off a judge, or if you lacked the resources for your daughter's wedding or to send a child to the university, your neighbors, friends and relatives would be there. There was no such thing as an immediate withdrawal of cash from the bank to dip into the savings account which not everybody had.

On the flip side of the same coin, however, having neighbors so close could also bring about some less-than-pleasant consequences. Neighbors would shamelessly indulge in terrible arguments over all manners of domestic matters, from the children to household duties such as cleaning the toilet and doing the laundry, and they would very often hurl the most vulgar insults at each other for everyone to overhear.

You would become aware of the petty grudges, some lasting generations, that neighboring families bore for one another. This was practically unavoidable in the summer, when people kept their windows and doors open. Domestic quarrels were heard all over the courtyard day and night, although in the evenings, after work ended for the day and alcohol began to be consumed, you would hear the drunks yelling and arguing the loudest. Invariably, you would discover things about your neighbors that you just as soon would rather not know, like who were the worst alcoholics. I became exposed to more Russian curse words as a child from one neighbor than I care to admit.

There was a cacophony of other sounds, as well, more pleasant and symphonic. The music of many different national traditions could be heard playing on radios and phonographs, all filling the air at once. Some people had their own musical instruments that they would play alone or in concert with others.

Besides these melodious sounds, the smells of cooking food representing a multi-national cuisine, wafted through the courtyard and mingled into one indistinguishable but intoxicating aroma. The Ukrainian downstairs may be cooking an Azerbaijani *sabzi pilaf* while the Azerbaijani across the hall prepared a Ukrainian *borsch*.

Baku had always been a city of many ethnic groups, people living side by side, with different languages, foods, festivals, religions, styles of etiquette, and national costumes. There was always some ceremony or a special event to celebrate. Weddings, anniversaries, "Sweet Sixteen" birthday parties, memorial dinners, good days and bad days—in Baku, both friends and the enemies were united. The very often mandatory first toast given at a wedding was to honor the neighbors, often quoting sayings:

"You will arrive first when there is trouble, even before the relatives."

"The friends come for the parties and the relatives for trouble."

There's an ancient Greek saying: Trouble is the measure of friendship.

Traditionally, every wedding in Baku was an international event and every guest would find his heritage represented in one form or another. You could expect all kinds of national dances and music; Jewish, Greek, Gypsy, Russian, Georgian, Azeri, as well as Armenian.

Hovering over all this was the unity of the Russian language, which by the second generation often supplanted all other languages: Armenian, Azeri, Yiddish, Ukrainian, Tatar, and Greek, and many others. After families migrated to the petroleum rich city of Baku, their native tongues were spoken only at home.

Certainly, before the catastrophe of the ethnic conflict of the 1980s and early 1990s, neighbors in Baku generously shared everything without rancor. It may seem hard to believe, but this was sometimes true even as war and secession fanned the flames of hatred against Armenians, who dominated Nagorno-Karabakh and voted to separate from the Azeri republic to join their confreres in next-door Armenia.

Street manifestations against Armenians were encouraged by the local government.

"Armenians, get out of Azerbaijan!" was the war cry in the streets, on the radio and television.

Despite the bitter atmosphere of animosity between Christian Armenians and Muslim Azeris in this Soviet republic, there were many strong friendships between individuals from these opposing ethnic groups that were able to survive. It's a true testament to the human condition and the ties that bind us all.

Our courtyard was colorful, as were many courtyards around Baku. The Azeri wife of the man who harbored us when we finally decided to leave Baku was a case in point. She had moved into what had been the apartment of the Jewish Smirnov family, where the mother Sonya was a judge, the daughter Zina a prosecutor and her son, Slava, was a defense attorney. The daughter's husband Artyusha was a leading ballet dancer, an Armenian. The daughter-in-law, Emilia was an engineer. Sometimes they were prosecutor and defense attorney for the same case and would argue the cases enthusiastically.

"Stop already!" the mother would yell, "Is it not enough that I have a court room family like this? Now, I never know whether I'm in court or home." She was petite with veined small hands which in spite of her wealth bore only a thin wedding ring of her late husband, waving the family members apart in their energetic verbal legal debates between brother and sister or prosecution and defense attorney.

"The only time I feel I have a family is when I am in a theatre and watch my son-in-law Artyusha perform on stage. Thank God we have him in the family!"

They never mentioned the clients' names, but more than once a client was astonished to see his defense attorney in the same courtyard as his prosecutor.

My father conversed with them, played backgammon, exchanged books and designed and made their shoes. Judge Sonia needed special footwear because of her bunions and was glad to have my father accommodate her needs.

———

It is worth mentioning another family next to us, a multiethnic couple, Valik, Azeri, and Alla, Armenian, his wife, both engineers, who had been living in the next apartment, and were another magnet for visitors, the Azeri engineer whose father was a composer of musical comedy and his sister, a well-known singer, heavy readers, and always speaking only Russian. It was the first chance I had to get a Solzhenitsyn book, *Cancer Ward*, from them when reading it was forbidden.

This group of "celebrities" attracted many clients and friends, keeping the Jewish Hanna busy peeping through her window at the elite attracted to this informal center of legal arguments, culture and commerce of Baku. What a disappointment it was for Hanna when they moved away and the eminence of the residents and visitors to the courtyard plummeted to a much lower level of culture and trade.

Our courtyard once had been a microcosm of happy childhood, culture, friendships, trust, support, looking after children, exchanging books, food, and being there for each other each other in time of need. Unfortunately, this happy saga came to an end with a terrible event of violence with the Baku Pogrom. An Armenian mother in her seventies lived with two her grown daughters, having lived not more than five years there before the catastrophe. On my last visit to Baku, I was disgusted to learn that in the pogrom time one of her daughters was gang-raped right in their apartment by roving gangs seeking violence against Armenians. When I learned that, it dismayed me and disgusted me. The images and bright memories of the happy courtyard disappeared and were erased. Like never before, I wanted to get away from Baku as soon as possible.

———

Perhaps the most wonderful example of the burning heartfelt love of an Azeri woman for our family was our neighbor Xalashka in our courtyard, what we affectionately called the *Italianate Kvartal*.

In many ways Xalashka was a stereotypical Azeri village woman. At the same time, she was an extraordinary person. She was petite, she had a mouth full of gold teeth and she always wore a necklace of round golden balls, evenly sized, which looked very heavy and were closely set around her neck. Her thin gray hair, cut short and parted in the middle, was held in the back of her head with hairpins. She still dressed in the typical garb of an old village woman with a short sleeved two-part dress in muted colors with a flowery pattern and an open collar leaving her necklace as a border around her throat. Her head was wrapped in the traditional kerchief. Her shoes were always black and flat which carried her comfortably through the city streets for her lonely nightly promenade for an hour every evening before it got dark, varying times with the seasons. If the weather was too cold, she avoided going out.

A simple woman who was difficult to comprehend, she was never very social, except with my family, especially my mother. They were long-time neighbors, and they conversed in Azeri.

Because my mother worked most of her adult life speaking with customers in the state grocery distribution store, she learned the Azerbaijani language very well. For Xalashka, despite living in a Russified country, where Russian was heavily imposed on the population by the government, she never learned Russian. She was born an Azeri village peasant and she died an Azeri village peasant, which was not uncommon.

Some Azeris who went to Russian language schools did learn the national language, but those who chose the Azeri *maktab* schools never or rarely did. Russian was a second language imperfectly taught in those schools and resentfully tolerated by the students and parents.

My family spoke Russian inside and outside the house, and because my brother and I had a grandmother who spoke only Armenian but understood some Russian, I was lucky to learn that language as well, which became useful later on when we had to flee to Armenia. However, I could only stammer in broken Azeri in response to Xalashka's extreme expressions of love for our children, so visible in her beaming face and the kisses and hugs she lavished upon them.

I found Xalashka to be a very unhappy and lonely woman. She never mentioned or shared anything about herself, and never afforded any opportunity to even ask her any personal questions. However, I noticed from time to time, when a neighbor engaged her in gossip about some other family, she would heatedly get involved, throwing out a few choice derogatory terms along with her advice.

"Throw out that prostitute!" she would scream. Or, "Send him to a sanitarium!" And, "If that no good bastard doesn't stop, she should divorce him!"

But about herself, Xalashka never gave anything away or provided background material in her own life that might be relatable. While she remained calm and laconic about her own past, she could suddenly burst out in very loud and aggressive diatribes about others.

She practically never smiled or showed her gold teeth, which was very typical in the village. She was exceedingly clean, and her house always sparkled. In the common Caucasian fashion, upon entering her apartment she would wipe her shoes with a damp cloth before slipping them off. The order in her home, however, was in stark contrast to her dearth of emotional harmony. Xalashka was irascible and demonstrative, which I always found very disconcerting and confounding. The smallest things would set her off. She was faster than matches. If she did not like something, which was quite often, she would suddenly start to shriek and say whatever was on her mind, completely uninhibited. You could see the veins in her neck bulging, ready to burst, as she screamed the most vulgar and obscene curses in Azeri.

She would scream at kids for playing and making noises as they ran around after one another or tossed a ball near her. And if one of their balls should accidentally reach her window, she would fly into a fury with a torrent of curses. Such episodes happened most often in the summer, when everyone spent time outside together. It made the contrast even starker compared with the tender affection this petite Azeri woman manifested towards my Armenian children.

One of the things that the children enjoyed most on a hot day was to cool off by pouring water on each other, as well as onto some of the adults, who also needed cooling off. The children would create their own water park, having a great time getting splashed and laughing. Everything would get soaked and the saturated ground would become an instant quagmire. The best part of the game for me was when the children, with the participation of the adults, would get up on the balcony of the second floor and throw water down onto the targets below.

Everyone enjoyed these activities, and no one complained except Xalashka. This was among the top issues that always seemed to set her off on her tirades. For her, fun and water did not go together. The water game relentlessly drove her into a fury. It was as if she simply could not tolerate any fun, any laughter, or any happiness. Her hysterical and choleric responses long puzzled me.

Always after these water games, everyone had to dry their clothes by hanging them on open windows and doors to be dried in the hot Baku summer sun and humid breeze that wafted in toward us from the Caspian Sea.

We called her Xalashka. In the Muslim language *Xal'* means an aunt. It is not necessarily a sign of being related by blood, but a sign of respect when talking to someone older than you, or someone with an official title or just unfamiliar to you. In many languages there is the formal part of grammar: speaking and writing as contrasted with the informal form which you use when talking to your parents, friends, animals, etc., like *tu* and *vous* in French.

Xalashka had one grandnephew, Samir, son of her niece, Salimah, who was notoriously the mistress of a noted Azeri prosecutor. Everyone in our "Italian quarter" knew everybody's private business and this clandestine relationship was not a secret, probably not even to his Azeri wife. It was not uncommon. In our courtyard there were two such Azeri cases.

Salimah used her aunt's apartment for her fortnightly trysts with her prosecutor lover. How did everyone in the courtyard know? In the hottest days of summer, the door was closed, and the curtains drawn on the site of their rendezvous. Hanna, our gossipy old Jewish neighbor, watching from her window, would see when Xalashka left, always with a rolled-up newspaper under her armpit.

Who knows why? Maybe, to fight off dogs?

She would return after a few hours with the same paper, as it was faithfully reported by Hanna.

People in the courtyard enjoyed playing a game in which they would walk by Hanna's window and suddenly spin around to catch her peeking out her window with curtain corner partly pulled aside. She would then come out and say, "I was just leaving." Then she would go back inside and then in thirty seconds she would do the same.

It was worth looking out the window if only because there were some prominent people living there, including a writer, a singer, a law enforcement family, a doctor, an engineer, and all had a parade of "famous" people visiting them. Hanna, acting as the courtyard archivist, would chronicle the names she recognized.

Almost every week, fourteen-year old, dark-eyed Samir came with his mother to visit Xalashka. He was very thin and tall for his age. Samir was from the village and his mother was trying to familiarize him in Baku with the ways of the city, where he was going to school, and introduce him to those among the upper levels of Azeri society where mother's lover held sway. As far as I remember, not one single visit of her niece and her son ever passed without some kind of clamorous conflict. Always, usually a very short time after they arrived at Xalashka's apartment, the visit would end in a raucous shouting match and invariably we would hear Salimah slam the door and leave with her son. Their departure did not prevent Xalashka from breaking out into even louder and more furious outbursts of anger.

We would hear and see these things, and some of them were hard to reconcile. There were times when we would see Samir running out of the apartment wailing as he rubbed his arms and yelled, "Ay Allah! Ay Allah! She pinched me! She bit me!"

These apparently were painful pinches and bites. We thought that the reason he might have spent any time at all with his great aunt was to fulfill the school district residency requirement. But we knew better, realizing that his mother's influential lover could have easily arranged residency for the young boy without putting him in harm's way, or more precisely in the way of Xalashka's ire.

They would stay away for a while until the next visit with the emotional fireworks display. Xalashka seemed to make no effort to compromise. It seemed to us that she would have been better off without them and she could enjoy that time alone, which was what Xalashka seemed to prefer anyway. She never visited any neighbors and absolutely never accepted any food, except from my family for some reason, yet she continued to maintain this singular, if contentious link to her own family. I never really understood this myself. It seemed completely pathological.

As if to coincide with her eccentric personality, Xalashka was afflicted by a very strange medical syndrome with consistent symptoms but no obvious etiology. Once every month, and every month it was, she would bleed profusely from her nose. These nose bleeds would last two or three days before tapering off. Many bath towels, old bed sheets or pillowcases were shredded and used to staunch the flow and keep the blood from soiling her house. After each episode, the pieces of red-stained rags were conspicuously tossed into the trash, which always left a trace of blood in the air, a lingering smell that Xalashka could never completely sanitize or cleanse away.

This may have been *psychosomatic epitaxis* caused by a neurosis like those classically described by Sigmund Freud whom Soviet society vehemently disparaged. One well-known historical example of this neurosis involves Maximilien Robespierre of the French Revolution who always bloodied his pillow with nosebleeds in times of stress.

My family helped her and supported her, but we knew that there was no possibility of intruding into her private life and getting her to see a doctor about this condition. For all we knew, maybe she did see one, though it was doubtful. It's easy for people like Xalashka to offer their opinions about what others should do to solve their quandary, but when it comes to their own problems; they never even talk about them, let alone try to solve them.

What was most baffling about Xalashka was that of all the fifty-six apartments in the unit, this Azeri woman socialized only with us Armenians. My mother was the sole human being allowed to help her and bring her food. I remember her looking frightfully ashen in the aftermath of the December bout, as if there was no blood in her body. Within a few days, some of the color returned to her face, but she still remained very strangely pale, like an old wall which did not get painted for many years, very faded and difficult to recognize the original hue.

Xalashka did not enjoy celebrating any of the annual holidays until my mother started to invite her to our New Year's celebration. Traditionally, people in Soviet Union celebrate the New Year around the holiday table with an abundance of different foods, champagne, and pastry. Preparation took a great deal of time. The New Year is a family secular holiday that all people looked forward to with great enthusiasm and pleasure. Xalashka never refused the invitation from my mother, who wanted to make sure her Azeri neighbor would not be left alone on New Year's Eve, a time when people reflect on the past and think about the future. My mother instinctively realized that the occasion was difficult for Xalashka, who would spend some time with us but always left as soon as the New Year was welcomed in at midnight.

It was not only baffling to us how much consideration and trust this querulous Azeri woman placed in us, her Armenian neighbors, and less to her own family. I remember one morning when Salimah, her niece, showed up while her aunt was on her walk. While she waited for Xalashka, I approached her and we had a brief conversation. It was one of the few times that I had ever spoken to her.

"I am surprised that she has such a close relationship with your family," Salimah stated plainly at one point. "She is a difficult person and she never associated with anyone before!"

Xalashka's fondness for my children, in particular, was evident, and she never made any effort to disguise the affection she had for them. Immediately after my daughter was born, and then my son, she came to visit them every day, sometimes two or three times a day. She would hold them and say nice and sweet things to them or sing an Azeri lullaby. I noticed that she was very protective of Arthur, whom she loved very much.

She used to say as she gesticulated with her hands, "I want to cut my heart open, put him inside, and keep him there."

During the days before the pogroms and the threat of Armenian genocide became a reality, Xalashka would take Arthur to school, despite how dangerous it was for us Armenians even to go outside. As things grew worse, the chances were good that you would meet someone looking for what the thugs called "adventure," which was really just the thrill of attacking Armenians after being riled up by the false stories of Armenian atrocities against Azerbaijanis in Karabakh. On one such perilous day, shortly after the Sumgait massacre, I recall that Xalashka volunteered to take my son to school. She walked in and announced, "It doesn't look good." She was fearful, but she was willing to do it.

At that time, I had been keeping Arthur out of school because of just such a threat, but he had missed so many calendar days already that when Xalashka said she would escort him, I considered it. Arthur wanted to go to school, and he got very excited, begging us to let her take him. In all probability, he was not really excited about school but by the chance to go out and escape from the boring house where we kept him sheltered.

I was torn, wondering how I could say "no" to a child who is so innocent, trusting, and possesses such a clean soul and explain to him that his only fault was being Armenian. How long could I keep the children prisoners in the house, where everything becomes colorless, uninteresting, tiresome and boring? How much of their childhood, of play time, of their youth could we take away from them? They were becoming adults too fast, and it was sad that they were learning how to hide from would-be attackers instead of playing without fear. They had to become adept at fighting and defending themselves and had to be careful what they said and where.

There had been a recent incident just two apartments away when my mother heard Arthur's voice crying. When she looked out into the courtyard, she heard an Azeri woman leaning over him screaming and shaking him by the front of his shirt. My mother, though not tall, was strong from lifting packages and boxes at her work, confronted the Azeri woman who was shouting anti-Armenian curses at the small boy. My mother grabbed the front of her dress and began pushing her repeatedly against the wall next to her own door. My mother held the woman there by force and would not let her go, but even as she reprimanded the Azeri woman for attacking a child, the woman continued to scream and yell out, "Dirty Armenian, dirty Armenian. Allah! Allah! ..."

As all the neighbors within earshot came rushing out, one Armenian old lady whispered into my mother's ear, "What are you doing? Don't you know what times we are living in? Tomorrow they can come and hurt you and your family. Let her go."

So it was with more than a little reluctance that I let Xalashka shepherd Arthur to school. She gripped his hand in hers and never let it go as they set out on the fifteen-minute walk to the school. It was not surprising that they quickly came across a group of Azeri toughs assembled on the sidewalk in front of the school. In those dangerous days, it was common to see young Azeris walking around in gangs looking for Armenian victims.

"This is an Armenian child and this woman is Azeri," one of the boys yelled out. "This is a humiliation for us. Why are you doing that, Xala?"

Xalashka turned very red and started screaming, "This is my baby, and you just try to come close to him. Just try it. Allah will curse you and your family. And I will curse you to become blind and not to see the funeral of your sisters and brothers!"

It was truly a wonder how a little old woman could exude such fury and inconceivable how frightening she could be perceived at the age of sixty-seven years old, especially considering that she appeared much older. But even this tough crowd backed off. Xalashka turned immediately around, gripping Arthur's hand tightly, and headed back home, never reaching the school. When they returned, I had a pretty good idea what had happened, but I didn't say anything. I kept looking out the window to make sure nobody had followed them.

We learned these details from Xalashka a short time later, and as she recounted the story she was trembling. I had a passing understanding of the Azeri language, which although it was a required subject in Russian schools, was not taken seriously by Russians, Armenians, and Jewish students.

I was never able to fully comprehend Xalashka's Azeri dialect, so my mother translated what she was saying into Russian for me.

"The boys on the corner," Xalashka said, "called me 'traitor' walking with dirty Armenian children who cut the hands off of our Azeri brothers in Karabakh."

After this incident, Xalashka never again offered to escort the children to school. She understood that it was no joke. We were now living in very perilous times.

It is absolutely reasonable for me to ask this question, which I have asked myself and others many times since this incident took place: Why would Xalashka take such a chance and risk her own life in those dangerous times? For this, she was seen as a traitor in the eyes of her own people, but she did it anyway.

Nobody had a good answer, and all I could do was hazard a wild guess. Maybe it was simply because Xalashka could not look away when she had such fond memories of us. Or perhaps it was due to her anti-violence stance and her strong opposition with all that was happening in Baku then. It could even be the horrific personal memory involving Xalashka's own dear children, a tragedy of which we were completely oblivious.

Many years passed before Xalashka revealed the entire dreadful story to my mother. It helped to explain a lot about this petulant Azeri woman and why she acted the way she did. It was a shocking revelation, even more so than the very notion that she had freely volunteered to impart such a personal and tragic story without being asked.

"I had three children," Xalashka began out of the blue as she sat with my mother over tea one typical morning.

"I lost all three of them in an instant. Two boys and a girl: Ali, Mostapha and Samirah. The range of their ages was only two or three years and they all were of school age."

My mother was shocked to hear this confession. "Oh, my God," was all she could say. "I'm so sorry."

"Bajim (Sister), this is the only time I will speak to you about this terrible tragedy of my life, and I will never mention it again. And, please, do not bring it up either. I carry it in my heart and mentioning it will make it burn in my breast. All I know is that I became a different person after the incident. In the name of Allah, I beg you never to mention it again to me!"

"I won't," my mother promised, both shocked and touched that Xalashka would confide in her. My mother, like the rest of us, thought that the details we were all begging to know about our Azeri neighbor were never going to be revealed and that Xalashka's secret would be buried with her. What was the date of the tragedy? Were the bodies of her children recovered? Where is their cemetery located? Did she ever visit them? Did she take any legal action? Was anybody found to blame or end up in jail? In all the years prior, Xalashka had never mentioned a single word about her husband, the father of her children. She never spoke about her marriage before or after the tragedy. But that was where her narration began the day she opened up to my mother.

"You know," Xalashka continued, "living in the village, children did not have many choices. No playground or park. Just the forest and swamp surrounded the village. It was during the school camping expedition. I am still not exactly sure how it happened, but they ended up on a patch of deep, swampy ground. One by one, the heavy, watery quagmire swallowed them all up, drowning them, and losing them forever to me. Don't ask what happened to me after. I don't know everything myself. When the terrible news reached me, I don't know what I did or said for a long time. They told me I went insane, and I had to stay in the hospital. I'm not sure which hospital I was confined to or for how long. Maybe I don't want to know."

My mother, aghast by Xalashka's confession, was practically shaking and unable to speak. It was too disturbing, too unsettling. She had never heard a tale more profoundly tragic and sad, and when my mother later told me and my family the story, none of us could believe it. Xalashka knew that we all wondered about her past, and she made it clear that she didn't mind my mother sharing the horror story with us.

"Because never in all these years did you ask me any questions, I volunteered it to you now," Xalashka told to my mother.

"One and only one time. That is the end of that!"

Xalashka did not know that my mother had a similar story of a lost child. The burden of guilt was heavier. My mother went to Armenia to visit her uncle and cousins. Next door, the daughter of the Armenian neighbors was dating an Azeri boy. She was forbidden to leave the house, under virtual house arrest.

She used the chance to trick my mother and her parents into letting her be a babysitter for Gurgyen, my mother's little boy, as an excuse to leave the house and have a chance to meet her boyfriend. Her parents never dreamed that she would be meeting a boyfriend while she was taking care of a baby. Neglecting Gurgyen, and too busy with her boyfriend, she allowed the little boy, to fall into a street trench and drown in a few inches of water. The uncle and cousins screamed at my mother and blamed her. But mostly my mother blamed herself.

Xalashka never spoke another word about any of it and my mother, true to her word, never asked her any questions, though we continued to ask ourselves questions through the years.

The definition of displacement in Freudian psychology is the transfer of an emotion from one object to another, good or bad. It is a defense mechanism which makes living with ourselves possible under adverse circumstances.

Could the hatred towards her nephew have been the displacement of her hatred of the reminders of her lost children who would be the age of the boy? Could her love for her children have been displaced onto love for my children? Could her hatred of water have been the reminder of the element that destroyed her young ones? Could her compulsive cleaning have been the displacement of her hatred of soil to scrub away the dirt that engulfed her children? All interesting questions to consider, though I did not know the answer.

The saga of Xalashka began to come to an end as we started to see less of her with the Azeri-Armenian conflict becoming more violent. It seemed clear to me that she was avoiding us at that time, which was understandable enough. In the final days before we left, Xalashka seemed to spend very little time at home, and we thought it was because it was hard for her to face us. The last time I saw Xalashka was the fateful day we were moving the children out of the city to relocate them to my aunt's. Xalashka seemed intent on avoiding us and was insistent that she needed to go for her walk after we had packed our things and were getting ready to leave. Just before we pulled away, Xalashka appeared and approached the car. She leaned into the open back window and whispered something softly to the children. I did not know what she said to them, and she did not exchange any words with the adults.

Even on the perpetually pale face that Xalashka bore, the parting moments showed her face flushed with emotion and sadness that her belligerent personality would ordinarily have hidden. Xalashka knew that she was not going to see the beloved children or any of us anymore. She was going to be lonely and losing her only support in Baku. Her expression reflected her extreme sadness.

Suddenly, without saying anything, Xalashka reached into one of the deep pockets of the typical flowery village housedress she wore and took out a heavy cup filled with water and cast it upon the family car. In Islam, water is important for cleansing and purifying and is used in several different ablution rituals. What Xalashka did was a gesture of good luck, but it was also ironic because she so hated it when the children played with water and splashed her, and now she was essentially doing the same thing to them. To me, it had an even deeper meaning.

Water is a good servant but is also a cruel master and a destroyer.

In Baku, we were drowning. If we didn't escape now, we never would. For Xalashka, old, alone and stuck in her ways, was no longer in a quagmire, she was trapped in quicksand.

She watched our car as we pulled away. We never heard anything about Xalashka after that day, but after many years in our exile in America, we telephoned an Armenian neighbor in the courtyard who informed us that Xalashka had passed away in an insane asylum. By the end of her life, she was unable to speak, though she would occasionally speak the word, "*Su, su, su*" over and over. It seems she could not escape the water and that quicksand was in her mind. *Su* means "water" in Azeri.

It was sad to learn of her passing, but we had lots of memories of her, the love she showed us and the courage she had to befriend an Armenian family that so many other Azeris considered their enemy.

In Jerusalem there is a monument and museum dedicated to the "Righteous Gentiles," those non-Jews who at great risk harbored and helped Jews avoid the Nazi killing machine at their own great risk. There is no such monument in Baku for people like Xalashka, but there should be.

CHAPTER 6

The End of Camelot

"**N**O MATTER HOW MUCH YOU FEED THE WOLF, HE STILL LOOKS TO *the Forest.*" This metaphor, with minor variation, credited to Ilse Lehiste, the noted Estonian-born American linguist, speaks to me of the tragedy of the multiethnic society that failed in Baku, even though there was much intermarriage.

At one time, the former capital of the Soviet Republic of Azerbaijan was heralded as a kind of Camelot, in part for just such diversity. With the city's wealth in petroleum, cotton, sturgeon, and caviar, along with industrial production, it had an abundance of resources that were exploited by Russians, Armenians and Jews alike, all of whom were attracted to this magnificent seaside city through the decades of boom times.

The native Azeris also prospered, though because they lagged behind in education, European training and certain progressive attitudes, they did not representatively fill the higher-level posts, and thus occupied the more menial positions.

Just as inner corruption destroyed Arthur's Court of the Knights of the Round Table, the once-resplendent Baku is gone forever. It made its riches in oil—there is a reason it is often referred to as "black gold." But because the Azeris in Baku wanted what they thought was rightfully theirs, they instituted a program many years before the massacres to remake Baku in the image of the Arab emirates. They constructed gaudy skyscrapers in bad taste, another indicator that the multi-cultural peace that Baku had so long enjoyed was soon to come to an end.

Evil is hard to confront. When the Sumgait massacre was happening, we had no idea. The Russian state media did not let on that devastation was happening so close to home. The only inkling was a cryptic phone call from the Azeri husband of a friend.

"Don't talk, listen to me!" the stern voice on my telephone intoned very firmly as I rubbed my eyes in confusion, still half asleep. Disoriented, I looked at the clock. It's midnight.

"Don't send the kids to school tomorrow!" the voice warned in conclusion.

My heart started to beat faster at the slightest indication of danger touching my children in what was already a highly toxic, poisonous atmosphere for us Armenians.

It was Vagif, I realized. He was a doctor, an internist, and an Azeri Muslim whom I knew. He was married to a friend of mine, Nonna, who was Jewish. Such interethnic marriages were not rare in Baku, but this late-night call was very odd.

"Why?" I screamed at him. "Why?"

He was no longer on the phone, however, so I was given no explanation. I was more confused than concerned when I dropped off to sleep, and when I awoke the next morning, I was puzzled by my decision to heed Vagif's advice and keep the kids home from school. I'm sure if it had been almost anyone else, someone I did not trust as much, I would have disregarded the warning.

I asked my mother to watch over the children that day while I went to work. It did not make sense for me to stay home. My mother was there, and the warning was not directed toward me. To save her from worrying, I did not tell her about the phone call. Neither of us had any intimation of the atrocities taking place in Sumgait at this time. My mother was shocked, unable to fathom any reason why the children should not go to school that morning. But she listened to me and stayed home with the children.

As I got on my bus and settled into a seat, I immediately perceived the uneasiness among the other passengers. People spoke in hushed conversations and looked suspiciously at each other.

There was a tangible tension which indicated to me that something was wrong.

Close to my stop, near the border of the industrial town of Sumgait, I saw two military tanks blocking the road.

"Did you hear what happened here in Sumgait?" I overheard one stocky older passenger whisper to no one in particular, but no one had the temerity to spell out the horrid facts right there.

What had occurred was that Armenians were butchered and violated, hacked to death with axes, women gang-raped in the open. Azeri crowds had gone on a rampage, destroying and looting, and only twenty miles from my Baku, the capital city of the "New Soviet Man."

It was inconceivable to me that such a thing could happen there. All my life, living in this "perfect" Communist system in Russia, nothing bad ever happened, certainly nothing as heinous as this kind of systematic massacre. Anything remotely bad was kept secret. Even after Chernobyl, when radioactive debris was spewing into the air and wafting along by the winds, poisoning vegetables and dropping venomous particles onto the grass that cows chomped on producing contaminated milk, the danger was downplayed. The nuclear accident turned out to be far worse than the Kremlin let on. The government lied to its citizens as deadly radiation invisibly damaged the ecosystem and threatened the health and lives and people all over Europe, not just the Soviet Union. Everything was reputed to be "fine," just as we were all trained to believe. It might be hard for capitalist countries, anyone outside the Iron Curtain, to take in, that you didn't believe in yourself; you believed in the government.

Over the course of the day, I would learn all about the violence in Sumgait, and when I got home, the first thing I wanted to do was to thank

Vagif for his late-night message. I immediately called his home and spoke to his wife Nonna, thanking her effusively for what her husband did.

I didn't have to say it, but we both understand how significant it had been for him as an Azeri man to give us that warning. He must have observed the results of the mayhem the night before while he was on call in the emergency room. The humanity he showed in going out of the way to think of me and my children showed that not all Azeris were members of the wolf pack.

"I actually had no idea he called you," Nonna confessed to me. "You know we don't really talk to each other much anymore. We used to arrange our hours so that we could be together. Now he works when I'm home. I work when he's home. Our excuse is my son."

At the moment, I was just glad he had been willing to talk to me. I will always consider it a blessing, and something that I will never forget.

Nonna, my Jewish friend and neighbor for twenty years, was an interesting woman. Like her husband, she was also a doctor, a cardiologist. She wore glasses, had these very thin legs and hands, and suffered from an unusual and maddening malady, minor though it was. Her joints made a loud cracking noise whenever she bent her wrists, elbows or knees. Every time she sat down or lifted things, even picking up a cup of tea, you would hear a loud crack.

"No cure," she had confided in me one day. "It's called *crepitus*. I have to live with it." She casually explained to me that there are no serious consequences. "It's like when people have a nervous habit of cracking their knuckles. A little bubble of air pops in between the joints."

I don't know if it had anything to do with her condition or not, but Nonna did not keep a very neat house. Her Azeri husband, however, assisted with the household chores. It is untypical for a man of Azerbaijani nationality to do so. Not too tall, a little chubby with dark hair, Vagif was by all accounts a nice man. He was genuinely concerned about Nonna, particularly her heavy smoking. He found for her what he called "healthier cigarettes."

Noisy joints and untidy house aside, she was a great friend.

Her one weakness, if it could be called that, was that she liked to go out to play cards with a mixed group of friends once a week until it was very late at night. She would not be averse to picking up the phone and calling her husband from her card party to ask him to bring over some cold champagne because it was hot, and she was thirsty.

"What a solicitous husband!" one of the women would invariably exclaim.

But when the psychic among them, Sopha was entreated by the group to "open the cards," it was always the same result when it was Nonna's turn to have her cards interpreted.

"You're not going to stay with your husband," Sopha would bluntly inform her.

"No way!"

"The cards never lie. The Queen of Hearts card is upside down in the family spot. The seven in black means seven months."

It was always upsetting for Nonna to hear this because it was her second marriage.

"I am a scientific woman," she would carp, "and I only go along with this nonsense for fun, but I don't set any store by it. Last time Sopha predicted I would meet a tall, dark and handsome stranger, the Jack of spades, and go on a long trip! What happened to that?"

Her son, Semyon, was from her prior marriage. At eleven years old, he was bordering on obese, and although Vagif was not the boy's father—he had two grown children from his own previous marriage many years before—he would look after the child when Nonna was at work.

For some reason that I can only speculate on, his Azeri ex-wife and her relatives had turned against him, though it seemed that they wanted to reconnect with him now that he was successful. When Nonna first came into his life, he was a wreck. He was paying alimony, losing the house and other properties to his ex-wife. His own Azeri relatives were unsupportive. He had only a part-time job. Nonna, a divorced Jewish woman with a son, receiving child support and an inheritance from her family, had a full-time job as a doctor, and was living in her own home in one of the best areas of Baku.

Nonna came into the picture for Vagif at just the right time and provided him firm guidance and support because he was a soul adrift. She accepted him in her house, improved how he dressed, taught him how to act in non-Azeri society, coaching him on his medical exams and assisting him in getting a full-time job as a physician.

It was the Greek myth of Pygmalion and Galatea, only in reverse. In this case, rather than sculptor falling in love with his creation, a beautiful stone statue of a woman, it is Jewish Nonna who molds Azeri Vagif into a successful physician in Baku through her contacts and financial backing. She introduced him to a separate world, taught him how to live, dress, comport himself and think in a different way from his Azeri village past. She married the statue she has sculpted and brought to life.

However, as he began getting drawn back into the lives of his grown children, Nonna observed this as a magnet slowly pulling him back into his old Azeri world. He, in contrast, started seeing her independence and freedom through the old eyes of the Azeri Muslim man who believes he has the entitlement and authority to maintain strict control of women.

When Sumgait happened, like others, I feared that this is only the beginning. Even though none of us believed it could ever happen in Baku, I paid attention to what people were doing. I made a trip to Moscow to get the "lay of the land," to see if immigration back to Armenia was even a possibility. There I learned about the long lines and whispers. You never knew when the KGB would appear and you would be carted away to parts unknown, branded a "traitor to the state," and conveniently disappear. It was September 1988, a year before Poland declared its independence in "Solidarity" and the fall of the Berlin Wall separating East and West Germany. In 1988, the "Iron Curtain," was still doing its best to hold strong. The official government stance was firm: there was nothing wrong with the mighty brotherhood of the USSR.

The Jewish community maintained a very different outlook, as they started to collectively whisper in one voice, *"When they are finished with the Armenians, they are coming after us!"*

Those who remained steadfast and decided to stay in Baku soon noticed that many important people in their lives were gone, having emigrated to

Israel, the United States, Holland, or Australia. Nonna herself had a sister in Australia who offered her the chance to get an entrance visa, not as a refugee like the Armenians, but as an emigrant. As the conflict in the streets become uglier and more vicious, Nonna started to observe Vagif revert back to the village Azeri of the old days, like the wolf reared as a tame pet dog reverts to the wild beast of the forest and attacks his masters. I didn't want to believe it. This is the man who called to warn me about Sumgait, who helped keep my family safe.

It was a crazy, mixed-up time, but I had to pay attention to my friend.

One day, I got a telephone call early in the morning. It was Nonna. She was calling from the Skoraya Pomoshch (Emergency Room) where she was on duty.

"Karina, Are you at home? Are you at home? Where have you been?" she asked me. "I've been calling you yesterday all night."

"Well, I went to bed early, Nonna, and unplugged the phone," I said, my voice agitated. "You know my mother has high blood pressure, and I don't want to disturb her."

"*Ungrateful! Moron! Son of a bitch! Bastard!*" the words shot out with machine-gun rapidity. I could tell that she was puffing heavily on her cigarette.

"Calm down, Nonna. Tell me what's going on."

"What's going on? You can't imagine what happened! Wait for me! I'm coming right over!" she shouted between coughs and tears of rage.

Since it was close by, she was in my apartment in a few minutes, trembling and coughing.

"That bastard! That fucking *Chooshka*! Vagif, he's turning into one of those Muslim genocidal terrorists. All they think of is killing. He told me, these are his exact words; he said,

"Hitler knew what he was doing, frying those Jews. Too bad he didn't get all of you and finish the job."

"What, Nonna? He told you that? And you, Jewish! And after eleven years of marriage? Not to mention all that you did for him, the high position he's reached with your help? Oh, my God, Nonna!"

"That fucking *Chooshka*!" she repeated, puffing away. "*Chooshka*" is the pejorative term used by themselves, the citified Azeris, and other nationalities alike for the village peasant Azeri, like in the United States: "redneck" or "hillbilly."

"We Armenians say, *The Chooshkas are good until they can be bad.*" I quoted the adage. "But Nonna, take it easy. Watch out. Don't follow your impulses. Don't throw him out of the house. God knows he can harm you and your son."

"I have such a headache!" Nonna moaned.

"Just take some medication; I have some here, Nonna. But you're a doctor. Try to calm down because you have your child involved," I warned her, "and an apartment to take care of; make your move very carefully. Do not let him know any plans you have."

"I know exactly what to do," Nonna said confidently, emphasizing each word with an ominous cadence separated by coughs.

It turns out that Nonna did know what to do, designing a bizarre plan to gain her freedom.

Months later, Nonna opened up to me, laying out the events, as she lifted a teacup in my kitchen to her lips with a loud crack of her joints. What she told me stunned me.

"You'll never believe what I did," she confided to me.

"This is what happened."

"As you know, my husband started reverting, acting and thinking more and more like one of the bloodthirsty Azeris. Those Azeris like him want to kill all the Armenians and next us, the Jews. I knew that our relationship was obviously fractured to the point where there is no saving it. An unexpected opportunity fell into my lap to set my plan into motion right in the hospital where I work."

"It all began when I was treating a young, handsome Armenian patient, Valerik Martirossov. While waiting for his medication to take effect we started talking.

"Well, Valerik, it looks okay, but we have to wait a few minutes more. Calm down. Let's chat about what everybody is talking about. Your situation as an Armenian here in Baku is more and more dangerous. I, too, have misgivings as a Jew. All the other nationalities in Baku are in danger from the Azeris, including my people. Tell me, Valerik, what are you going to do?"

"I knew America was accepting Armenians as refugees. I submitted all the paperwork, and I've been waiting for almost two years now," Valerik told me.

"A friend of mine got a fast okay and already has left with his family to America. He had an application pending. The Armenians are luckily zipping along fast to America without all the holdups and delays to other countries."

He turned to me and asked, "And you and your husband, what are you going to do, Doctor?"

"He's not Jewish and not Armenian. He is Azeri and he does not want to leave Baku. He tells me, '*I am your husband. Nobody will do anything to you.*'"

"If you can believe that," Valerik said, then added,

"Would this be satisfactory to you living in a world of Azeri enemies?"

I looked at the young man and said,

"Let me tell you a story.

"Rabbi Shmuel on his deathbed said, 'My children. Come close. I have something very important to tell you.'

'What, Papa? What? What?'

"The children came close and the rabbi whispered, 'Remember ... keep ... Armenians!'

'What do you mean, papa? What do you mean?'

Valerik shook his head and smiled, "We have the same story. An old Armenian is on his deathbed said, 'My children remember to defend the Jews.'

'Why Jews?'

'Because when they finish with Jews; they are coming after us! We will be next.'"

I told Valerik, "It's not just that, I have to confess to you that our marriage is on the rocks. He's becoming more and more the *Chooshka* I first met and helped educate to be a modern Soviet citizen and doctor. I am afraid for myself and my Jewish little boy."

"Do you want to move to another part of USSR?" Valeriy asked me.

"I don't know. I have my married sister in Australia. She's trying to facilitate the process to get us out of this degenerate country. Here, I am a human doctor. There, I can be a kangaroo cardiologist. My husband as an internist can treat the koala bears."

Later that evening, to her husband, Nonna would say, "We're getting ready to move to Australia. We have to change our plans. We were under the impression we have to restore our relationship. But my sister says that to proceed with the Australian government paperwork we have to come as a divorced couple. On top of that, you know my sister is against you. After a few months in Melbourne, I can take control out of my sister's hands and get a visa for you. While you are waiting here in Baku, we have our nice apartment here which you can put up for sale."

"Nonna, you are a fabulous actress if you can carry this crazy plan out," I told her.

She sighed and answered only, "God, I hate him!"

However, I only heard part of her master plan.

Initially, Vagif reacted in shock as he deliberately considered Nonna's proposition. During this time, she stopped by my apartment often to talk with me while she was awaiting Vagif's decision. I could tell she was nervous, tense. She wanted very badly to be rid of Vagif for good. She was practically chain-smoking by this point. I had to ask her not to smoke with my baby daughter, Ani, in my apartment. I continued to warn her to keep cool and stay in control. One mistake and she would lose everything. I wanted to help ensure that she did not open the Pandora's Box and tell her husband anything. Nonna referred to our talks as "psychological torture chambers."

When Vagif finally agreed to the divorce because it was one of "convenience," Nonna was suspicious and not able to enjoy this good news fully. "Maybe he has something in mind for his own sweet reasons," Nonna cynically confided to me. "The divorce is easy. We will have it in a few weeks."

I was an amazed witness to the convoluted happenings in this surreal drama and tried to be supportive to my good friend Nonna, but what realistic advice could I give in an unrealistic topsy-turvy world all around us? Moreover, I was not aware of the fully bizarre nature of her plans.

It was almost too good to be true, but Nonna began the next phase of her carefully thought-out plan. She placed a phone call to Valerik, the handsome young Armenian patient, the teacher of mechanical drawing whom she had treated at the emergency room.

"Valerik, can you come and meet me in the Polyklinika Medical Center? It's important!"

"What?" he reacted with nervous tension. "Why? What's wrong with me?"

"It has nothing to do with your health. Just come."

He did and over a cup of tea, she offered him her shocking business proposition.

"We don't know each other very well, Valerik," she began, "but I'm going to tell you something strange and maybe you are not going to think very well of me."

"Tell me the truth. Is there something seriously wrong with me?" Valerik pleaded.

"No. Not at all. Trust me. There is nothing wrong with your health. You know all the rules are broken in this crazy situation in Baku. We have to do what we have to do to survive. I am married to an Azeri who is treating me badly. I want to get away. You showed up as a patient, and I am desperate to escape. You have a golden key to escape as an Armenian refugee going to America. I have divorced my husband. He thinks it's a way to get our papers to go to Australia. It opens a door for me to get the hell out of here with the Armenians getting killed and raped every day, and we Jews are next."

"What door?" Valerik asks, confused. "I don't understand. You're not Armenian."

"Yes, but if I marry you, I become an Armenian refugee as the wife of an Armenian refugee. Don't say anything till I explain further. I'm referring to a commercial marriage only, Valerik, or *mariage de convenance* as they say in French. Don't worry about anything. As soon as we get to America as

Armenian refugees, you go your way and I go my way. I believe divorce is just as easy in America. Their movie stars are getting divorced every minute."

"And do not worry about my husband. He's not my husband in my mind or in my heart, and now not even on our passports now. He thinks our divorce is a formality to get us out of here faster. He doesn't know this to be true or not, but I just want to forget him and wipe off his name from my life. I told you that all my close friends have moved to America. I have relatives there. I think I'd be lonely in Australia, full of snakes and deserts. I don't know, I just want to get out. I want to get out as soon as possible. The fastest way now is to go to America with that precious label you have: "Armenian refugee status."

Valerik sighs. "Yes, I see. This is very bad."

It is very unusual for a Russian interchange to put all the cards on the table. The Queen of Hearts may have been dealt face up now in the gypsy fortune cards layout.

"I've had enough!" Nonna exclaimed. "I could wait for Australia with my sister's help, Valerik, but I'm desperate to get away as fast as possible. You are my only hope to get out quickly. My Azeri husband is treating me and my son badly. I am Jewish; my son is Jewish. There is no future for us in this country."

Valerik's face showed hesitation.

"If you are worried about any expenses," Nonna offered, "I'll take care of myself and my son, and I am willing to offer you money, as well." Nonna reached over and patted him on the back of his hand.

Her hand movement brought forth a noisy crack in her arm joints which startled Valerik and as he suddenly drew back, he spilled his tea. Nonna mumbled an uncomfortable apology as she sopped up the spill with a napkin from his lap.

"Valerik, what do you have to lose except gaining an unwanted wife on paper?" she continued.

"Think about it. It would be really be a big help for me. It will also make things a little smoother for you."

Afterward, Nonna came to visit me at my apartment and told me everything.

"I can't believe that I did that," she said, "or that I could ever do that. But I did. I did!" she kept trying to light her cigarette with the lighter in her shaking hands. My daughter wasn't there so I permitted her to smoke.

A few days later, Valerik called with his reply and accepted her marriage proposal. They went for a speedy civil marriage with only an office employee as witness. No picture of the bride in the paper. No wedding march. No publicity. No banquet, just an official marriage license.

I knew the routine of signing up with the American Embassy in Moscow because of the trip I had made some months prior to find out what I needed to do and start the initial process of getting declared "refugee." I gave Nonna a step-by-step account of everything she needed to know, from the waiting line to the machine that gives you the number in line. I even described the color of the rug.

She told her now ex-husband that she would take care of everything on her trip to Moscow at the Australian Embassy. He wanted to come along, but she argued about the expense, losing time at his job, and needing to take care of her son, Semyon. He swallowed it hook, line, and sinker.

Valerik, her co-conspirator, made the trip on his own to the Moscow embassy. He was an unmarried man who was waiting for years to leave. It is quite natural that in the meantime he had taken a wife. It was nothing unusual. The embassy now viewed the two of them as a married couple falling under the category of "Armenian refugees from Baku," which made the case of emergency even stronger because it was an Armenian and Jewish mixed couple, both threatened by the same enemy.

Before they left for Moscow, they had made arrangements to speedily fly to their safe haven in New York, sponsored by one of Valerik's cousins. Our family was still on the waiting list to go to America when we learned that the newlyweds were out of the country and safely in New York City.

I was kept informed by mail and telephone of this bizarre adventure of my friend Nonna.

Shortly after arriving in America, Nonna called to inform me of something her sister in Australia told her. Her sister, who knew of the plan all along, milked the situation fully to vent her hatred on the Azeri Vagif when he telephoned her in Melbourne expecting to hear Nonna's voice.

"She's not here right now," she told him.

"Where is she?" Vagif demanded.

"I'm not sure," she answered with a stabbing vagueness that she knew would cut Vagif.

"The world is a big place."

"Isn't she with you?"

"No, not with me," she says, then, twisting the knife.

"With her husband."

"Husband? I'm her husband!"

"Not anymore, sweetheart. She's in America married to a young, handsome Armenian who you want to kill. Catch her if you can." She laughed and gleefully slammed the telephone down.

Behind Vagif's back, Nonna had made arrangements to "sell" their home to the neighbors. The apartment had always been in her name, and he never thought to change it after the divorce. Since all property belonged to the government, paperwork for residency in a nice apartment was a tangible asset with transfers involving exchange of money and calling up favors owed to connections. With her prompt action, Nonna had sabotaged any possible hope of Vagif being listed as the owner.

She told me with triumph in her voice, "Vagif will be lucky if he can beg to stay in the apartment as a tenant." Shortly afterwards, I heard that Vagif, indeed, had to vacate and move everything of his out of the apartment.

Three months later, I received a call from Moscow, where I maintained a temporary mailing address. I was informed that I had letters waiting for me there. I retrieved them and searched for a hopeful response from the American Embassy in the pile of mail, but there is none to be found yet.

Among the mail items, however, was a colorful picture postcard from Nonna. It showed the famous water fountain and statue in front of Rockefeller Center on the front. On the verso, the postmark was stamped New York City, and in the small space on the left was a message.

'Karina, this is a copy for you of what I wrote on the postcard I sent to Vagif from here in New York City:

Dear Vagif,

I wish you would be in Hell. You were born an animal and you will die an animal. And you are staying where you belong in that shit. Fuck you and your ethnicity.

Regards,
Your JEWISH ex-wife.'

My close friend Nonna behaved cruelly, perhaps deservedly, to Vagif, the same man who took a risk warning me on the telephone to protect my children when the atrocities of Sumgait were taking place. Here is another face of this terrible human tragedy. I sympathized with my friend for her hateful predicament, fearing for herself, and her son from a man who deteriorated under the violent influence of his countrymen and the environment of hatred. But I still harbor feelings of gratitude to him for what he did that night with his telephone call warning me not to take my children to school that terrible day. This shows how violent times of ethnic conflict can summon up the best and the worst in people.

CHAPTER 7

Soviet Mentality

S OVIET MENTALITY IS A TERM OFTEN USED BUT UNEXPLAINABLE TO readers of other cultures. It was only seventy-odd years from the time Stalin's forces won their revolution in 1917 to the Fall of the Berlin Wall in 1989. But in the span of one generation, the Soviet mindset had become pervasive.

It was pretty straightforward. The government would take care of everything for you — and I mean everything. In exchange you were to never question its almighty power. No one would dare challenge it — or if they did, there was always some sort of hell to pay.

A small but significant incident when I was still in school will shed some light on what I mean.

Many societies have rigid standards for schooling. The story of the bureaucrat in Paris who opens a logbook and states, "Everywhere in France at this moment, at 2:30 p.m.," looking at his pocket watch, "in the fourth grade, the students are studying the agreement of the past participle in gender and number with the preceding direct object." This Napoleonic system influenced the education systems of all Continental Europe, trickling down to the Russian Empire, then the Soviet Empire wherever it was in power.

In the Soviet Union, the rigidity was of tempered steel. I as a young girl and being a voracious reader made the mistake of making a personal comment about the demigod of Russian poetry, Alexander Pushkin. His novel in verse, *Eugene Onegin*, concerns the love story of a young girl in eighteenth century Russia. I made the mistake of writing down a comment that "nowadays no young girl would act as obediently to her parents' wishes" as in this masterpiece of Russian verse.

I was called out of class to the headmaster's office to the stares and giggles of my fellow students. Going to the principal's office is never treated lightly. In his office, there circled around me, with sour faces, two teachers of literature and my home room teacher. They read aloud my composition. "It is not according to the study guide," one teacher said.

"Where did you get that idea to criticize Russia's greatest literary genius, Pushkin? The glory of our nation! (Which means Russia, not the Azerbaijani Republic.) The glory of the world!"

The idea came from reality. Our European Jewish neighbors in the courtyard next door would sound through the paper-thin walls their yelling and screaming at Olga, their daughter, a friend of mine but much older than me, a young teenager. She was going out with a boy they did not approve of. He was a Tat, or Mountain Jew. They looked down on them because they acted more like village Azeris than European Jews.

Olga retorted, "You are still living in the past. These old-fashioned ideas don't apply anymore!"

I, as an inexperienced young girl was fascinated by the drama of my older neighbor girlfriend challenging her parents.

It made a great influence on me and was in the back of my mind as I read the poem of the strict parents exerting their will on Tatiana in the novel. No way! Not in this modern world. Not in Baku, even with the Moslem Azeris who forced marriages on their daughters, and certainly not with modernized city Armenian or Jewish families.

Why do you disagree with her mother's decision?" a teacher on her break sitting in the office interjected. Expressing your own opinion in a composition, even though the instructions were to state what you think of this masterpiece of Russian literature was all right, but my neighbor's situation made a much stronger impression on me than this classic novel.

They very gently tried to change my mind and tried to find out where it was coming from. I could not tell them what I was feeling after hearing all the drama coming from the other side of the wall sympathizing with my young neighbor. It was very intriguing for me as an inexperienced young girl.

It was the first real love story I had heard in my life and the parallel with Tatiana in Pushkin's novel was too close to reality. I don't know why I was called to the office. Maybe it was disagreeing with the great writer. But I sympathized with my neighbor who shared her secrets with me. It made me feel very important and involved that I as a much younger girl had someone sharing conflict and drama with me. My personal reaction to Tatiana's dilemma did not fit in with the standard composition: she must obey her parents, marry their choice and be happy.

If the same thing occurred in America, my parents could have taken it up at a Parent/Teachers meeting or a visit to the principal, and I am sure some do exactly that today. Jehovah's Witnesses refuse to pledge allegiance to the flag. That is their religious right guaranteed by the U. S. Constitution. In the sixties some hippy parents challenged the antiquated political clichés in the old textbooks and the antiquated teachers in their children's schools.

We were not raised to question anything. For many years, because we had nothing different, I thought what we grew up with was "good." It was an eye-opening experience to find out about my old school.

"Don't even think about that!" Elmira Rubenovna leaned over and firmly spoke into my ear, not wanting anyone in those dangerous times to hear her words on the main shopping street of Baku, Torgovaya Ulitsa.

I told her excitedly that I wanted to switch my kids to my old school in the city where I graduated, and she had been a teacher of literature. I was still living in Baku and there was still strong belief that the horrors of Sumgait would never happen in Baku. By that time most of the teachers had left the school, Russians, Jewish, Armenians, and even some Moslems. The Azeris were taking over all the good things: Armenian jobs, Armenians' properties, Armenian belongings, and Armenian lives. But I was one of many that believed Sumgait atrocities would never take place in Baku and things would go back to normal. The military was there to protect us.

They pretended protecting; we pretended believing.

I saw her hesitate for thirty or forty seconds trying to decide how to respond.

"Should I slap her face to wake her up? Should I say something rude and swear at her? … Are you stupid or do you live on the moon?"

"The school you remember which was number one in quality is not what you remember. It's not what you think. It is not Number One School anymore. It's become a typical *maktab*, a Moslem village school."

The impact of her words and her rigid posture drove me to walk one street away to take a look at the school I had gone to for ten years. I wanted to give my beloved school the benefit of the doubt. The building itself had a sad gray look as if it were crying. The students who were walking out were all dark, the girls with Moslem scarves on their heads. Students in my day always had worn starched white blouses and shirts, but the students now wore gray or black and their stance and movements were gloomy. I was convinced that Elmira Rubenovna was right.

We had had the typical conversation then of Armenians and Jews, "Are you going? Are you staying? What are you doing?" It was hard for Elmira Rubenovna because she had old parents.

I met her the following year in Moscow at a session preparing Baku exiles to learn how to move to America as refugees. "I'm here to find out, but it's difficult." She seemed to be occupied with not being able to break her loyalty to Communist ideology; the transition was very difficult for her.

The school was the best in the city and proud of it. Everybody referred to it as "the Jewish school" It had a staff mostly of Jewish and Armenian teachers.

I remember the day the director walked into our classroom to announce, "Comrade Isaak Einemer, head of the Department of Russian Language and Literature, is no longer teaching at our school. The poor misguided creature decided to betray us. We hear that he is washing dishes in the back of a Tel Aviv restaurant in Israel."

Many of our teachers had titles of merit as outstanding teachers. One of these looked like Stalin. He had been injured in the war and always showed up late for class. We could hear his heavy stumbling steps echoing in the empty corridor as he approached. He was big, handsome, with hair combed back on his head. Everyone was afraid of him. In the middle of a world history class, he caught a girl, Khaimovich, in front of me sneakily reading a book in her lap.

Russian teachers never hesitated to humiliate students in front of the class with sarcasm.

"What are you reading there? Tell us about your interesting book, more interesting than our class!"

She stood up.

"Give it to me!" The girl reluctantly handed the book over to our formidable teacher. "Aha, George Sand's *Consuelo*."

Then after a short pause, he asked, "Who is George Sand?"

I in a moment of mischievous fun, I leaned forward and sabotaged her with a whispered falsity which she repeated, "He is a man, a French writer."

The class burst into laughter.

"So, the writer of intimate love stories of women's sensibilities is a *man*?! What a revelation! You have to send your discovery to *Literaturnaya Gazeta*. Sit down! And read books you can understand!"

Fifty percent of students between classes would be reading. One day, near the end of the quarter, I was caught up with all my assignments. At that stage, usually the teacher would only call on students who were falling behind. I felt confident. I would not be called on, and I was in the back near the wall covered with portraits of Einstein, Newton, and Galileo. I suddenly heard the silence all around me. Pavel Mikhailovich, the physics teacher, came silently and stood next to me. If I had known he was coming, I would have hidden the book. He caught me at my desk reading the Hindu manual of love, *The Kama Sutra*, very interesting for a sixteen-year-old.

He took the book walked to his desk.

Some of the students knew what I was reading and started giggling. The book was circulating around in our unofficial book club of unofficial books.

"See me after class," he said, pinching his nose, a habit of his.

After class he said to me, "What are you reading? It must be interesting, more interesting than physics."

"Oh, I just started it. I don't know."

"You're on page 42. You just started?"

I apologized. "No."

"I have to talk to your parents." My teacher was emphatic.

My mother threatened me. "It's bad enough I have to go to school about your brother all the time and now for you. No phone calls. No friends' visits. Where did you get that shit?"

Pavel Mikhailovich never returned the confiscated book to me. He must have read it himself.

Also in the curriculum was the necessary teaching of the language of the Azerbaijan Republic, a Turkic language, Azeri, which was written in Russian alphabet with a few added artificially constructed symbols. I never paid attention to the class and had no interest in it. Nobody paid attention. It was like a singing class, easy to pass.

Who were these Azeris was a joke to us Armenians. Our alphabet was one of the first in Europe and Asia. The very name "Azeri" for our Moslem neighbors was a recent invention. They had been called "Caucasian Turks," "Caucasian Tatars," and finally named after a neighboring province in Iran called Azerbaijan where a Turkic minority lived. My mother and father spoke fluent Azeri to pursue their occupations and deal with customers in their jobs but as far as reading Azeri literature, it was not a concept.

Another class we did not take seriously was Political Economy. It was Marxism-Leninism with a touch of Engels and Stalin. I took it as "gut course" elective. Nina Federovna was the Russian teacher who caught me reading a newspaper *Arguments and Facts,* a kind of Russian *Believe it or Not!* She called me to the front and asked, "Did you do your homework?"

"No."

"Tell us about what you are reading."

About three times I answered no.

"Tell us."

I talked to the class about an article in this scarce newspaper that my father subscribed to and received because of a "connection." I talked about unusual complications of law and juicy, unusual historical facts. I held the class in fascination and the teacher herself was in rapt attention. After twenty minutes there was a bell.

"Well, I have to give you 5 (*equivalent to A+*)," she said. "Not because you know anything about Political Economy. But your tongue is hanging in the right place."

School Number One is one point of evidence about the partial success of the "New Soviet Man" in Baku. Classes were delivered in Russian. We were all avid readers in the Russian language.

In 2004 an international reunion of graduates of Baku School Number One took place in New York City. They came from Australia, France, United Kingdom, Canada, New Zealand, Germany, Italy, all successful in their exile, still loyal to their memories of a quality educational institution that is no more. The same can be said about the city of Baku. We heard the joke in New York: Baku lost the gold hands and minds and welcomed instead gold teeth. They lost the Jews and Armenians and got instead the village Moslem peasants of the countryside.

In the Soviet Union there was no leeway. There wasn't even any concept of "leeway." The government controlled who received what benefits. It made sure only "good" news was broadcast on the national media. It was supposed to free us from the "capitalist" mentality, and we were "free" because we supposedly had no worries. We had plenty of worries. It was a time of immorality—where bribes were the name of the game and where massive atrocities could be perpetrated on an individual or a group of people because they did not "follow the party line."

The friction between Armenia and Azerbaijan had been seething for some time when the Armenian majority in the enclave of Nagorno-Karabakh voted to secede from the government of Azerbaijan. It was not unlike the American Civil War, or the "War Between the States," where Northern whites fought Southern whites after South Carolina seceded from the nation. Secession is often a cause of the bitterest wars.

A tragic aspect of the Armenian-Azeri conflict that is often overlooked is that it all took place in the hypnotic propaganda never-never land of the Soviet Union, where this national struggle was publicly downplayed to the point where it was all but disbelieved. Still, it was a war between the states and, predictably, the result was the imposing of an embargo and a full-scale military conflict. Further fueling the embers of war, was that the enemy combatants were of two different religions, Christian Armenians and Muslim Turkic Azeris, with a bloody history still burning in the living memory of the 1915 Turkish Ottoman genocide that left 1,500,000 Armenians dead.

The local Azeri Communist Party was successful at fomenting hatred and violence against the Armenians as a cover for their greedy, power-hungry bid to break away from the Soviet Union. It was the way all the Baltic countries were rising up at the time. This situation offered party leaders an opportunity they could not pass up, a promise of power, money and largesse for their families. Armenian possessions could be seized and distributed to friends and relatives.

Ethnic cleansing would open job opportunities in positions vacated by the better-educated Armenians to be filled by the lesser educated Azeris, many of them running away from Karabakh and Armenia, fleeing to their co-religionists, embittered and inflamed by the State propaganda.

These runaways are what renowned sociologist Dr. Georgi Derlughian came to refer to as "subproletarians," and what Karl Marx has called *Lumpenproletaren* (rag proletarians), people without education, training, social stability or European attitudes and culture. These are the young Azeris who attacked my aunt's apartment in Musabekovo.

They had one thing going for them. They were unified in their quest for freedom. Make no mistake about it: the USSR was the most *unfree* place on earth—and any form of socialist government that seeks to recreate the "Soviet Mentality" is doomed to the same violent chasms that we experienced in Azerbaijan and throughout the USSR as the Iron Curtain was rent, irrevocably, by people seeking true freedom.

What will always sadden me the most is that Baku was such a beautiful city, one of great diversity. So many nationalities lived together peacefully until this conflict in Nagorno-Karabakh stirred up the tempest. It is like a small seed dropped into a bell jar in a chemistry class demonstration where the chemicals in the air suddenly and violently combine with a blast and drop down to the bottom in a splash of color. However the violent explosion did not produce something beautiful—rather, quite the opposite.

I must say this here. The divisiveness that is happening now in the United States has the same feel, the look and smell of what I experienced in Baku. The United States is more racially divided now than it has been in decades. There is a massive fear of immigrants. The threat of Islamic *jihad* is constantly with us. The bitter political rivalries between left and right over practically everything from gun rights to property is tearing this wonderful nation apart. Violence has shattered the comfortable safety of schools, churches, and public gatherings.

After Sumgait, I started to wonder what was really going on. I knew the government wouldn't tell us anything. I remembered how confused I felt after I was so severely reprimanded for challenging the system with my spot-on comment on the *Eugene Onegin* epic poem. I had made trips to Moscow to lay the foundation for my family to emigrate from Baku to Armenia, but all the while I continued to doubt myself, wondering if what I was doing was truly the right thing to do. The lessons of the state ran deep, and that is the only justification I have in hindsight for holding out hope that the atrocities of Sumgait would never happen in my beloved city.

CHAPTER 8

The Great Armenian Earthquake

IMMEDIATELY FOLLOWING THE ATTACK AT MY AUNT'S APARTMENT, MY mother took it upon herself to take the children out of Azerbaijan for their own safety. This would be the second time in the past ten months that she had come to this decision. After the Sumgait Pogrom on February 28 that same year, she personally escorted the children to Armenia.

After the first exodus from Baku, my mother and children stayed with relatives for a short time in Armenia and returned to Baku after the violence subsided. It turned out to be a false lull. My mother fully understood, as I did then, that the botched attack on the family in Musabekovo was part of a growing pogrom that had now progressed into our city, Baku. Who would have known that my mother and children would have to confront death in twice as many days?

Not everyone agreed that departure was the only option this time, and this caused some turmoil in the family. Some were still in denial and wanted to stay, believing they would be safe. Others were more rushed and scared. They just wanted to leave. But this was not the time for a family conference.

I may have been one of the last Armenians to finally accept the hopelessness of the situation, but after this assault, everyone in Baku realized that the prospect for any kind of future there was bleak, at best, and that drastic measures had to be taken. Even the passive Soviet government in Moscow felt obligated to declare a "state of emergency," sending tanks and troops into the streets to quell the violence with options to shoot to kill. Luckily, their action temporarily foiled the assault on our family.

We at first discussed all leaving Baku together. But packing up and leaving your life completely behind is obviously easier said than done. It was critical that we escape the hostility and bloodshed, but there were inherent logistical considerations that needed to be worked out. The mindset of Armenians in Azerbaijan at that time was typical of Soviet society. We cherished our possessions, perhaps because they were so difficult to accumulate: our furniture, our cars, our homes, jewelry, knickknacks, and books, whatever. It is not a familiar concept to start over from scratch.

You may ask, why not sell your summer house with all its beautiful trees planted so many years ago. Why not sell your cars? We thought the same thing; however, we did not see the inherent flaw in this logic right away.

Were there any Azeris naïve enough to purchase our possessions knowing that after they chased us out of the country everything would be there free for the taking? After offering a little bribe to local politicians, that is. I recall one Azeri friend of my husband's—a man who had always appreciated our house with its fruit trees, shade trees, plants and flowers—making a ridiculously low offer to us to purchase the property.

"No," was Anatoliy's resounding response.

Later, he would grumble to me, "I would pour gasoline over all the trees and the house and burn everything to the ground rather than give it all away for practically nothing."

He did not do that, of course. He did not have the heart to destroy something we both loved so much, but I understood the sentiment.

"How are we going to live in Armenia?" I asked him. "We still need to sell our things and get some cash."

This was a problem with no immediate or simple solution. In a time of great danger, sometimes decisions are made in haste. My mother, who had been taking care of the children, was determined to protect them. She advocated for the immediate exodus of our entire family, and she spoke up firmly: "I'm going to take the children with me to Armenia," she told me emphatically. "You can stay here to do what you need to do, but I want the children to get away to a safe place as soon as possible."

That's what we decided to do. We certainly are not the only ones who saw the writing on the wall.

For most, it was not a question of if they should get out of the city, but of when. The traffic leaving Baku that day was so heavy the streets were almost impassable. Many people were headed for the airport like us.

We were lucky to get tickets, lucky to have friends who could help us. We managed to get on the next flight out of Baku to Yerevan. While about thirty rubles is the ordinary fare, the price-gougers made us pay ten times as much, and we did so without hesitation. The enemy republic was Armenia, but the air routes remained open with the heavy protection of the Soviet army. Still, we dared not make it obvious in this hostile environment that we were buying tickets to fly to Armenia. Everything was based on connections in USSR, so we purchased our tickets from a government agency called "Vogzal," where we had some friends.

We hurriedly helped the children pack only what was essential and headed to the airport. We said very little during the twenty-five-minute drive, my husband behind the wheel, my mother in the passenger seat and my two children in the back of the car with me. We were worried about being stopped on the way. We were always worried about police trying to shake us down, but in the present atmosphere, with all the ethnic conflict, the result could be far worse than just paying a bribe. We thought we would be safe now because we could see all the military patrols and emplacements at the airport. As soon as we arrived the children started crying.

"Where are we going now?" Arthur asked.

"Why are we going?" asks his older and more mature sister.

"It's only for a short time!" I said, evading the question.

"Why aren't you coming with us?" Ani astutely asked.

"We have to pack the rest of our belongings. We'll bring the rest of your toys. As soon as we finish, we will come and join you. I promise."

I honestly did believe the separation would be temporary. It may be naïveté, but I still expected that Anatoliy and I would be able to sell some property, raise sufficient funds and then join our family in Yerevan, the capital of Armenia, in a relatively short period of time. I did not want to simply abandon everything and allow pillagers to take whatever they wanted in this chaotic and lawless world where nothing belongs to you anymore, not even your life.

We met-up with the other family members who were also booked on the next scheduled flight to Armenia; my mom's sisters, Ella and Lyalya, along with my cousin Alec, who was carrying his pet parrot in a covered cage. It was by sheer luck that we found them in the massive crowds talking with friends and neighbors carrying luggage for a one-way trip. Apparently, along with my aunts, a large contingency of survivors of the Musabekovo attack had also found their way to the airport.

The loading of passengers, however, did not begin for two more hours. There were massive delays as the airport tried to deal with the huge volume of travelers. The extra time was bittersweet. I wanted to spend more time with my children, but it would only make it harder when it came time for them to leave.

When they finally announced the departure of their flight, more passengers attempted to board than the plane could handle, which took further time to sort out. There were other Armenian families like ours trying to get their children out of harm's way. Eventually, they began to call the names of the passengers who started boarding one by one.

Suddenly, a bunch of people whose names had not been called rushed forward and tried to force their way onto the plane, reminding me of the Titanic in its final moments, everyone trying to escape from this foundering ship, the "S.S. Baku," and find a spot on a lifeboat that will keep them alive.

Standing in line with my family, I watched this scene unfold with a sense of helplessness and dread, a combination that left me feeling nauseous, and I questioned if we were doing the right thing. There was no sign whatsoever of patience or civilized order. Everyone was pushing and shoving to save their children, just as we were trying to do.

Although the plane was surrounded by the military, people were climbing right onto the wings and fuselage of the plane. I couldn't believe it. The soldiers repeatedly pushed them off, their weapons drawn, recalling for me the videos shown of the last days of the fall of Saigon and the end of the Vietnam War with people hanging off the helicopters rescuing the fleeing, now-desperate friends of the United States forces. We saw depictions like this on the news in other countries all the time, but now it was happening right in front of me—on the flight my children were on to take them to safety!

People desperately continued trying to get aboard. The children were crying. I felt Ani's little hand squeezing mine hard as the surge of the frantic bodies tried to squeeze by us. Soldiers in uniforms did their best to keep the crowds in reasonable order by shouting threats and brandishing their M16s.

It was a sad sight; the children clutching us, the shoving and confusion of the desperate crowd rushing to get on the plane. It became more frightening for everyone as we neared the airplane stairway and we had to part. My family began preparing to embark on their journey amid chaotic screams and shouts, and we all shed a lot of tears.

I didn't like to be separated from my children any more than they did, but I knew it was the right thing to do. Finally, we had to say our sorrowful goodbyes. As I watched them board, standing on the runway waiting for the plane to take off, I felt a sudden and unexpected rush of relief. In a sense, it was the happiest moment for me to see my two children and relatives take off and escape the dangers of our chaotic homeland. Once they were safely on the plane, Anatoliy and I turned and reluctantly left the airport. After spending most of day there, we barely got home before the nine o'clock military curfew.

The next morning we were both emotionally exhausted but overjoyed to receive a brief phone call from my mother in Yerevan, Armenia. She reported that they had arrived safely, and everything was fine. We were immensely reassured by this notification, but never in our wildest dreams could we have anticipated the new dangers our loved ones would face in the next few hours.

My family arrived safely in Yerevan around midnight. My mother, Ani, Arthur, Aunt Ella, Aunt Lyalya and Alec, and the parrot Mimi were all together. Nobody had slept and the children were cranky. Representatives at the airport showed great hospitality to them and the other refugee Armenians, greeting them with flowers, music, and rousing speeches. They provided food, instructions, arranged transportation and invited them to start a new life in Armenia.

Unlike many of the other refugees, my mother had a relative in the Armenian capital city; her only uncle, Harutun, who is her mother's brother. It was about an hour's commute to her Uncle's home, but because of the late hour they were forced to spend the night on benches inside the airport.

They huddled close and leaned on each other, trying to sleep, and hoping that the whole nightmare of the previous evening at my Aunt's house in Musabekovo, still fresh in their minds, was behind them forever.

In the morning, my mother wanted to get everyone to her Uncle's in Yerevan, but government officials requested that refugees stay in nearby cities where there existed empty homes abandoned by the Azeris who fled to Azerbaijan to be with their fellow Azeris.

My mother tried to explain to the officials that she had relatives in Yerevan, and they did not need special accommodations. However, because the Armenian government was so kind and caring, my mother and aunts decided to show their appreciation and accept their hospitality.

Numerous buses were provided as one by one the Armenian refugees, and all of their possessions, filled every seat and empty place. They were transported to Leninakan, now renamed Gyumri, the second largest city in Armenia and the capital of the Shirak Province in the northwestern part of the country. It is about 126 km north of the capital, but my mother believed they would be there only briefly, confident in the knowledge that they would be in Yerevan with relatives before too long.

Upon their arrival, they were driven to a staging area where there was an organized welcoming reception for all the displaced Azerbaijan Armenians. They were greeted with open arms by Armenians of the Republic. Following official procedure, everyone had to register in the town of Akhuryan, a suburb of Leninakan, about 6 km from the airport.

Even before they reached their final refugee destination, the parrot that Alec had been carrying since leaving Baku began to violently strike the inside of the cage with its body and scream shrilly. The bird, which had been well-behaved up until their arrival in Yerevan, started to become increasingly agitated.

It had behaved similarly the night before, during the Musabekovo attack, throwing itself against the cage and screeching. At first, Alec thought it was the stress of the flight, but it soon became apparent that something was troubling Mimi. Passengers on the bus were so nervous about leaving Baku under so much strife that they ignored the avian noise amid the din and nervous chatter of their fellow refugees. The bird, however, quickly used up its vocabulary of swear words, and it no longer continued to be entertaining.

"Shut that goddamned bird up," one passenger shouted

"We're upset enough without that racket!"

But nothing Alec did could calm the parrot. It was like trying to pacify a baby in a temper tantrum. Since it was December, a heavy cloth lay draped over the cage. The covering usually kept the bird not only warm, but passive and quiet, except on this occasion.

Finally, upon arrival at the check-in center, while everyone went into the office to register, Alec remained in his seat with the cage on his lap watching over the unruly parrot. Inside the three-story management building, the adults filled out forms and answered all the pertinent questions, providing their name, age, and address for themselves and their children.

The registration was fast and easy and my entire family, including Alec, was processed quickly. With this simple method, the government was able to accurately keep track of the number of refugees arriving in Armenia and where they were sent. One of the possible places that my family offered to stay was right on these premises, in a new nine-story apartment housing complex adjacent to the smaller management building.

After signing up, my family, mostly my aunts, begin talking with other refugees they met and shared their thoughts about how relieved they were to be away from Baku and its murderous gangs.

Suddenly, as they were all leaving the registration center and heading toward the buses parked outside, there arose a faint but frightening hum, like the buzzing of a million bees or the extreme bass on a car loudspeaker blaring hip-hop music. The unusual sound continued to grow louder, quickly swelling into a tremendous roar that reverberated through their bodies. They felt unsteady on their feet as the very ground beneath them started to move and shake.

Clutching each other, my family could only watch in shock as the brick-and-mortar building they had just walked out of, as well as the nine-story apartment complex behind it, began to fracture, then buckle and collapse backwards, strewing bits of concrete and broken glass into the air. The sound was deafening, and just like that, in a matter of moments, the buildings were gone, transformed into a heaping pile of steaming and smoking rubble.

My mother momentarily let go of Arthur's hand to wipe her cheek when she felt something small and sharp strike the left side of her face. She did not panic when saw a spot of blood on her fingers, not wanting to scare the children, but it was impossible for her to disguise her emotions after the terrifying and incomprehensible sight they just had observed. A dark cloud of debris was steadily rising from the crumbled remains of the buildings. In the swirling wind, it moved slowly toward them, enveloping them.

My mother had never experienced an earthquake before, but even as she made the children cover their mouths with their shirts to protect their lungs from the choking miasma, she realized how lucky they were. Only a fortunate twist of fate had saved their lives. (It was the third brush with death.) Had the large apartment complex fallen in the other direction, it would have landed right on top of them, as well as the bus, killing everyone.

At first, few seemed to comprehend exactly what was taking place. Screams and shouts of terror were everywhere. Some people thought they were under military or militia attack. As everyone instinctively rushed toward the bus, Aunt Ella began screaming when her foot slid into a crack that had opened in the heaving ground. The maw of concrete closed onto her foot and she could not move. She could feel the hot temperature due to escaping gas and pressure coming from deep within the bowels of the earth. Several men came to her aid and managed to free her foot, though in the process she lost her shoe to the crevasse.

Like other families, mine tried to locate one another, which by now was a real challenge because it was impossible to see anything in the thick cloud of dust and debris. There was screaming, crying, shouting.

"I'm here!" Ani cried because she could not see her grandmother even though she was holding her grandmother's hand.

While the ground shook, it was hard to tell if it had started again or if it had never stopped. Clearly, the bus was rocking from side to side despite the effort of several men outside who tried to steady it and keep it from swaying.

"Get on!" the driver shouted "Get on! Everyone! Get on the bus!"

My family got aboard safely, and the bus pulled away from this scene of destruction, tires screeching, as if they might be able to drive somewhere that had not been impacted by this seismic event. Just then, however, as if they were extras in some B-horror movie, the ground in front of the bus literally opened up as if someone had taken a giant razor and cut a straight slice into the road.

The driver had to swerve violently, sending the bus careening off the road to avoid the crater. At that same moment, the hysterical parrot escaped from its cage, which had broken wide open. Alec managed to enfold Mimi in his arms as she squawked and flung her colorful feathers around the dust-filled air inside the bus. There may have been others besides Alec who realized at that point that Mimi had predicted the earthquake with her bizarre behavior earlier, but no one had understood these warning signs at the time.

Mimi might very well have been named "Cassandra" after the character in the Iliad, Homer's classic Trojan War epic. Cassandra had warned against the trick of the Greek wooden horse, but no one would believe her. Similarly, we understood what Mimi felt only instinctively. Animals are often said to be harbingers of natural disasters, and in the aftermath of this quake there were reports that Armenia had seen the appearance of an unusual number of snakes everywhere, supposedly materializing from the cracks in the ground produced by the tremors.

The escaping bus was not harmed and was back on the road, but the driver was forced to travel blindly through what appeared to be a virtual wasteland. The dust outside the windows provided only limited visibility. None of the terrified travelers, including the feathered passenger, had any way of knowing just how bad things were. Everything was in chaos, too horrific to imagine, but the chilling reality was evidenced all around.

Seated just a few rows down from my family on the bus was a man named Gregory. He appeared to be in shock. Gregory was a shoemaker we all knew from Baku. Because my father's name was Gregory and he was also a shoemaker, there had been a closeness between our families. Tragically, this man's wife and two sons had entered the doomed nine-story structure to inspect an apartment offered to them while Gregory waited outside smoking his cigarette. When the earthquake struck, he could only watch in abject horror as the edifice toppled down on his entire family, killing them instantly.

The trauma had a profound effect on him, to the point where he was not able to function with the pain and heartbreak of his loss. He would be institutionalized at a facility in Yerevan, where he would die a short time later. This is just one of many tragic stories that resulted from what has become known as the Great Armenian Earthquake. The world had not seen a catastrophe of this nature in a major city since the San Francisco earthquake in 1906.

All I wanted was for my family to be safe and together. I didn't know what the future had in store, but they were far from safe. And we were not all together, that was the worst thing.

It was one of the world's most historic earthquakes, a magnitude 6.9 to 7.0 on the Richter Scale with a death count that reached 55,000-60,000 souls and an additional 500,000 injuries.

Blithely unaware of this disaster at the time it occurred, Anatoliy and I kept close to home in Baku most of the day, wary of the roving gangs of Azeris who were on the lookout for Armenians to hunt and kill. Anatoliy didn't go to work. Because it was winter, turning dark early, this is the time we tried to circulate without being conspicuous.

We were surprised by the flickering of lights all around the city. There was no special event or holiday to celebrate, yet there were bonfires blazing everywhere. Fireworks exploded colorfully in the sky, exploding and shaking the windows where their flashes were reflected all across the streets of Baku. We were greatly puzzled to see Azeris gathered together outside joyfully drinking and eating, cooking meat on skewers over open flames. Crude signs were displayed here and there:

"ALLAH HU AKBAR," the battle cry of the jihadists. (God is great!)

It is only when we turned on the television later that evening that we learned why the Azeri population was rejoicing and praising God. My heart instantly sank when I heard the terrible announcement:

"MAJOR EARTHQUAKE IN ARMENIA." The Azeri newsman's voice is unabashedly jubilant as she relayed the initial reports that more than 20,000 Armenians had been killed.

"Allah has punished our infidel enemies, the Armenians!" she announced.

While my husband and I sympathized with the many victims and survivors of the earthquake, we were not worried about our children and family at this time because we believed that they were in Yerevan, Armenia's capital city, an area which we knew had not been affected by the disaster. Of course, we had no way of knowing that the Armenian government had assembled many Armenians at official refugee facilities near Leninakan or that my mother had accepted this kind but unknowingly perilous offer. It was an out-of-the-frying-pan-into-the-fire situation for my family, as they went from the violence in Musabekovo to the center of the earthquake.

We continued to watch this sad news along with the rest of the world, following the developments with solemn interest and concern, hoping that Armenia would be able to rise up quickly from the ruins. We lowered the volume on the TV and sat very close to the set so that we could still hear every word without attracting attention from neighbors or passersby on the street.

Sadly, the numbers of victims being announced kept increasing. Every hour there were more and more casualties. I still hoped to get a reassuring call from Yerevan and a chance to talk to my mother and the children. No call came, however, so I tried to reach them but could not get through. I presumed that this was because of the disaster and the overwhelming number of emergency calls disrupting the communications lines all around the devastated country. After hearing nothing for two days, I remained uneasy, still unable to get through.

On the third day, I became more anxious and frustrated. I was also annoyed at my husband for spending the afternoon hosing down the plants and flowers and grass in the backyard. He soaked everything. I didn't understand why he was doing that, and he offered no explanation. I thought he had lost his mind. That evening, however, bottles of gasoline with flaming cloths in the openings were hurled into our yard. Of course these are known as "Molotov Cocktails," a primitive and cheap firebomb. We had all seen them being tossed around in places of unrest around the world on the evening news for as long as there had been broadcast television. Because my husband had saturated everything all day, he was able to easily put out the fires.

I realized that his actions that day had been a defensive measure. He obviously anticipated the firebombing, and not informing me of his reasoning was his way of protecting me. I was a nervous wreck to begin with, my stress level increasing by the minute. I needed to hear some good news. I needed to hear from my children in Yerevan. That was all that mattered.

In those days, to make a long-distance phone call you had to dial 07 and first speak to an Operator, who would then connect you. At least that was how it was supposed to work. I kept calling the relatives in Yerevan, but the female operator would just laugh at me and sneer.

"Allah is punishing you Armenians!" she told me to my utter astonishment. I called again and again, only to receive more insults and curses from Azeri telephone operators praising Allah for chastening the despised infidels. They played patriotic music and refused my further requests. I continued to call, begging them in the name of their Allah, but they scoffed and exulted in their divine victory and glee in the suffering of Armenians.

"Allah will continue to punish you. You have to beg me. Ha! Ha! Listen to this Azerbaijani music: 'We are dancing to the blood of Armenians!' our victory song!"

I refused to stop trying, hoping that the next operator would be better, more sympathetic, more human. They were not. I started to believe strongly that something terrible has occurred to my family, and I had lost all of them. By the fourth day, I was not eating, not sleeping. I was convinced twice in as many days that something bad had happened.

At the end of the fourth day, the sound of the phone ringing startled me. I jumped, in part because I was aware that the phone only rang rarely these days, and when it did it was usually bad news being transmitted, informing us that someone had been stabbed or killed.

I hoped that it was from Yerevan, but this was a local call. Zhana, the second wife of my brother-in-law, Shurik, astonished me with a curt and abrupt message.

"Your mother and children are all right."

"What kind of game are you playing?" I exclaimed rudely.

"How do you know that?"

"I spoke with them," Zhana told me.

"I found them. They were in the earthquake, but they are okay. They are okay."

"No!" I screamed.

"It's impossible. Are you kidding?"

I refuse to believe that they had been in the quake. It is easier for me to deny the whole thing than to confront the terrifying reality. I ask her to swear on the grave of her brother who had recently died.

"I have to go now," she said softly.

"I can't talk."

I did not fully appreciate the chance she was taking talking to me, and I continued to repeat my recriminations, unsatisfied with her laconic answers. Zhana told me, "I can't talk any more. They're listening."

She repeated that she could not continue speaking and hung up.

"HELLO!" I yelled with indignation, but the line was dead. I hung up the phone, realizing that my instincts had been correct. Even though my kids were supposed to be far away from the epicenter of the quake, no relatives in Yerevan had confirmed that they were there.

Maybe they had been in the earthquake after all, but Zhana said they were safe. What does that mean? How safe? Partially? Was anyone injured? They had to be terrified. I could not believe that in all the chaos of such a great disaster I had been so lucky to have my children spared, and for the second time in as many nights.

⸺

A moment later, after considering all this, I felt bad for the way I had reacted. The relief, the calm, and the hope I now felt, I owe all to Zhana, my sister in-law, who took such a great personal risk to inform me that my children were safe. She was like an angel sent down from Heaven, and I was so grateful.

Zhana lived close to our apartment and was one of the few Armenians still working in a State organization in Baku, though only part-time. AZE-RIGAZ at the time was a national company dedicated to petroleum sales. Zhana was a petite woman with dark eyes and equally dark facial hair who looked just like Alice B. Toklas, friend of Gertrude Stein. Like Alice, she had fashionable tastes. In Zhana's case, she liked to wear nice hats.

Then I remembered that she had special resources at her fingertips to make long-distance calls. Azerigaz was a large company posessing a special communications system, called a "Teletype," for doing business with other Soviet republics

My conjecture was that Zhana, knowing the name and address of our relative in Yerevan, possessed enough information to secure a personal telephone number with her privileged access to business technology. I wondered if Zhana spoke in Armenian to the local operator. Did she speak in Russian when Azeri employees nearby could hear her, this hated Armenian, dealing with the reviled enemy?

Tragically, a few months later, while Zhana was walking along the streets of Baku after leaving work, she was viciously attacked by three Azeris. They happened to be strolling by and without warning one of them swung his arm up. He was holding a knife, and he stabbed her repeatedly. She was left on the sidewalk for dead, bleeding profusely. Fortunately, because of the presence of the soldiers in the state of emergency, she was rescued by a military tank platoon and taken to the hospital, where she was treated for a punctured liver and other internal injuries.

Her family did not know what had happened for several days. They were not immediately notified, and she was considered missing. Her purse, along with all her valuables and identification, had been stolen.

Just as Zhana had come to my aid in my time of desperation to tell me what she knew about the well-being of my children, now others were being asked to come forward on her behalf. Her sick parents, whom Zhana had been caring for at the time, called out desperately everywhere for help in locating their daughter after she had gone missing. But who could they rely on? Neighbors of twenty, thirty years? Co-workers who despised her? Fearful witnesses? The Azeri police, who stood idly by while Armenians were attacked?

Zhana was finally discovered in a nearby hospital and eventually returned home, but she was never the same again, walking slowly, bent over, and appearing much older than her years.

It was one of thousands of tragedies, and it was indicative of the time. We were crippled beyond our years because of the great misfortune that befell Armenians both in Azerbaijan and Armenia at this time. In one place, we were under constant attack. In the other, the land was torn apart from below the ground, and the government, barely able to care for its own citizens, was even less capable of supporting the influx of refugees. Utter chaos reigned for months and months afterwards.

Because Armenia was so devastated by the earthquake, I implored my mother to bring my children back to me. How could they survive such utter devastation without their mother? It was bad enough in Armenia that my mother relented and flew back. It wasn't long after when the final incident occurred that made me "pick my poison." In Armenia, they may face hardship. Here in Baku, they would end up dead or badly maimed like their Aunt Zhana. It was really no choice at all.

CHAPTER 9

The Toilet

EVERYTHING WAS STARTING TO ADD UP—AND NOT TO ANYTHING GOOD. My mother had brought my children back to Baku. I thought they were "safely" at home with me, away from the massive devastation in Armenia. How could I let my children live in a place without clean water and a working sanitation system—at least that was my justification.

But it was also clear that nothing in Baku was safe either. The incidents of violence against Armenians were escalating. I was becoming increasingly alarmed about my children and their safety. But no matter how much you worry and work to keep them safe, when the very fabric of your society is unraveling, you sometimes can never know how fast the last threads will detach and fall away.

It was a regular early winter school day in Baku—except the violence against the Armenians was increasing and becoming so obvious we could no longer disbelieve it.

Even after seeing and experiencing Azeri anger and aggression firsthand, it never occurred to us that our children would become targets, certainly not in the schools, especially kindergarten. We were wrong about that. Very, very wrong.

One day, I was surprised to see my Azeri neighbor, Elya, through the window in the courtyard with her two daughters. They went to the same school as my children. Normally, she escorted my children home with her own children. Sometimes I did the same with her children. She is a housewife and I work, so we arranged a schedule between us. That day it was strange to see only her children and not mine with her.

"Elya," I called to her as I walked outside. "The school day is over?"

She looked frustrated and scared as she ushered her kids toward the doorway of her apartment.

"Go, go. Go in, children." Turning to me, she said, "Yes, they let them go home early."

"Why?" I asked.

She turned her head away from me. "I don't know. There are a lot of people there."

She did not make eye contact with me as she herded her children into the apartment and quickly pushed the door shut behind them. The exchange we just had was unusual enough to make me nervous, and it was obvious she was trying to avoid me. I was about to ask her what's wrong when she suddenly turned her head and waved her hand dismissively in the air.

"Go, go," she ordered me brusquely, the tone in her voice changing completely. "Quick. Pick up your kids."

I was instantly seized by panic and I rushed straight to the school without saying another word to my neighbor. I tried not to think about what may have happened at the school, and just focused on getting there as fast as I could.

I had not considered the possibility that one of the wandering bands of thugs could actually be a threat to the most pure and innocent creations in the world—little children. They truly are nature's finest products. I could not comprehend how anyone could ever harm them, no matter what religion, ethnicity and heritage they might be. Who could punish a child so severely for something that they do not even comprehend?

The school was about a twenty-minute walk away. I made it in ten. It still felt like hours. I was so terrified that I did not even feel the ground under my feet. By the time I arrived at the school, I was numb all over. I just wanted my kids, but I knew that something was awry right away because it was too quiet. It did not even look like the same school. It appeared deserted.

Usually at this time in the school schedule, recess was over, and classes had resumed, while some of the rooms between first and fourth grade would already be dismissing the students. The children would be leaving the school to go home, some running, some skipping, excited voices calling out to one another. Parents would be standing outside the building waiting for their sons and daughters to emerge. But not today.

I started to see other people rushing towards the school and children being escorted one at a time to the gate by teachers who then shooed them outside and into the open arms of their relieved parents.

I made my way up to the main entrance only to be confronted by a new door monitor, one I had never seen before.

"Where is the regular monitor?" I asked

"She's sick," the Azeri woman responded stoically.

"What's going on?"

I got no response.

"Is it a committee meeting?" I continued to press the Azeri woman for an answer.

"No."

"An accident?"

"No."

"Is it construction?"

"No."

"Is it a teacher sick and no substitute?"

"No."

"Are they getting ready for some event?"

"No."

All these negative responses only served to increase my anxiety. With the crowds of Azeris marching in Baku and screaming against Armenians at this time, I did not need any further explanation, or lack thereof.

Only a week before, while driving home from a downtown hospital after having taken chest X-rays that were required by the application to the American Embassy to emigrate, our car became stalled in a crowd of people made up mostly of unshaved, angry-looking young men dressed in black. They were chanting and shouting slogans against Armenians, the target of their hatred.

I did not feel safe as I realized the dangerous situation we were in, with my husband and I stuck in traffic with a swarming sea of Azeris screaming, "Death to Armenians!" Instinctively, we both began to raise our arms and shake our fists in unison, trying to blend in with the others and mimic their hateful chants to hide our nationality. It was a matter of survival, and we did what we had to do. My husband could effectively yell hateful Azeri words out the window and be heard as we move at a snail's pace among the throngs of Azeri berserkers. We knew we could not escape until the rally was over. At one point my arm became so tired that I had to rest it

"Put your arms up in the air and shake them," my husband commanded, and I painfully complied.

Now, as I was allowed into the school, I hurried down the corridors where the classrooms are located and encountered a group of about twenty or so of these enraged, disheveled young Azeris, exactly like the ones that had surrounded our car just a few days before.

I realized that they were cornering and questioning children they saw It was clear that they were looking for Armenian children. Who else? They appeared so busy, promenading together and possessed with the same dark thought in their heads and a similar grim expression on their faces. They seem to be fired with a malicious hatred, eager to disavow all of humanity, proud of their cruelty and brutality, behaving like fur trappers who catch animals with steel teeth, callously crushing their legs and leaving them to die in agony.

Here, I want to take a moment to explain the sign of a person's national identity in Azerbaijan as displayed in the last name. Armenians typically have the surname ending in "ian" or "yan." The last segment means son of the preceding male name. The Russian name typically ends in "ov" or "ev," following the same idea. Some Armenians assimilated their last names to terminate in the Russian endings. For example, Minassian became Minassov. These are analogous to English names like Peterson, Jackson and Harrison where the first part is a common given name, son of Peter, son of Jack, and son of Harry. The common Spanish family names end in "es" or "ez" like Rodriguez, son of Rodrigo, or Perez, son of Pedro.

My children's last name is Khachatorian a pure "ian" ending, leaving no doubt as to their Armenian nationality, whereas the assimilated family names with Russian endings might be a safe shield for them. But, one way or another, the Azeris living with us as neighbors know who is who. In my case, there can be no doubt that my children are Armenian, bearing such a strikingly well-known Armenian surname like the famous composer of the "Sabre Dance," Aram Khachaturian.

Looking at them, I envisage the worst as a worried and frantic mother. I see these ugly, viperous faces are filled with venom and they are intent on performing evil acts, desperate to find what they came here seeking: innocent Armenian children whom they could make victims of atrocities.

And two of the children are mine, trapped somewhere in the building where these marauders are sniffing around like a pack of hyenas on the open prairie looking for the kill. To me, they are worse than beasts because at least a hunting animal is hungry for food. These are not animals of prey, but hungry for vengeance and excited to show off to one another just how cruel and violent they can be.

I climbed to the second floor and found some of the classrooms empty, even though the school day was not over yet, but now I knew the reason. The majority of children had left, most of the Armenians among them. There was no sign of Ani or Arthur, so I decided to go back and find the school monitor, whose job is to ring a bell at the end of every class period, which lasts forty-five minutes.

Next to the monitor I saw the small closet where the coats, hats and other garments for the younger children in the primary grades were kept. My thought was to first grab my son's coat and then find my children and take them home. I visually searched the cloak room for Arthur's coat, which my mother had ordered special for my son. It was very distinctive, but I did not see it. I wondered if it might have been stolen. It was rather expensive, made of chamois and very fashionable, not often found in children's clothing. It was styled more like an adult's, with all the accessories. Whenever my son wore the coat, many people admired it and complimented him, and we called him, "our little man."

"Where is my son's chamois coat?" I ask the Azeri monitor, trying hard to appear casual and not show my fear. I also intentionally held myself back from mentioning his name, particularly his Armenian surname.

"What's your son's name and who is his teacher?" she sharply snapped at me.

I simply pretended that I did not hear her and continued tenaciously searching for the coat myself, in case I had overlooked it. I wondered if she could be cooperating with that Azeri group of thugs searching the school for Armenian children to harm.

I tried to think logically, which was a challenge because of the stress of the situation, and I determined that not being able to find Arthur's coat is an indication that he and his sister are still in school somewhere.

But where?

I couldn't help feeling that if the regular monitor had been here, she might have helped me find my children. Then I started to think that maybe I was lucky that this Azeri monitor did not know me or my children and wouldn't expose me as a hated Armenian.

The situation of these thugs running through the halls gave them the chance to seize whatever they thought was valuable and apparently the chamois coat caught the eye of one of the thugs. In every war ever fought throughout history, from ancient Egypt to modern Iraq, conquering soldiers in enemy territory are on the lookout for hidden treasures to loot. This is their glory day.

I began walking faster through the halls, back and forth, looking for my children, while at the same time trying to appear unconcerned and inconspicuous. Suddenly, I was startled when I felt a hand squeeze my left shoulder very hard from behind. At first I thought it was one of the hooligans attacking me.

A woman's voice softly but very firmly repeated in a hushed emphasis, "Don't say anything! Don't say anything! Don't say anything!"

I turned around and recognized her as one of the other mothers. I did not know her name. I knew her only by sight and I felt safe knowing that she was not Azeri. I think she was "Mountain Jewish" or what the Jews called "Tat." They keep their village traditions in contrast to the Baku urbanized Jews mostly originating from Russia or Eastern Europe. Some people confuse them with Azeris from the villages since they seem to dress and act the same way and are often engaged in illicit street business instead of education or trades like their more sophisticated co-religionists.

She is a tall woman with, what one could say, a sort of masculine look. She was wearing a man's style watch which was once fashionable on her left hand. She was carrying a broom in her other hand along with a large checkered rag, as if she were a cleaning lady or a volunteer mother. She suddenly thrust the broom at me in an obvious attempt to make it appear as if I were also functioning as a volunteer at the school.

As we walked along together, pretending to clean as we went, she whispered, "Your kids, you know what happened?"

I felt panic rising once again. "My kids? Where are my kids? Where are my kids?" I kept asking her in a loud voice until I got a response.

"*Tikho, Tikho. Tikho*," is all she said. It is Russian for "Shush, Shush, Shush."

We continued along with her controlling hand still squeezing my shoulder firmly and guiding me down the corridor. With each step I grew more impatient with her and my dread mounted because I still did not know where my children were or where this woman was leading me. I expected the worst.

"They're behind the locked door of the toilet," she finally disclosed. "Don't let them hear you or they'll start yelling and answering you, and then you'll never see them again."

These stunning words pierced my soul.

I knew that the toilet was upstairs. I am familiar with the long, narrow room with gray slate floors that echo when you walk on them. I have taken the children in many times there, and now I desperately yearned to go there and hear their sweet voices.

"*Tikho. Tikho.* Be patient!"

I did as she said, and we kept on with our mock cleaning.

"Tatyana Mikhailovna," the woman whispered softly in my ear, "herded them into the toilet and locked the door." Tatyana Mikhailovna, I know, is Ani's third grade teacher.

I could see the door ahead and the big metal lock securing it. I had many questions that I began to ask her because all I wanted to do was get to my kids and hold them in my arms.

"If you want to see your kids you must settle down. Play this game. Clean and you will save your children. Clean. Clean."

I was numb and petrified, and I tried to channel all my energy into "playing this game," but it is a game of life and death, and it scared me.

My mannish protectress continued to whisper gruffly one-word instructions to me, and when I asked her any questions, she responded with the minimum number of words possible. It was frustrating and in such a nervous state I found myself talking and asking even more questions.

"Don't know. Don't know," she repeated. "Stop asking! Wanna see your kids again or not?"

When she muttered this ghastly question, I felt sick and could not think of anything else.

Just then three vigilantes appeared running back and forth past us in search of victims.

"Hold on," she cautioned me. "Patience! Wanna see your kids, so don't do or say anything to endanger them. And us."

We could hear the intruders shouting, cursing and arguing in the Azeri language. They were clearly frustrated because they could not accomplish their evil mission.

One of the Azeris suddenly stopped in front of us. He was tall and bearded and looked to be the leader of this group. He stopped. The other two men with him halted as well. The leader at the toilet door affixed with a huge shiny lock securing it and then looked at us.

"Why lock there?" he asked in heavily accented broken Russian.

Neither of us responded right away. He glanced back at the lock and turned his gaze upon me.

"Lock, there why?" he asked again, expecting an answer this time. He pointed to the door beyond the anteroom with sinks where the entrance to the toilet area is located.

At that moment, we were surprised to see Tatyana Mikhailovna appear next to us. Perhaps she noticed the thugs had stopped moving and she bravely came out of the classroom to see what she could do to help. She walked toward the washroom as if to wash her hands, brusquely pushing us two "cleaning women" aside and coolly taking over, acting like what a typical school professional would do.

She answered his question in an official voice, preventing us two "cleaning ladies" from showing our emotions. She was a better actress than either of us because surely, she had to be just as nervous and afraid as we were.

"We always lock the door when the school is closed," she told the barely Russian-speaking

Azeri. "Kids can do bad things in there, smoking, something inappropriate."

"Who key has?" came from his twisted mouth displaying a row of gold teeth, typical of Azeris from the villages.

"I don't know," she answered. "The principal. Somebody who is on duty."

I felt threatened just by his proximity. He was so close to us as he stood there staring at the lock. There was obvious doubt on his hateful face as he considered his dark options. Neither of us knew what he was going to do. He could come back with a tool to break the lock and find my children hiding there.

Then, he joined the next group that passed by, still with doubt on his face but a confident smirk as well. He believed, we hoped, that there was no one in the locked bathroom. He did not realize how close he was to fulfilling his dirty, bloody mission. Not ready to give up, the marauders divided into small squads and dispersed like scurrying rats going floor to floor, room to room, looking for victims, slamming doors and shouting in Azeri.

"We gotta get out of here," she whispered to me. "There is nothing for us to clean here anymore. Let's go."

"No," I yelled in protest. "I want my children. I'm not leaving without them."

"We have to move on," I was told. "We have to clean down this corridor." Then she repeated that dreadful question that instantly froze my blood, "You wanna see your kids again or not?"

She grabbed my hand and had to forcefully pull me away as tears rolled down my cheeks. We began to wipe down the radiators in the corridor, kicking up dust. That induced the coughing which conveniently hid my sobbing. I realized that this woman was controlling me because she thought that I could not handle the pressure of what was going on, and she was afraid I would do something stupid. I now understood that we could not unlock the toilet door or even let on that there are children hiding inside until the marauders have left.

In this moment of privacy, she confided and told me what had happened.

Tatyana Mikhailovna knew Ani as her own third grade student, recognizing that she was a clever girl and could understand the danger. The teacher told her, "Keep quiet. Don't cry. There are bad people here who want to do bad things to you." Her instructions to have the children hide in the toilet and lock it was wise, and Ani and Arthur did as they were told.

We continued to clean the corridor. It seemed to take forever because the marauders wouldn't give up. They continued along, yelling and arguing as new ones entered the school with the same behavior and goal in mind: to harm Armenian children.

I held back so many questions that were on my mind. "Why can't I hear their voices? Are they hungry? Are they on the dirty floor? Are they cold? Are they getting sick from the foul smell?"

The toilet was an "Asian toilet," which is nothing more than a series of holes in the floor with two depressions on each side in which to place your feet.

"How is my daughter managing her little brother?" I worried.

As we continued our pretense of cleaning, we kept returning to check on the toilet to be sure that the heavy metal lock still hung in place on the door. However, I sensed that my protector was agitated with me for failing to keep in step with her military decrees and was concerned that our ruse was starting to become obvious. She maintained an aggressive and controlling manner with me, speaking in broken sentences.

"Whatcha want? You wanna see your kids? Can all be in trouble!" She barked these staccato words out at me in a husky whisper.

Two hours after school had been formally dismissed, the marauders were still stampeding through the halls. I perceived Tatyana Mikhailovna sitting in an empty classroom crouched over her desk. She was holding a ball point pen either grading or pretending to be grading papers. She turned her face away from us and did not speak a single word. She is usually very affable and chats with me about my children. This time, however, she did not even make eye contact and looked away from me to her paperwork without inviting me to enter the classroom or to come over to her desk to talk. She was trembling and was afraid, but she was the brave heroine who was standing guard to rescue my children.

This went on for some time as we all waited until the troublemakers would tire, grow bored or become disappointed and leave the school. Now, very timidly some school administrators started to take an active stance and appeal to them to get them to depart.

"It's time to lock up the school. Nobody's here."

I really don't know if there was any truth to it or if the school officials were just protecting some children still trapped inside, but the raiders seem to believe it. One by one they started to abandon the building. Workers in the school, however, were not willing to leave immediately, and I recognized that the heroic Russian third grade teacher of my Ani was lingering behind because she still kept hold of the key to the heavy lock on the toilet door that shielded my children from these rampaging murderers.

After the last of the bandits left the building, the front door was bolted and everyone remaining in the school, about eight or ten people, came together to console one another, some crying in relief.

"Everybody evacuate the school!" someone commanded, "Let's get everyone out. There's always a chance these vermin will come back, and we will all be in danger."

They all rushed upstairs at once to unlock the toilet door and release my children, who were still trapped in the toilet. When my Ani and Arthur were finally freed, they rushed headlong into my waiting arms. I embraced them feeling a joy like no other I can recall besides the day they were born and I saw them for the first time.

The first thing my son says to me is,

"Pee-eeew! It was stinky there!" he complained.

Still shaking, Ani related to me what she kept whispering to her brother the entire time they were in the toilet. She said she instructed Arthur not to cry or make noise because if they were found, the men looking for them would kill them.

"I'm proud of you both," I told them. "You were very brave."

I was elated, but still worried because I knew that we were not completely out of danger. We could not be sure if the vigilantes would return or not, so we hurried away toward an exit, escaping through a back door where just two weeks before a young Armenian boy was stabbed to death by an Azeri student. We were offered a ride home by the husband of one of the teachers, and I was grateful. But being enclosed in the car with two kids who had been trapped in the toilet all afternoon, they were, as my son said, "stinky."

As I reflected over what happened that day in the children's school, I came to recognize that I was very lucky, in spite of everything, not to be observed clutching Arthur's expensive coat, which had been my intent. My masquerade as a cleaning woman would have been revealed; who knows what would have happened after that.

Like other survivors of a disaster, we have asked ourselves the dreaded question with guilt-heavy hearts, "Why us?"

As my grandmother used to say, after we found our asylum in the United States, "To be rewarded thus we must have given a needy person a piece of bread."

She often related this story to us; "One rare snowy day in Baku, a bedraggled man came to the door and asked for bread. I gave him a *byutterbrot* (a sandwich). When I looked out the door afterwards to give him something more, I did not see him or any trace of footprints in the snow!"

Angels in Eastern art are not fluttery ladies in pink dresses with wings, but bearded men of athletic build as depicted in early church art and in Rembrandt.

"I am convinced that he was an angel testing us," she said of the bedraggled stranger. "And we, praise God, passed the test."

As they say in Italian, *Se non e vero, e ben trovato.* If it isn't true, at least it is well founded.

But the gruesome fact was now very clear to me. My children had been spared death three times: once at my aunt's apartment at M. The next day in the aftermath of the Armenian earthquake, and finally from roving bands of thugs threatening them at the one place I thought they would be safe. Nothing was sacred to the Azeris bent on blood.

I couldn't justify any of it any longer. It was time to go.

PART TWO ——

Fleeing Baku

The Appointment in Samarra (as retold by W. Somerset Maugham [1933])

THE SPEAKER IS DEATH:
    There was a merchant in Bagdad who sent his servant to market to buy provisions and in a little while the servant came back, white and trembling, and said, "Master, just now when I was in the marketplace I was jostled by a woman in the crowd, and when I turned I saw it was Death that jostled me. She looked at me and made a threatening gesture. Now, lend me your horse, and I will ride away from this city and avoid my fate. I will go to Samarra and there, Death will not find me."

    The merchant lent him his horse, and the servant mounted it, and he dug his spurs in its flanks and as fast as the horse could gallop, he went. Then the merchant went down to the marketplace and he saw me standing in the crowd and he came to me and said, "Why did you make a threatening gesture to my servant when you saw him this morning?"

    "That was not a threatening gesture," I said, it was only a start of surprise. I was astonished to see him in Bagdad, for I had an appointment with him tonight in Samarra."

While the children and my mother were finally relatively safe in Armenia—and never to return to Baku—our situation as Armenians staying among the Azeris in the future breakaway Soviet Republic of Azerbaijan was more perilous than ever. Between the two halves of my family lie the Caucasus Mountains where the Titan Prometheus in Greek mythology was chained to a rock after being condemned by the gods for giving mankind the gift of fire. Whenever we look up in that direction, we would see eagles circling over the heights like the one who feasted on Prometheus' liver every day as punishment from the gods for doing good. Were they set to feast on ours?

But we knew we must leave and that means leaving *all* our possessions, our beautiful summer home with its lovely orchards of the apples, dates, walnuts, apricots, figs., white and black blackberries, plums, and pomegranates—seemingly every bounty one could imagine—for good.

All the bounty in the world would mean nothing if we didn't survive. We didn't know where death was set to meet us, but one thing was certain, our lives were in the balance in Baku.

CHAPTER 10

The Mysterious Four X's

WHEN YOU FLEE YOUR COUNTRY FOR GOOD, WHAT DO YOU TAKE WITH you in the car?

Take extra tires and tools for emergency repairs?

Cans of gasoline?

Take an overnight suitcase?

Some snacks for the trip?

Change of clothes and some personal documents?

It is not something an average person ever has to think about in his lifetime, but it was the only topic of conversation between me and my husband. It may have been bizarre, but since nobody worked, shopped, or did anything normal anymore—who's to say that conversation wasn't "normal" given the circumstance?

We left our beloved apartment with barely anything. We have to make it look like we're only going to visit a friend.

So that's what we do. Our first stop on our way out of Baku was at a good Azeri friend, Omar. Like the Germans who housed Jews during their holocaust, there were so many Azeris who risked their lives helping Armenians escape.

Omar had a big Azeri family. We were only there one day and one night, but it still caused consternation, for Omar had relatives who wanted to visit. Omar and his wife had to make excuses to keep the relatives from discovering their contraband guests. We were very lucky because people usually just drop in anytime without warning. In this part of the world, particularly in the Caucasus, where hospitality is so important, family and friends do not call in advance because they know they are always welcome.

Only one man, Enver, who was an Azeri friend of Anatoliy's, visited and found us staying with Omar and his family. He would play an important role in our escape. Omar's wife, the lady of the house, was a tall, heavy, and dark-skinned woman. She shuffled about quietly in slippers and never dressed up. She had never really learned any Russian or lost her village peasant ways.

Omar, also tall, chubby, with a mustache and mesmerizing black eyes that sparkled when he drank vodka, spoke Azeri all the time even though he was a major government official and his Russian was good. He had been a close friend for many years and my husband spent many enjoyable times with him at our homes and in his office. He usually came to our house alone, but sometimes with his wife, although he was more usually accompanied by his mistress, whom he would introduce as his cousin, even though we knew she was his girlfriend.

"This is my cousin," he told us the first time we met her. "I invited her to come with me and visit you, and then I can take her home."

The next time the story was, "Remember, this is my sister, I saw her near here. She didn't want to come to meet my old friend Anatoliy, but I convinced her."

Still another time: "Now she lives close by," he lied. "I had to force her to come."

"Yes," the girlfriend assented to this claim with conviction. "I happened to meet him on the street."

After a while the stories were no longer necessary, though they persisted and continued to prevaricate. After a while, when she stopped coming, we heard that another woman had taken her place, but the second woman did not visit us.

Later on, when we came to America it was a surprise for us to learn that Azeris (who devoutly follow the Koran) do not cheat on their wives, do not eat pork and do not drink vodka. In our experience, Omar, like so many of the Azeris we knew, had a mistress, ate "white pork" which was an excuse for eating domestic pork by claiming it was game meat from hunting wild boars. They told us it was okay in the dietary rules of Islam. He had no compunction whatsoever about drinking alcohol.

I can only speculate that perhaps Omar took us in because he felt a kind of obligation to us for being diplomatic when he found out that his wife was considerably in debt to me and was playing a Ponzi scheme in the bazaars. That whole sordid business started innocently enough, with her asking me to bake pastries to sell in her children's school. Soon after she asked to borrow money but then began to make excuses for not being able to pay me back, which she did typically in the Azeri way by beating her ample bosom histrionically and swearing the excuses on the grave of her mother and on the lives of her three children.

In *The Arab Mind*, Raphael Patai's classic study of Arab culture and society, the author analyzes this attitude of constant lying. Lying to a non-Azeri is not considered a sin. Look at promises of Azeri leaders in recent history as examples. I was used to being confronted with this behavior among the Azeri women street vendors. Once, such an Azeri woman, who happened to move into the same courtyard apartment complex where we used to live, displayed a classic case of the culture of fabrication.

This woman was a wheeler-dealer (*spekulyanka*) in the bazaar. She would look in your eyes, pull open her blouse aside and beat her chest till the skin burned red, swearing for a measly ten dollars, saying, "*Bu ölsün (May my heart die)* if I am lying. I am selling it to you for exactly what I paid for it. Let all my six children die right here and be buried side by side." She gesticulated toward an imaginary row of coffins but would not give you a chance to say anything about this ghastly promise. She would do that every time when she has a customer in front of her.

As a mother, hearing these awful words, I felt chills up and down my spine as she imperturbably and graphically condemned her babies. All for ten dollars. We heard this all-too-often but we never got completely used to it. Indeed, in the minority Shi'a sect of Islam, the religious disposition of Azeris in Azerbaijan, were persecuted so many times by the majority Sunni sect of Islam, that they have a notorious special dispensation to lie about their oppressed religious affiliation in order to survive. It's called *taqiyya*, and I suspect it has percolated into other aspects of life.

We were nervous throughout the day and night, and the time passed under enormous pressure. We saw the effect all this had on our kind hosts. Their own children did not understand why they were forbidden to go outside.

"Don't you see?" my husband explained to me. "They are even more afraid than we are. We're not going to give them more trouble. It's time to go."

I realized he was right, as did our hosts. Early the next morning we stole down the stairs one by one to the car so as not to arouse the suspicions of the Azeri neighbors. No suitcases, no boxes filled with personal effects in our hands. Omar went first and started the car, then Anatoliy, me, and then Enver.

The plan was to have Omar, wearing his officer's cap to impress the soldiers at roadblocks, drive us in our car to the border town of Mahachkala, with Enver following behind us in Omar's car. At the border, Anatoliy was to take the wheel of our car and have Omar get out and take a seat next to Enver and be driven home. It was a short trip, but it was not safe. At the border, we quickly shook hands and said goodbye before going off in opposite directions. Omar and Enver went back the Azerbaijan Republic way. My husband and I went toward the Armenian way.

So as not to attract undo attention to myself, I tried to bear a resemblance to a typical Azeri woman. I fixed my hair tightly and covered my head with some kind of scarf. I wore no makeup. At this stage, I didn't want to take any chances.

The shortest and most direct road from Baku to Yerevan, Armenia, winds through Azeri villages, a demographic consideration that would have made it exceedingly dangerous for us. As a result, we opted instead to take a more circuitous route, heading further to the north along the Caspian Sea and past the old city of Derbent on the ancient Chinese Silk Road to the city of Mahachkala, which is near the Russian border and the Socialist Republic of Daghistan at this time. We then swung west to the Soviet Socialist Republic of Georgia and its capital Tiflis, before we finally turned south toward Armenia and its capital city of Yerevan. On a map it would look like going up the right side of a tall rectangle, turning left at the top, and down the left parallel side, instead of taking the short base of the rectangle, going directly to the left.

This is not an arbitrary route, and it is not the first time that my husband drove this roundabout course to Armenia. On another occasion previously, he and I were driving this way with relatives in our car when we had to stop at an Azeri village to gas up. While I conscientiously tried to hide our Armenian nationality, my cousin Armen who was with us stupidly played a loud tape of Armenian music, which instantly let the cat out of the bag and enraged the hostile Azeris at the gas station. We tried to escape as quickly as we could, but it was difficult. The road was strewn with stones, which Azeris had thrown at us while running after our car and screaming profanities and pledges of death. We accelerated up a dangerous mountain road, hurling up black dust into their twisted faces full of hatred as we made our escape.

On still another past trip to Armenia we drove in our "Zhiguli," a French-manufactured FIAT 124. At that point, in the dead of winter, my husband asserted to the border guard that, "rear wheel drive is necessary for the perilous snow-covered roads in the Caucasus Mountains."

"Are you people crazy?" the border guard questioned us. "Do you have chains and nails?" he asked, as if he is concerned about our safety. A bribe, however, instantly put his mind at ease and he let us pass.

"God bless you!" he called after us as he pocketed the cash.

The guard's warning that the roads were dangerous was far from amiss. Shortly after, my husband's driving skills and experience came to our rescue. In the past he had often driven trucks through treacherous mountainous regions like this and on roads in similar conditions. Clearly navigating such snowy mountain passes demands great skill and nerves of steel. Snow is everywhere and there is little room for error.

The surface was glazed in a thin layer of ice, but there were no visible signs of these treacherous slippery spots, called "black ice" in New England. No external electric lights exposed our way. No roadway reflectors or cat's eyes to display the borders of the cliffs. Precipitous drops on the side of the road loomed without fencing. Sharp, sudden curves taken at low speed were still jarring and knocked us from side to side. Several times we skidded towards the edges of the abyss.

Now, again, on our final escape from Azerbaijan, we had to maneuver what turned out to be the narrow mountain Georgian Military Road to Armenia. We had been afraid it would be officially closed, but it was open. Who knows? Maybe in all the political confusion, it got ignored. Maybe the "oversight" was a Russian official who had a heart and knew it would be a way for Armenians to escape. Whatever the reason, we were blessed to be able to use it.

It wasn't easy travel. It was raining hard and who knows if it would turn into ice high in the mountains on those dangerous winding roads? I wondered. *Did we come here, escaping from the murderers in Baku, only to die falling off this slippery road into the void and be lost and forgotten below?*

Our ears popped from the high altitude, like on an ascending airplane takeoff. As we descended in altitude on the other side our ears popped once again as we felt ourselves careening downwards at a sharp angle. Finally, we saw the lights of civilization. Armenia! I was very thankful. Unfortunately, after the great Armenian earthquake, there was not as much civilization to behold as there once had been. We should be happy, we were safe, after all, but we were without our relatives and friends. We were without jobs, without our home. And though we were safer, we were not safe. The only thing that truly made us happy was that we would soon be able to see our children. A part of us realized that during this brief period of time we had been face to face with death, but we were determined to find a way to make it through this and survive.

Not surprisingly, our happiness was short-lived. We were filled with uncertainty from the very beginning. There was no way to ask someone for help, no emotional support, no financial relief. Armenia was still in turmoil after the earthquake—still very little power and sanitation.

It was almost surreal. We had left genocide only to come to a place—my ancestral homeland, Armenia—that could barely take care of its own, the people who already lived there, let alone thousands of refugees. After the earthquake, all the services one takes for granted were shut down: no electricity or running water; working telephone lines all but non-existent. The Great Armenian Earthquake had rendered my homeland a virtual third-world country.

Every person was in every way on his own, and each and every person had to deal with the challenges and turmoil of daily life himself. In moments that were particularly difficult or tragic, I would raise my arms to the heavens and ask the powers that be, *"Why did this happen to me?"* But then I looked around; I could see that there were others, many others, who were just like me, in difficult predicaments of their own.

Thoreau in his striking example of emotional relativity in *Walden* describes a woman after a great earthquake in Italy inconsolable with the loss of her home until she looks and sees the disaster everywhere around her. Then, she raises herself up and begins the cleanup and recovery.

The reason for this disillusionment is that there was no open communication—anywhere, between the government and its people, between people in the community. We barely even knew our neighbors in our new Armenian home, which was completely anathema to how we lived in Baku.

It makes sense, however. People in the Soviet Union were not taught how to act in emergency situations. For a generation, we were in fear of our lives if we talked about anything bad happening. Sure, there was always gossip. But "officially," everything was always "sweetness and light"—even when the world was falling apart around you. After the Second World War, the refugees, the broken families—no one mentioned the people who were killed. It was a taboo and a lie. It was all, in fact, one lie after another, so no one was prepared to pick up and start all over again from scratch. And that was what made this situation all the more difficult for me and my family as well as all the other people fleeing Baku.

Our quarters looked like a soldier's barracks, one room opening onto another. It was a house that one of my many aunts, Galla, bought after she left Baku. She was one of the first ones to leave and luckily purchased the huge home, which we call a "railroad flat," at a bargain price which could accommodate so many of us relatives. Because my aunt was one of five sisters, all with large families of their own, there were about sixty people living there. Many of us slept on the floor or on the chairs because there were not nearly enough beds or sofas for everyone. Nonetheless, Aunt Galla was our angel. We had a place for all of us to stay together, support each other, and try to find a way to survive.

We quickly established a routine: starting at five o'clock in the morning, we passed the only hot iron around to make the children's school uniforms presentable. Five dozen eggs were boiled for breakfast every morning. By the time one meal was eaten and everything was cleaned up, it was time to get started on the next meal. After the kids were put to bed for the night, the adults had a moment to relax, laugh, and dream about getting away and going to America. I don't think anyone believed this fantasy as strongly as I did. I knew that Yerevan was not our final destination.

Life was very tough in the capital of Armenia. Yerevan, the capital, was spared but a good part of the country had been destroyed by the earthquake and jobs were scarce. Everywhere you looked you could see injured people, some very seriously so. Almost every family had a lost member in the earthquake.

No resources seemed to exist, even though the entire world was sending aid. Moreover, typical of the corrupt Soviet Union, the government bureaucrats commandeered the foreign aid and sent the generous gifts of syringes, medicine, bandages and emergency food rations conspicuously labeled in English to be displayed on the bargain tables of the black-market bazaars to send the profits back into their own pockets.

We had a limited amount of cash with us and it was used up very fast. Fortunately, all her life my mother had been a collector of crystal, porcelain cups and saucers, brass, and chinaware that she purchased on her trips during the good times in the Soviet Union. I had purchased some items on my trips abroad, as well, but nothing compared to what my mother had accumulated. Though she loved these pieces, she did not hesitate to sell them. We had to survive. They were sold at far less than top value, but money is money.

We soon became aware that we refugee Armenians from Baku were not accepted in Armenia precisely because we spoke Russian and not the national Armenian language.

My mother tearfully reported how our daughter Ani had gone to the defense of her brother, Arthur, who was being picked on and beaten by the other children.

"You are fake Armenians," they shouted at her. "You come from Baku. You speak Russian." Our children were five and six years old at the time. We told them why they needed to leave their home—but to be ripped from all that they knew, survived all that they did, only to be bullied in this manner. It was heartbreaking.

We were fortunate to find a way to send the children to School Number 35. Amazingly, luck would have it, a friend of mine, also from Baku, who had married and moved to Yerevan years before, happened to teach history in that school and helped us enroll them. There, the language of instruction was Russian, and they could continue their education without a break neither in the language nor the educational system they were used to.

The institute was directly across from the Market downtown where there was a large department store. Anatoliy drove them to school because they were too young to take the bus alone in a big city, especially in the winter. Just as I had to take the official state Azeri language as one of my minor required courses in School Number One in Baku, my children going to the Russian language school struggled with classes in the official state language, Armenian, with an unfamiliar writing system, as a required second language.

Ironically, it was not until we came to America, and the children enrolled in Armenian language classes in Rhode Island churches, that they became fluent in the language of their heritage. Even in the United States the local

Armenian-Americans are mostly from the Middle East, Egypt and Lebanon, or Marseilles. They are not completely comfortable with our idiom. We still speak Russian, and our Armenian is a different dialect from their language—the language that is spoken in Yerevan. To compound the issue, I am unable to read the Armenian alphabet.

Because of our accents, on the streets of Yerevan we were cast as outsiders. But there were other reasons for this as well. When you have more than sixty people living like livestock in overcrowded quarters, then people notice. That and in a million other ways, we were constantly reminded that we were refugees, even though Armenia was our "home."

To say that it was a confusing time is a gross understatement. We had escaped rape, torture, and murder—only to find that we weren't truly welcome in our ancestral homeland.

Armenia was a homogeneous country of one nation and one language that was able to retain its own ancient language and culture. It was technically part of the USSR, but it somehow escaped the extreme pressure of "Russification" from Moscow. People in Armenia did not understand that in Baku, although it was a super-multicultural city, Russian was the dominant tongue that unified the socialist republic and strengthened ties to Mother Russia. I find this best exemplified by the many puzzled looks of the faces of Yerevan people who kept asking us, "You are Armenians, but why don't you know the Armenian language?"

These people did not know that in Baku, it was because of the government, under the orders from the Kremlin, which closed down the Armenian schools, newspapers, theatre and churches. These extreme measures were almost certainly taken out of the fear Moscow had of nationalist movements, particularly with regard to wealthy Baku's highly diversified society, which was located on a seaport in the Caspian Sea in the center of an extremely important economic and military resource: petroleum.

I can remember as a child seeing people visiting our courtyard and asking for help because they were shutting down the Armenian newspaper.

Then in adult conversations later on, I overheard that a theatre and school for Armenian language and culture had been closed. I remember people ordering subscriptions to Armenian newspapers even though they could not read the language. It was a show of support.

In a mono-cultural society like Armenia, there was no fear of a nationalist movement from a minority. So there was a completely different mindset there. Immediately upon our arrival in Yerevan, we had to endure the culture shock of meeting Armenian nationals who first welcome us and then later criticized and picked on us for speaking in Russian. I could understand the indifference of our compatriots in Yerevan to some degree, as they were a country still reeling from the Great Armenian Earthquake and were having trouble taking care of their own citizens, let alone the tens of thousands of Armenian refugees coming in from Azerbaijan. The mountainous country itself simply did not have the plentiful resources of petroleum-rich Azerbaijan, with its additional cotton agriculture, harbor on the Caspian Sea and exotic caviar and sturgeon.

This culture shock we experienced was made more difficult because we had been assimilated to the Russian language and the multicultural ambiance of Baku. Plunged into this alien monolithic world with its singular language, unfamiliar alphabet and culture, I felt fortunate that my family and I had had a grandmother who stubbornly spoke to us all our lives in Armenian. In doing so, she prepared us for this unexpected and unplanned transition. It may not have been all that unexpected for my grandmother, however, as she clearly saw the bloody future.

"Get me out of here!" she screamed at us which still rings in my ears when the attacks against Armenians in Sumgait, suburb of Baku, first began. "I saw it before! It's coming again!"

We would laugh at her, believing that our great Soviet Union would be there to protect us and never allow any bad things to happen. Now, we knew that she was right, and we all had the same unhappy, uncertain expression on our faces. We still wanted to go to America, the thought of which had always been a bright light at the end of a long tunnel. What made it more difficult for us was that in Baku, at least, we lived with the illusion that maybe the situation could improve, and all these troubles would pass. In Yerevan, the flame of hope was a cold, bleak glimmer.

To rub salt into the wounds, even in Yerevan, we were not free of tribulations from people who shared the religion of those enemies who attacked us and our kinfolk. We humans tend to generalize our antipathies just as the pigeon in the psychology laboratory experiment can be trained to fear the sound of a bell just before they administer an electric shock.

One afternoon, upstairs, above us in the college hostel, some students from Afghanistan tossed a large mutton bone with scraps of meat attached out the window. There were children playing outside below, including my son. The large bone struck Arthur on the left temple, over his eyebrow. My mother tried to staunch the bleeding and we took him to what might be called an emergency room, albeit a somewhat primitive one, where the medical staff stitched the wound closed. My son still carries the scar with him to this day.

When we got home, I immediately went upstairs to vent my fury at the students for the harm they inflicted on my child. The maintenance man of the hostel saw me and followed me up. As soon as I set my eyes on the students, the rancor I harbored against Azeris and anyone associated with them suddenly exploded when I thought about how close it was to Arthur's eye and that he could have been blinded forever.

"I wish you would die!" I screamed. "We ran away from you and you still are pursuing us!"

The maintenance man was also enraged and shrieked at them, "I can't get rid of you till you graduate. Is this how you handle garbage in your country? Out the window? Is this what you learn here in a civilized country? You are animals! I'd like to throw you bastards out the window like your garbage!"

Not a concept to these young men from who knows where in the mountains of Afghanistan.

I took my son to have the stitches removed and a motherly nurse from Tashkent of the same faith as theirs and of the Azeris hugged, kissed, and consoled my little boy in Russian through the whole process. I thanked her and felt ashamed of painting everyone with the same brush.

But trying times can bring out the resourcefulness in a person. My mother was one of the best. She found what turned out to be a student hostel for us to inhabit. It was a short distance from where the rest of my family was staying, and my husband, my kids, and I were anxious to move in. Before we arrived, my mother opened a can of kerosene to sanitize and deodorize the place. Wearing a protective shower cap to shield her hair and scalp, she closed the windows and fumigated every room one at a time. She followed up opening and closing the windows and cleaned each room again and again to eliminate the vermin. It was still difficult there: no lights, no gas, sleeping with all our clothes on in the cold, but it was an improvement from the crowded swarm where we had been staying. And it was clean.

The disruption of gas and electricity service made everything a challenge. With the shortages of fuel, the power was spotty, and blackouts were common. The capital city escaped the major earthquake, but because of war, blockade, trade embargos, manpower pulled away to serve in the army, and no money or supplies for street repair, we suffered through general disintegration of all living conditions.

The roads and sidewalks, like everything else, were in shambles. It was the dead of winter, and with so much rain, snow and mud, it was hard to navigate the streets and get the children to school. Their boots, even though I covered them with plastic bags that I bound to their lower pant legs, nevertheless filled with mud. Each day when they returned from school, I attempted to clean the footgear as best I could without proper cleaning supplies—or even hot water for that matter.

It was an exercise in futility that was disheartening, like trying to walk on quicksand. Armenia was at war and blockaded by Azerbaijan, which shut down what had always been the main highway and rail entrance to the country. There was a sense of being cornered, but I still saw the light of promise of America at the end of this dark tunnel. I steadfastly refused to turn away from that promise, no matter how dire our situation was.

Our new home was located in an old college dormitory, which still housed university students from abroad. There were no bathrooms, only Asian style toilets. These are merely holes in the floor. The raw electric wires nailed haphazardly to the walls and under open wooden slats were exposed to water that dripped down from the walls everywhere. After periods of blackouts when the electric current was suddenly restored, we were startled by the sight of crackling electrical sparks and the smell of acrid ozone. The pungent odor reminded me instantly of the Baku trolley cars when the sparks from the long electric poles above the cars snap and emit flashes of a bluish light.

We had to take care when we made our way to wash our hands or go to the toilet, treading gingerly on wooden slats that were laid above live electric wires sagging in puddles of water. We had only one pair of rubber galoshes to wear as possible protection for this dangerous trip. It was like navigating a deathtrap, and we could not allow the children to go there alone. If you saw a rat, you had to control your response and not jump or run because you could wind up stepping into an electrified pool. Our constant fear was the looming threat of death by electrocution.

My mother's constant effort to keep everything as clean and sanitary as possible was practically obsessive. We had rats, mice, bedbugs, and cockroaches. The kerosene sitting in a pail with perforated holes which she continually whirled around her head on a rope was our only hope to eliminate the threat of contagious infections from vermin. The constant smell of kerosene gave us headaches, but it was better than the alternative.

A misery that everyone had to endure was standing in long lines for everything—food, clothing, shoes, anything you might need. Even in cosmopolitan Baku, we had long lines for food. But here in Yerevan, a country under a boycott, we suffered from shortages of everything. I remember one day when my husband came home with some odd-looking sausages, which my mother unsuccessfully tried to fry. We were aware of the unscrupulous practices of post-earthquake hoarders and speculators, who during the blockade period would adulterate food to sell on the black market. They would pump liquids into the sausages with who-knows-what to swell them up and make them look plump. The greasy smell of paper that was burning inside the sausages was overwhelmingly nauseating, and my mother had to throw them in the garbage.

So we stood in lines and waited—and waited. It was a dreadful chore. Sometimes you could wait in line all day and come away with nothing because there was not enough to go around. You dreaded the crush of the crowd breaking the precious eggs you carried. The crazed people, some desperate and dangerous, were enough to drive you away from the lines. But the smell alone could do that.

Once my husband reported to me a stench so wretched and foul that he left a line he had been standing in for two hours. As miserable as this was, it was better than starving to death. There was even some delight when my husband found several glass jars of eggplant preserves that could spread on bread morning, noon, and night for us and the children.

While we waited expectantly for news from the American Embassy, we were asked to show our passports whenever we sought jobs, or if we wanted to send the children to a different school, or if we asked for help of any kind. It is as if we had to provide proof that we were not dead.

It's 1990. You would think that we would have had some sort of identification papers. But we don't. We are refugees. We left all of it left behind in Azerbaijan. Here's the catch: in the Soviet Union, they admitted to no such persons as refugees.

In Armenia, things were very different. They had suffered a major earthquake. They had a domestic population of their own people who were refugees without papers. Understanding our situation, that we had recently escaped from Baku where we had no chance of obtaining documents from the enemy Azerbaijan, the Armenian officials were more tolerant and sympathetic. So we were able to get by with very little.

Amazingly, when I was in Baku, I had a "job" helping people fill out applications to go to America, so by the time I reached Armenia, I had become somewhat of an expert on this process and helped others fill out their paperwork—for money. It was what I could do. My husband, who was able to find work here and there, discovered a friend, a shoemaker from Baku, and began to serve as his helper. It was a craft that my husband knew something about. When Anatoliy was serving as a young man in the Soviet army, he was assigned a cobbler's job while deployed in East Germany.

Émigrés do what they can to survive. The aristocratic writer Vladimir Nabokov of *Lolita* fame was a refugee from the Russian Revolution. He survived by giving lessons in tennis, chess, and boxing in Germany, France, and England. Whatever skill or talent you have, you try to exploit to put food on the table.

We stayed at the youth hostel for more than two years, and as the conflict with Azerbaijan worsened, Armenians who had not thought up to that time about leaving the country now became disposed to the radical idea of immigrating to a capitalist land. Each day was a struggle, waiting and hoping, while the tension and fear seems to have followed us all the way from Baku like a fog, a long shadow casting us in darkness.

Because our car still carried the recognizable license plates from the hated Azerbaijani enemy capital city of Baku, it became a target, like my son and the rest of us. Scratches and dents appeared. The tires were slashed. The vandals apparently did not appreciate the immense difficulty of filling out all the necessary paperwork to transfer automobile registrations when you cannot even prove your own identity. Even though everyone knew the situation, we could not prove anything, including our own existence. Azerbaijan would never transmit documents to assist us, the hated Armenian enemy.

"Go back to Baku," people coldly advised us.

The country was in denial and the same old Soviet bureaucratic system continued.

I went back and forth to Moscow often during our stay in Yerevan. Every time I went to the American Embassy to check our emigration status, I returned feeling numb. I kept imagining the possible negative answers that might greet me:

"The Armenian refugee program is over," or

"Unfortunately, the country is not giving you permission to leave," or

"You don't have proper proof of your refugee status."

There existed a lot of gossip and speculation and some of it was completely confusing.

One time, I asked my cousin Tamara to do me a favor on her trip on personal business to Moscow, "Please, do me a favor and telephone the American Embassy while you're there," I asked her.

Calling Moscow from earthquake-ravaged Armenia was very expensive and difficult, so I gave Tamara the phone number of the American Embassy along with our case number so that she might check on our status while she was there.

"I got it!" Tamara exultantly announced to me when she got back to Yerevan.

"Your case has Four X's!"

I didn't know what she was talking about at first. I asked a small favor of her, to contact the American Embassy in Moscow to check our status, and I get this inscrutable reference of "Four X's."

Then it hit me. Four X's represents the last deadly stage of syphilis!

This is something I recalled from a book that I had treasured years prior. It was a very scarce and suppressed text about the history of psychology I read clandestinely as a young girl, with the warning:

"For Educated People Only" on the title page. It was written by the eminent Swiss psychiatrist Dr. August Forel, whose portrait is on the Swiss one-hundred Franc note.

"With all the trouble I have in my life recently," I ask Tamara facetiously,

"Do I really need to be diagnosed with late stage syphilis, too?"

Her brow furrowed.

"What are you talking about?

I laughed.

"Did you call the American Embassy, or did you call the STD Hospital for Sexually Transmitted Diseases?"

"Which hospital are you talking about?" Tamara asked, completely mystified.

"You're better off not knowing." I countered.

She still didn't-follow me. I guess she didn't read Forel's book.

Perhaps the interlocutor at the American Embassy spoke poor Russian over the telephone, I speculated and this confused Tamara even more. Most likely it was a box, or boxes, on a form that were checked with a typed "X." Possibly it was an embassy code which they did not explain. Maybe, not.

Whatever. Obviously, I should not depend on anyone else to obtain such vital information. But I thanked her for her effort anyway.

I preferred to go to Moscow myself, and I did a total of seven times in the two years plus we were in Yerevan. I could not trust anyone for information unless I saw it with my own eyes and heard it with my own ears.

People now wanted to believe that the impossible would happen—that they could leave the USSR. That's the sense I started to get at this time. They believed more and more, but they were still afraid. I myself also sometimes had doubts, but in my mind's eye, on the edge of the horizon, I could still see a faint light in the distance. It was the shore of America, and I believed that very soon our ship would arrive and dock at that safe harbor. However, there remained a piece of my brain, that latent Soviet mindset, that had me programmed to believe that the great Soviet Union would protect us and that all this was just a nightmare from which we would wake up safe and snug in our beds.

But in my heart, I knew that we must leave here and go far away to save ourselves. Our only real hope remained in that fabled land which we were taught to despise while growing up, America, the capitalist enemy.

CHAPTER 11

Drama of Errors

THERE WAS A REASON WHY MY FAMILY AND I WERE A BIT MORE FOR-
tunate than the other Armenian refugees from Baku. We could speak
the language because of our infamous grandmother who refused to learn
Russian or Azeri. It was Armenian or nothing for her. Her insistence on the
"old way," I think helped us in many ways as we fled our home and found
an unwelcoming reception in our homeland. For this grandmother also
helped us learn how to stand up for ourselves.

If you study folklore in the history of literature, you will be reminded
in the stories of my family and many of the universal themes that anthropologists turn up time and time again in *all* societies. These archetypes of
international folktales are even cataloged by codes in the Aarne-Thompson
index, which is a classification system devised by Finnish folklorist Antti
Aarne and American folklorist Stith Thompson. The catalogue system is
useful in comparing the tales of different countries and cultures.

Among many, you will find such motifs as the *abandoned child, the
abducted bride, the adopted child, the hateful mother-in-law, the journey
escaping from persecution, the overbearing wife, the overbearing husband,
hidden treasure discovered, rescue and loss,* and looming over it all, always,

the fear of the powers of darkness, *the evil eye*. These themes surfaced in the stories of my family, just as they appear in folktales, operas, and literature around the world. Life imitates art, only in the case of my family; no witness took down their words or noticed their parting last words.

There have certainly been enough family dramas, sudden deaths and tragedies, which have been intentionally downplayed or omitted altogether from this book because they did not deal directly with the political and social dimensions as related to the persecutions and other reasons that prompted our flight from our country.

Some of the incidents I've left out include my mother's loss of a son named, Gurgyen, in a drowning, a child carrying the name in honor of an uncle of mine. The latter went missing in action in the Second World War. There was also an aunt, who, two days before her wedding, died from a reaction to an inoculation, turning a village celebration into a funeral.

My own father, first becoming a political prisoner in the army of his own country for being found with a contraband document, then being rehabilitated and going on to take part in the march of the victorious Red Army in Poland and then capturing the *Reichstag* of Hitler.

But some stories bear repeating because even though they are not directly related, they give glimpses into the complex world in which we lived—and survived.

My maternal grandmother, Arusak, was such a story. What makes it remarkable is not that anything "out of the ordinary" happened to her. It's because she was so much more like the Azeri peasant women that I have talked about (and even derided) throughout the book. She was not, by any stretch of the imagination, "nice." But she was a character.

Arusak had a very strong earthy village peasant personality. She was, without doubt, a harridan (a strict, bossy, belligerent old woman) who wielded her words like a shotgun. She would discipline everyone around her, including her own husband. She was taller than my grandfather and certainly outweighed him. She had a pockmarked face, liked to dance and had a regal look. She dominated her husband; he could not leave the house without Arusak's emptying his pockets of every penny.

No matter how old her daughters were, she expected absolute obedience and respect. Each daughter had to follow a list of assignments before Arusak's going "on vacation" to visit her village. She took full provisions, even a whole chicken cooked and clarified butter to show off that she came from the big city. One daughter, a tailor, had to make two or three new dresses for her mother, as if in tribute.

Her daughter asked, "Ma, you're an old lady, why do you want the skirt so short? You can see the petticoat."

"Eat shit! None of your business! I paid good money for it. Let it show."

Arusak had a way with words.

She once said to me, "If you marry that guy, I will cut you into little pieces and feed you to the hungry dogs in the street, and not one piece for your husband."

We had learned to ignore her harsh, extreme peasant metaphors, which she tossed like Molotov cocktails with impunity whenever things did not go her way. This was the accepted mode of village talk. Arusak once said to her husband, "You are not a man. A man like you I can find on every corner."

She told her grandson, when he crossed her, "I want to see you begging in the street for a crumb of bread and no one giving you a drop of water and spitting in your face."

Everything had to be her way. She was never satisfied with anyone. Everything had to be her way and no other.

But the golden virtues of the village were also Arusak's: the extreme cleanliness; loyalty to family; protection of her name and reputation of the family; avoidance of scandal. She indiscriminately hurled epithets of "prostitute" at females in the family, forbidding them from going to an innocuous movie that she deemed as offensive. Then, however, she would secretly go to see the movie herself, while misinterpreting the title, such as *Prostitute of Casablanca*.

Arusak had lived through the Ottoman Turkish massacres in Armenia—of that we have no doubt simply because of her age. She would narrate a story that she remembered as a girl involving people on horses attacking everybody. In her Armenian village in Adana—a part of the Ottoman Empire that was heavily populated by Armenians—each house had a small cellar nook where the preserves were kept. This was where she hid. Not knowing anything more than this, it is difficult trying to determine exactly when and where the attack she described actually took place. When we fled Baku, we left without family documents, though her passport put her at about a hundred years old when she died in California in 1997. Her marriage, at age fourteen or fifteen, was not uncommon.

With such a string of Turkish anti-Armenian attacks in village after village, town after town, the when and where this one took place remains clouded in mystery. However, using what we do know and doing our arithmetic we can determine that the attack by the horsemen would have been around 1911. The massacres of Adana took place in 1909, and Arusak would have been twelve years old at the time. It is also worth noting that lying about one's age was a universal tradition. However, it is certainly a possibility that she lived through that massacre in Adana. Furthermore, while the distance of Adana from Armenia is great, we now see refugees from Africa crossing great distances to try to reach Europe. So it is very possible that she had lived in Adana for a time. We will never know anything with certainty.

At any rate, there were great Armenian massacres in 1895, which in the Turkish Pasha's eyes justified as precedent for the killings in 1909. That Arusak witnessed horsemen storming into the village and killing Armenians in Turkey while she was a teenage girl seems quite believable as fact and not just another one of her vociferous rants.

There is an old anecdote which reminds me of my grandmother Arusak's character. The story goes that when the Mongols or Tartars invaded Europe on their fast, short-legged horses in the thirteenth century, one woman of grandmother's formidable personality answered back to her husband who had warned her to hide.

"Shut up!" she told him. "I want to see what these Mongols look like."

Suddenly, one of the Tartars wrapped his arm around her waist and swept her up onto the back of his saddle and rode off with her into the horizon. Her husband, after watching them disappearing in the distance, exclaimed,

"Poor Tartar!"

Even after immigrating to California, her six daughters dared not speak openly in front of Arusak. Even this raised her hackles.

"Why are you whispering?" she would interrogate.

"What secrets are you trying to hide from me?"

The transition from village to capital city to Los Angeles was painless for her almost right up until she entered her tenth decade on this planet. The colorful pages of the history of her life moved by like flipping the leaves of a picture book: from medieval village, to modern city, to megalopolis. One day in California, the daughters wanted to go to a birthday party without her. They turned the clocks in their house ahead to fool her.

"Ma, time to go to bed," they told her.

"Funny, I don't feel sleepy!" she responded with suspicion. Not fooled, she quickly discovered the trick and there was hell to pay.

In Baku, at the start of the Azerbaijani massacres of Armenians in the suburb of Sumgait, my Grandma Arusak prophetically yelled to us all, "Get me out of here! I've seen it before! It's coming again!"

"Oh, Grandma," we entreated. "This is Baku, the beautiful exceptional city. That can never happen here. Our country will protect us. The Soviet government will never let it happen. We are all brother citizens in the strongest country in the world. We went up first into space. Our government is there to take care of us. Gorbachev will not permit such a scandal to happen again like it did in Sumgait. That was an exception."

"Grandma, we have small children here and grandchildren," one daughter emphasized. "We have to take care of them first. We can't spend money to set you up in another republic."

"No, get me out of here! I know what's coming. I saw it before! Get me a plane ticket to Armenia or Russia. I want out! I saw it before! I don't want to see it again." She railed incessantly, voicing her thoughts in her own inimitable way.

"If you want your heads smashed into the shit on the street and flies eating your face, go ahead and stay! I want out! You can wait and see it. Not me!"

She was right. It came sooner than we could ever have believed.

One day I went to a beauty salon in Baku and saw two old ladies sitting there with the beauty-masks plastered on their faces. One was my grandmother Arusak, but because of the mask I didn't recognize her. Of course, she recognized me immediately as her young granddaughter. Before she left, she walked up to me and wagged her finger at me. "Don't tell anyone that you saw me," she warned, "Or, I'll tear you apart one leg after the other. Put your tongue in the proper place!"

Then she left by the back door and resumed her charade of limping and moaning like a real old lady is supposed to do.

Before she went to the next annual visit to her village, Arusak called together a family meeting where she made excessive demands on her daughters. "I need clothes and underwear to go visit my village. I need to take plenty of presents. Daughters, respect your mother!"

"But, Ma, we have families of our own. We have expenses."

"I don't care. Your first responsibility is to your mother!" she said. "And don't let me hear complaints from your asshole husbands, either. I arranged good marriages for you, but you picked those losers."

We immediately protested that some of the "losers" were husbands that she herself had picked out for her daughters.

"I guess I didn't beat you enough!" was Arusak's reply.

Grandmother Arusak bore twelve children, six girls, six boys. When someone would ask why she had so many babies, she'd tilt her head, smile, and answer in Armenian, "No TV, no radio. What else to do?"

Only the two older girls were born in Armenia, including my mother, Zhenya, and a younger sister. The others were all born in Azerbaijan, in Baku, where the family settled.

Later, when we found our children suffering from the usual childhood diseases, Arusak insisted that it was the "Evil Eye." (Remember, she was a peasant villager to her core) I can't fault her completely. She was a superstitious woman because all her boys died—a tragedy no mother should have to endure.

We all knew grandmother's story of her putting her little boy to bed and finding him dead in the morning. Today, we know it as "crib death" and seek logical medical answers, but then it was obviously a case of the "Evil Eye," a generational and cultural superstition.

Italians often wear a twisted golden tooth around their necks to poke out the *malocchio* or evil eye. Greeks spit three times on the bride at a wedding to ward off supernatural danger of jealousy. Argentines pay a man to sleep in the new house before anyone else so that he may absorb the malignant forces of jealousy. The pricks of envy are a tangible force of nature. In Spanish they say, *Los celos te matan.* (Envy kills you).

One day, my son went along with my husband and me to the marketplace to purchase a black sheep, which was brought back home to the courtyard where it was slaughtered. With its legs tied, my husband sliced the animal's throat in Arthur's presence. The sheep quickly died and its blood was gathered into a bowl. A ceremonial sign of the cross was painted on my little boy's forehead with the hot blood. This was followed by the summoning of an Azeri woman who burned salt three times to poke out the evil eye. I still remember her prayers repeated over and over in Azeri. I also remember my little boy asking, "Why is the sheep crying?"

Barbaric by today's standards perhaps, these rituals are common in many cultures, and are still in practice today. This was similar to *kaporah*, the Jewish sacrificial offering whereby a squawking chicken is sacrificed to transfer the bad vibrations from the child into the bird.

Amulets and incantations did not lessen the tangible danger of the Armenians from the Azeris. The only answer was to get out of there, leave Baku, even though we Armenians had helped build up this once-backwoods mining town of oil derricks and peat marshes into a great cosmopolitan city. And it was grandma who saw the familiar signs of resentment and murderous intent.

"I saw it before!" She reiterated the mantra.

"No, grandma, it will never happen here."

"No! Get me out of here!"

Arusak came from the village of Litzen in Armenia from a rich family. Her father kept their wealth in a large jug, the sort that milkmaids carry on their shoulders. It was full of gold coins, some bearing the faces and names of Czars dating back to the seventeenth century. On his deathbed, my grandmother's father advised his daughter, Arusak, that he had hidden the gold coins in the house.

Some years later, Arusak's niece, her brother's daughter, got married and decided to start construction, enlarging the house for herself and her parents. The news soon leaked back to Arusak in Baku that a large cache of gold had been discovered in one of the walls. Grandma immediately took a trip to Armenia to claim what was hers.

"This is my father's savings," she told her niece.

"I don't want it all, but at least give me part."

The family completely denied finding any treasure and there was nothing Grandma could do. Arusak went back to Baku with empty hands and a heavy heart. Nothing, however, can be kept secret in the village; everything argued in favor of the rumor of a substantial windfall.

As Armenians say,

"Go to a friend for advice,

To a woman for love,

To strangers for charity,

To relatives for nothing."

We owe to this woman the valuable gift of teaching us Armenian. Arusak demanded we speak with her in Armenian. Even if we were hungry, it didn't matter. We had to voice the request for food in Armenian. She did not understand Russian or Azeri and had no desire to learn the languages. When we were refugees in Armenia, our family was conspicuous as some of the few Baku Armenians who could speak the language.

Most of Baku Armenians spoke only Russian, a notable success of the Russification program from the government in Moscow. Yerevan Armenians were always puzzled by us Baku Armenians not knowing the language of their heritage. But Baku Jews did not know Yiddish or Hebrew, either. In a city of forty nationalities, many spoke only Russian, thanks in part to the proscription of ethnic language schools. No Armenian schools. No Yiddish schools. No Hebrew Schools. Everything was taught in standard Russian.

On the other hand, there were "maktab" religious schools allowed for the Muslim Azeris since the Azerbaijan Soviet Socialist Republic was created in their name. In the villages, the Azeris did not speak Russian, only Azeri, a dialect of Turkish, and that was the language of their schools. Probably, Russian was taught as a second language, and played the same disregarded secondary role as the required Azeri lessons thrust on us in our Baku schools. However, most of the Azeris of the cosmopolitan oil-rich capital city of Baku did speak and understand Russian.

Grandmother Arusak knew neither Azeri nor Russian, kept a firm hand on all her daughters, whipping out commands in the most biting and indecent Armenian, untranslatable, needing to be bleeped out.

So many other refugees were questioned or taunted, "If you are really Armenian, why can't you speak it?"

In America, my children understood Armenian from their great-grandmother, and we saw to it that in the school of the Armenian Apostolic Church they learned to read and write the language of their heritage. In Rhode Island, I found work as an interpreter, as did my daughter, utilizing this specialized language skill, where I earned an income as well as contributed to our community. Grandma's stubbornness paid off.

Arusak received a medal as a *Heroic Mother of the Soviet Union* for bearing twelve children. In the USSR, mothers were rewarded for increasing the population, particularly after the devastating losses of war. Arusak had worked for the city of Baku to be on a waiting list for a new apartment. It took many years to achieve that goal. With her husband, she lived with the two yet unmarried daughters.

Grandfather was in his early seventies when he died and afterward Arusak continued in the apartment for many years until we had to run away from Baku.

If it were not for the genocide of Armenians in Baku, and the eventual writing of this book, I would never have pursued looking into the history of my maternal grandfather's escaping to Armenia from Turkey.

My mother's father's name was Kapriel (they called him Kapo). He was their eldest of two boys. His younger brother was called Reuben. As the family narrative went, Kapo also came to Armenia with his brother, his parents and his sister, Tamar, who was about fourteen-years old.

They all crossed the mountains into Armenia to escape from the Turkish Empire. On reaching Uz, that village in Armenia, they settled down hoping for some stability. The people of the village made assumptions about these new people who came with some money and built a house. In those days a wife aged fourteen years old was not unusual, and Tamar, they thought was his wife. She was in reality his younger and only sister.

Only the mountains separated them from Turkey, and they imagined they were more secure, but there were local Turks around, who were harassing Armenians. They were stealing animals, burning houses, and kidnapped Armenian girls. They were called in our family narrative "Kochars."

Mothers would hide girls in underground niches and dress them shabbily to make them look unattractive. They always came "like a storm" and the day came that they kidnapped Tamar. Kapo went searching everywhere for his sister and sought her for three days with his younger brother, Reuben, but to no avail. Then Kapo happened on a helpful Turk who through some gifts of sheep, large wheels of cheese, and fresh butter became cooperative.

That man, who by tradition in the family stories was called "Kochar" (a term which research has now come to show is the name of a tribe of pastoral Turks), told Kapo that the girl was with a clan and she was under constant observation, but she was not allowed to leave. Many nations abduct brides, literally, or go through the traditional ritual of a kidnapping.

"I still want my sister back," Kapo said, and promised to do whatever it took to rescue her. He bribed the "Kochar," who was lame and played a humble role of village guard in the tribe, the gift of two sheep. Then the Kochar told him that if Kapo and his men of the village will pass in the mountains at night, he would set up for them a conspicuously burning torch. It would be their signal that the chief of the tribe was away, and it was safe for Kapo to come forward and fetch his sister. They waited three days watching from below until they observed Kochar's promised torch flaring high on the mountainside. This accommodating Turk helped bring Tamar down the rugged trail from the Turkish camp into their welcoming arms.

Upon returning to the village, they happily feted Tamar with a two-day celebration of food and music. Unfortunately, the merriment was short-lived when after several days she was abducted again. Kochar later reported that Tamar was no longer there and that she was pregnant. The helpful young Kochar was rumored to have been killed for his cooperating with us. Later, we heard that Tamar was also dead. The family reluctantly held an Armenian funeral service in absentia for Tamar, all the while hoping that a miracle would bring her back to us alive and well.

It was like the stories of colonial New England's and Virginia's girls being carried off in Indian raids from the early settlements in North America. Unaccountably, mysterious blond and blue-eyed Native Americans began turning up generations later, no doubt descendants of these captive women. Such may have been the fate of my great aunt Tamar.

My grandfather finally settled in Uz and married an Armenian woman there. It was the earthy Arusak, my grandmother of redoubtable fame, a match with her husband in rugged fortitude. The story goes that they traveled on horseback from Uz over the mountains into Azerbaijan when my mother, Zhenya, was five or six. My mother remembered riding on horseback in her mother's arms at night half asleep under a crescent moon and dozing under the noonday sun. They rode day and night.

He found work in furniture stores, and he would carry the heavy tables and cabinets strapped across his shoulders, without the benefit of modern delivery equipment. This was the husband that Arusak accused of not doing enough as the man of the house.

The year would have been 1937 when Armenia won its separation from the Caucasian Federation under Stalin's control of the Soviet Union. The notorious Beria and Stalin are said to have wanted to reduce the population of Armenia and let them be absorbed into Georgia. One way to lower de-mographics was to exile thousands to Siberia. Armenia was still suffering economically after trying to accommodate all the exiled Armenians who were fleeing persecution from the Ottoman Empire.

When I asked my aunts why they left Armenia, they all said it was impossible to live there anymore. There was a lot of pressure both economically and socially from the highhanded imposition of Communism, and Stalin looked with suspicion on the Armenian Communist Party and those who returned from exile in foreign countries "tainted by capitalist ideas." Under Beria's command, police terror was used to strengthen the party's political hold on the population and suppress all expressions of nationalism. He suppressed the Armenian Apostolic Church and executed thousands by the firing squad in the years 1937-38 alone.

Do we need to seek a reason for trying to escape from these conditions? What was the lure of Azerbaijan, one may ask? Economically, it was in far better shape with its oil wells and caviar. There was a long history of enterprising Armenians achieving fabulous wealth in the petroleum and related industries, such as the fabled international millionaire, Calouste Gulbenkian. Stalin might have been less suspicious of potential nationalist uprisings in the potpourri of nationalities in Azerbaijan than what prevailed in Armenia. With the ghastly situation in Armenia, what neighboring border was open for them to flee to? Russia would be the same politically. Turkey was out of the question as an enemy of the Armenians. Georgia was the motherland of Stalin and not particularly friendly to their fellow Christian Armenians.

My mother, Zhenya, was born in Armenia and married my father, Grigori in Baku, Azerbaijan.

He was also born in Armenia. His own history is a tale of wandering, confusion, and mystery. The story of the family was always strange, unexplained really, but we grew up with it and accepted without questioning the bizarre tale about our father Grigori as an infant, the details about which we were cautioned to keep secret.

This story started to unravel as we strolled along the streets of downtown Baku. I was puzzled to witness an old woman often come up and hug and kiss my father, stroke his cheeks, and call him, "My real son! Grigori!"

She sold loose sunflower seeds in rollup paper cones on a street corner. She was not my grandmother. I knew that.

"Who was she?"

I was too young to understand the strange story and maybe even today, as an adult, I still do not completely understand it.

On the long, arduous trip from Armenia, my paternal grandfather and grandmother, Sümbül, traveled with a newborn child, my father. I used to think of them as the Biblical paintings of the Holy Family pausing on their flight to Egypt. The harshness of the mountain climate, being burdened with a child, and the fear of a child's crying attracting danger, all these things I speculated about. The inexplicable fact was that they dropped the baby at the side of the road "next to a big stone" and moved on.

The whole village of the sunflower seed vendor knew my grandfather Grigori's story. My other grandparents knew his story. The child, like Moses abandoned in a boat of reeds in the Nile, was saved, only not by a Pharaoh's princess, but a village peasant woman who fed him and cared for him until the news from the village reached my grandparents in the big city. She was the sunflower seed lady.

Now, my grandparents were the subject of scandal by people in Baku who came from the same part of Armenia and knew the story of the abandoned baby. They went to confront the woman and there was a big conflict.

"Give my baby back!"

"Which baby? You dumped him. Now, you want the baby back?"

"How can you sleep at night? How can you live with yourself? And your husband is the same. If that would be me, I'd rather hang myself! But you don't have a shame or heart!"

Did you care if there was a wet nurse for the baby? Did you care if he had milk? Or you were hoping he would die there and not be a burden to you?"

The conflict went on for almost a month with cursing, crying and screaming involving families and relatives on both sides. Finally, the wisdom of old people was heard and accepted. The baby was returned to my grandmother.

When I asked about how that baby was cared for, they said, "At that time every second woman in that village was pregnant and there was plenty of mother's milk to go around."

This doesn't completely solve the mystery, as many unanswered questions remain.

When my mother complained about Sümbül, her mother-in-law, my mother brought up this family scandal. The one time, as an adult, I approached my grandmother Sümbül about the truth she avoided giving me a straight answer.

I even asked my father what happened to him as a baby on the road to Baku. What kind of mother could she be? What was my father's answer when I brought up the question about his fairy-tale history of abandonment as a baby?

"I know all about it," he said, waving his hand in the air.

"Whatcha gonna do?"

Another time, as a child, I witnessed a heated argument in the family. My grandmother, Sümbül, was upset or jealous about something my grandfather did, and he flung out at her.

"If you were a good mother, you would never have left your son on the roadside!"

"If *you* were a good father," she echoed back, "You never would have allowed your son to be left on the roadside! You want me to tell you what kind of a good father you are?"

"Go ahead and say it! Say it!" he raised his fist,

"Don't raise your voice to me or I'll punch you."

"You think I don't know what you are doing behind my back? I knew all the time. But today you made a shit of your own wife."

"What are you talking about? You're crazy!"

"No, you're crazy. You even have the nerve to bring that woman to the Armenian theater where she sits right next to you. You have your wife on one side of you and your girlfriend on the other side. What kind of father are you?"

"You're imagining things!"

"That prostitute! I even know her name—Vartush."

"You're crazy," he waved his arm in disdain and left.

She never could prove anything. Who knows if it was true, but as a child I remember that episode which I only half understood. Life continues in the same way.

Children observe and hear more than adults suspect. The vision of the abandoned child left on the road haunted my childhood dreams, but I was afraid to ask any questions about it.

"Would I or my brother be abandoned on the edge of the road by a large stone when we went on a trip?"

My father always lingered by the doting seed vendor and accepted her caresses, but he did not share the scandalous story with me. Everything was kept secret. Adults did not share many stories with children, or even other adults, for that matter. It is truly a scandal and a mystery, but when you hear the story all your life you learn to accept the unacceptable.

You could probably challenge me about why I did not know. I can only say that such a thing is not unique to the society where I grew up. After I arrived in Rhode Island, I audited a college course on women's literature. One of the stories concerned a deeply held family secret.

A student challenged the teacher that such a fact could not be hidden. In response, the professor asked the class,

"Don't tell me the secret, but have you been warned not to reveal something in your family to anyone? Raise your hand if it happened to you." Almost all the hands in the class shot up.

In times of unrest and danger, the most helpless get waylaid and misplaced: children, the handicapped and the elderly. Babies throughout history have been saved and adopted by tender-hearted men and women. Every society has a legend of an abandoned child. Yes, my grandmother abandoned her own child. However, perhaps it was to make atonement for this unimaginable sin that Grandmother Sümbül went and adopted and raised an orphaned Armenian teenage girl, Nadya. When I was young, my grandmother Sümbül would take me and my younger brother Raphael on a train trip to Surakhani to visit Nadya, her adopted daughter, now grown, a petite Armenian woman married to an Azeri. We received a huge welcome. My grandmother was treated like a queen. We returned home carrying large bags of walnuts, chestnuts, hazelnuts, and dates back with us on the train. These were gifts of appreciation for my Grandmother Sümbül who had adopted and raised Nadya.

When Nadya finished eighth grade and this pretty girl was on her way to trade school, she was kidnapped and carried away by an Azeri, Mamet Kulí. She became his wife and bore him nine children. The shame of marrying a Muslim kept her from coming back. She worked the farm, performing the chores of feeding chickens, cleaning, cooking, and fetching water and firewood, never a moment to rest. I spoke in Russian to her young children who were learning the language in school, but they also spoke perfect Armenian because my grandmother Sümbül had insisted on speaking Armenian to their mother, and following the family tradition, Nadya did the same to her own children, with an Azeri father or no.

Nadya never had a smile on her face, her brow was always furrowed. She displayed a constant look of shocked sadness in her tearful eyes, like the paintings of Mary Magdalene gazing up at the crucified Christ. With slanted eyebrows and her down-turned mouth, she sat on the floor in the Azeri way, looking sad and complaining about Mamet constantly beating her. In addition, he was unfaithful to her. My grandmother wanted to reproach him about his infidelity, but Nadya begged her not to say anything because he would beat her even more severely. In sharp contrast to his occupation as a bookkeeper, he was a big, large-boned man with huge hands, which he clearly was not averse to using on her in anger. Grandmother did speak to him about his philandering anyway, but to no one's surprise he vehemently denied everything.

One of Nadya's boys was a talented drawer. The walls of his small room were covered with his sketches. They were very good. He was surprised when I, as a young girl, recognized one sketch as looking like a Rembrandt. He showed me the original picture he copied from one of his art books and I told him that I had been reading about the life of Rembrandt. He wanted to go to art school, but his Azeri father was unsupportive and put him down for his artistic ambition. "It is woman's work," he would tell his son. These two Armenian families were permanently joined by my parents, Zhenya and Grigori, in Baku. Arusak, my maternal grandmother, the demanding harridan, in colonial New England villages would have had her hands locked in holes in the stock and a sign displayed over her head as "a common scold."

<hr />

Turn left out of the main gate of our courtyard in Baku and you came upon the home of my father's parents. Friends had talked to them about a woman, Arusak, with six daughters nearby. One of them was named Zhenya, who was just right for their son Grigori. These were destined to be my father and mother. It was not the old-fashioned arranged marriage precipitated by the parents, but others set up the meeting.

This grandmother, Sümbül, was a schemer seeking to find an adequate bride for her son, one who was acceptable to her. She paid no attention to his marriage, even while my mother was pregnant with me. So Grandmother Sümbül, around the corner, busily pursued an arranged marriage for her son behind his back with a bride who was suitable in *her* eyes.

Sümbül settled on an Armenian girl of "good family." The family was later appalled to find out that this potential suitor, Grigori, was already married with a visibly pregnant wife. Grandmother Sümbül was cavalier about legal and formal details: she had abandoned a child, welcomed him back, and now tried to dump Zhenya his pregnant wife (whom she did not like) to fix him up with a potential fiancée preferable over my mother.

Living with this mother-in-law would not be easy for my mother right up to Sümbül's death in her eighties. She insisted that my mother do all the laundry herself, which at that time was an exhausting series of operations. Every batch was boiled first, then washed, wrung dry by hand, starched and whitened with bluing. Every birthday occasion saw Sümbül raid my mother's gifts and hand them over to her own sickly daughter. My mother, Zhenya, out of the iron tradition of respect for the mother-in-law, had to bite her tongue. Sümbül insisted that my brother and I, as children, address her and her husband as Mom and Dad, and required us to call our own parents by their formal names, Zhenya and Grigori. Imagine my mother's living with this harridan who tried to divide the closeness of mother and child. It was not only the family and birthday presents that Sümbül tried to control, but even my mother's hard-earned salary.

The paymaster after the bookkeeper's serious complaint finally refused to hand over my mother's pay in cash when Sümbül showed up on payday. She had been appropriating my mother's earnings for herself and her sickly daughter.

"You have no right to get Zhenya's money!" the paymaster told Sümbül to her face, "You witch, don't you ever come here again!"

This mother-in-law overworked my mother like a scullery maid and continued to drain her energy. Finally, my young mother had enough and tearfully opened up and shared her health concerns with her own doctor. The doctor was dismayed. The pediatricians making house visits for me and my brother had noticed a young woman living there who exhibited the suspicious symptoms of tuberculosis.

It was Sümbül's daughter with her dark family secret. My aunt, though it was endangering the family and my brother and me, kept my mother in the dark. She was formally registered with the Health Department as a tubercular patient, which could not be covered up. The physician recognized that there were serious medical infractions in this household and urged my mother to tell her mother-in-law, which my mother did, much to Sümbül's fury.

"My doctor forbids your daughter living here with her tuberculosis while we have my young children here. He doesn't care if she has a separate room," my mother told her. This earned the eternal hatred of Sümbül for my mother.

As a result, the city medical committee made an official visit to our house and demanded separate housing immediately for the children away from Sümbül and her contagious daughter. The secret scandal was out. The committee gave our family the priority status on the waiting list and the opportunity to obtain a good apartment in Musabekovo, a new development, finally giving relief to my beleaguered mother from her overbearing mother-in-law.

Strangely, my grandmother Sümbül softened in old age. She voiced her appreciation that my mother never spoke against her and was kind to her in spite of all the dreadful past history. The tubercular daughter, my aunt, died young. But, even here, there was a story that exceeds believability. That sick girl delivered a baby boy, with no husband. The son did not know that a neighbor across the street that he passed by daily was his own father. It was only revealed to him when he was thirty years-old and the fact that he was half Jewish, clouded in secret by my manipulative grandmother Sümbül. The tradition of family secrets continued through four generations.

Both extreme grandmothers agreed on one thing at least that proved useful to us: honoring their heritage by speaking Armenian and teaching it to their children and grandchildren. Their fortitude (even though it was highly overbearing at times), was what I called upon time and again, to carry us through the very difficult years of fleeing Baku, living in Armenia, and then finally making it to America. Their legacy has endured and sustained us, and I have come to be very proud that these are my ancestors.

CHAPTER 12

Lost Sapphires

IT IS LIKE BEING HIT BY A CAR. YOU GET UP AND SAY, "THANK GOD, I'M alive." You have broken bones but no pain. You are in a state of shock and think, *"How am I going to get back on my feet?"*

Everything we worked for all our life, we had to leave behind in Azerbaijan under the threat of Azeri persecutions of Armenians.

Or did we?

I learned that a girlfriend of mine, who had flown with me to the American Embassy in Moscow in order to request refugee status for Baku Armenians, was now flying from our exile in Yerevan, Armenia, back to Baku to try to sell her house. There was a rumor that we could travel safely back to Baku. There were other Armenians taking the same dangerous chance of going back to the Azeri city where they had grown up but had also recently escaped, like us as exiles.

I had the illusory hope that I could do the same, and that I could successfully sell one of our houses along with anything else that I might still find in our apartment after some time settling in Armenia. We knew that the Soviet government, upon an order that came directly from the Kremlin, sent the MVD forces to Baku, ostensibly to protect us Armenians. When it came to the Ministry of Internal Affairs, the very name induced fear in everyone, yet we still trusted the Soviet government to safeguard us from harm with its military power despite how they let us down in the attacks on Armenians in Sumgait and Baku not too long before.

My girlfriend told me that her Azeri fiancé, Fuad, was living at her house in the capital city Baku, and she could provide me with an "Azeri shield." Fuad spoke fluent Azeri, which now seized the reins as the dominant language of the Republic of Azerbaijan. It was another ever-widening fissure in the Iron Curtain. With countries exerting their freedom of choosing their language, the collapse of the entire USSR was imminent.

It was more than a little frightening. The super-patriotic audience thirsting for an independent sovereign Azerbaijan nation shouted down their government officials: "Don't speak Russian to us! Speak Azeri!" But I was going on a mission, and Fuad's mother tongue was a major advantage for my girlfriend in retaining her belongings and getting some compensation for the property she and Fuad owned.

After seeing my mother crying night and day, but not saying why, I thought, *maybe I could benefit from knowing Fuad, as well.* I knew what was bothering my mother, who worked hard all her life for what she had; she did not want to leave behind everything she knew and held dear. None of us did. We all lamented leaving on these terms, even if we did not cry openly. When I sought the help of my friend and her Azeri fiancé's in order to minimize our losses, my old grandmother, my mother, and the whole family was against it. It was not unlike my superstitious grandmother who lived her life according to bad dreams and would often warn us, "Don't leave the house today." We used to laugh at her, but I was not laughing now, living in this reality of nightmares.

My husband felt the same way. I tried hard to convince him that it was easier for me, as a woman, to go on this "mission," but he remained very uneasy about it. He knew the sister of my girlfriend, who carried an Azeri last name from a previous marriage. She spoke Azeri fluently. At that time, we still did not harbor hatred and fear of all Azeris, growing up among them as we did, sharing entertainments with them, and being protected and sheltered by some of them in these times of danger. All was happening, and it was happening fast. It was a confusing time. We were in a state of shock and we still had hope that it all would just pass.

Eventually, my girlfriend and I left on our excursion, taking a roundabout route by plane from Armenia to Georgia and from there flying to Baku. It was still internal travel in one country, the Soviet Union, but the two provinces of Azerbaijan and Armenia were *de facto* at war. Firstly, planes were not flying directly from Armenia to Baku, and for good reason: who would want to be pointed out as coming from the enemy republic of Armenia?

Fuad took a plane halfway to meet us in Tiflis, Georgia, and then accompanied us to Baku Airport where his personal taxi was waiting. As a cab driver, he made it more secure for us. He was living with my girlfriend in her apartment and I stayed there with them. We knew it would only be for a few days.

It had been enough time since I had been away from Baku, but already everything looked different. I remember looking out the window in disbelief, wondering if this was the same city. There was a palpable sadness there. Everything looked so gray. Even some of the trees looked woeful and sad, with many, in fact, having been burned by tank fire when Soviet troops rolled into Azerbaijan to quell the unrest, a display of might that was likely meant more to keep the Communist Party in power than to protect us Armenians.

Just as noticeable was the unequal population exchange. Armenians and Jews with their culture and education had been exchanged for peasant village Azeris who were streaming in from the Azerbaijan countryside and out of Armenia. These people were not even walking in the same way. The men had dark beards and shuffled along the streets slowly, not with the former big-city rush. The influence of the ayatollahs of Iran was evident. Everything was dark and heavy.

The first two days that I spent with my girlfriend and her fiancé, I did not leave the house. Fuad needed to coordinate his work schedule with ours while we needed to defuse, fearing that someone would harm us every day.

On the third day, Fuad and I got into the taxicab and drove along Tolstoy Street, where School Number One was located at one end and School Number fifty-two at the other. The temporary emergency headquarters of the combined police, military, and State investigative and security force was located there, in the empty school. The site was in the middle of the neighborhood where the Armenian population had been concentrated. It was only a fifteen-minute walk from where I grew up.

I felt unsafe standing in front of this school, which was so familiar to me, even with the three branches of Soviet homeland security concentrated inside:

1. The formidable MVD, a Soviet military force, whose charge is to crush internal conflicts was present.
2. So was the secret police, KGB, feared the most.
3. But it also had the Azeri *militsia,* or local police, the same local police who had stood by with hands folded while violent acts against us Armenians were being committed in front of their eyes.

It was about 9:30 in the morning as I entered the school, now housing the "SHTAB" or Central Soviet Criminal Investigation Headquarters. Their mission was to investigate crimes against Armenians and to help Armenians leave alive and retrieve what they could from their possessions. I inquired about the procedure to request permission for providing me with an armed escort to visit my house to see what I could salvage.

Their response was, "We don't have the extra manpower right now. You can come back in the morning, and we will escort you to see what you can find then."

I was disappointed that I could not take care of everything right away. It did not sink in immediately that this incredibly powerful force, comprised of three major units of Soviet authority, was helpless to protect us Armenians. All they really could do was speed our exiting from this city and this country.

Fuad then informed me that he could not help me the next morning because he was busy, having several errands to attend to with his fiancée. However, he managed to reserve another cab for me in the morning under the pseudonymous Azeri female name, "Aliyeva." That night, I practiced pronouncing the word, "yes" in Azeri.

The plan was for me to answer "yes" in Azeri when the phone call in the morning and the taxi driver asked, "Are you Aliyeva?"

"Let's practice," Fuad said. "Say, *bali*." He enunciated it very clearly for me.

"*Bali*," I repeated in turn.

"No, *baaaali!*"

There is an ancient tradition of asking a suspected enemy to pronounce a word in order to assess his or her nationality by even the slightest variations from the "correct" phonology. In the Bible, the Hebrews tested questionable soldiers with the word for wheat, *shibboleth*. The enemy could not pronounce "sh" and said *SIbboleth*, which sealed their horrible fate. That was what differentiated the Ephraimites from the Gileadites and the Bible records 32,000 killed. Thus, the word *shibboleth* denotes this ancient trick in many histories of conflict through the centuries.

In Baku, the Azeri mobs would pull people off buses and asked them to pronounce the word for "hazelnut," which is *fhundux*. Those who pronounced it with an unaspirated pure "f," *fendex*, were instantly revealed as the hated Armenians and suffered the consequences as a result. That was the Azerbaijani *shibboleth*, as it were.

Despite my coaching, I fell short in stretching out the word for yes, *baaaali*, unable to pronounce it to Fuad's satisfaction no matter how much I tried. Azeri did not flow effortlessly off my tongue, even though it was a required second language in school. None of us took seriously the Azerbaijani Socialist People's Republic's official language. We never thought that we had any need to know this dialect of the Turkish language, which we deemed to have little history or culture. In fact, we looked upon it as a joke.

Some relatives and neighbors did learn the language through work, where the need arose, but that was about the extent of it. Each Soviet state educational code demanded classes in the official language of its own Socialist Republic, but for all intents and purposes, they may have been neglected "gut courses" just like in Azerbaijan.

To be fair, if Russian had not been so well disseminated in the Central Asian republics, perhaps their local tongue might have been more meaningful. But Russian was so heavily established in Azerbaijan as a standard language at home, in the family, in the street and in commerce, at least in the capital city, Baku, that the influence of the Turkish dialect was minimal among non-Azeris. Likewise, the influence of school-requisite Russian was minimal among the Turkish-speaking Azeris in the countryside, outside the cosmopolitan city of Baku. A trip to a deep village, where they never went to school, where they never needed school, you would find little or no Russian.

This situation is analogous to the United States educational situation in one of its territories. The Free Associated State of Puerto Rico, which has essentially been a colony of the United States since 1899, is a Spanish-speaking territory. Everyone there has gained U. S. citizenship and English is a requirement in schools, but how many can pass a *shibboleth* test? I can attest to that fact in Rhode Island. I noticed many Puerto Rican neighbors lacked English. The colonial master's language, in this case English, is still not widely known. Similarly, the case is the same in the countryside in Azerbaijan.

In desperation, meeting the challenge of my hopelessly accented Azeri pronunciation, we decided that the best approach was to put a cloth over the mouthpiece of the phone when I spoke in order to fake a bad connection.

Simplistic, yes, but it worked. That morning, alone in the house as I was waiting for the cab to arrive, I felt completely isolated. It was like being in the middle of the ocean without knowing how to swim. I couldn't help but worry.

I will be alone in a taxi. I have to convince myself that I am Azeri. I am in my own city, and I must make myself believe that there is nothing for me to be afraid of in spite of all I know.

I was nervous as I got into the taxi wearing a stark Azeri disguise, no makeup and no special clothes. I sat quietly on the right side of the back seat. The driver greeted me in Russian,

"*Dobroye utro!*" (Good morning).

I just nodded and thought it could be a trick because so many Azeris now hate to speak Russian and my name on his manifest is Aliyeva. I felt unsafe and tried not to look out the window.

Who could see me? Whom could I meet and might recognize me and greet me and expose my cover?

I finally took a brief sideways glance at him. He was tall and physically in good shape, wearing an open black leather jacket. Then I noticed his hand on the steering wheel, focusing on the impression of a wedding band that had clearly been on his finger for a long time, but was removed now.

Could he have had an Armenian wife and now disowned her?

I wondered this and all sorts of other wild possibilities.

When he started to drive, he said in Azeri, "Bajim (*sister*), are you going to Tolstoy Street?"

I answered simply, "Uh-huh."

I perceived that his accent did not quite sound like Azeri to me, but the trip was long and to avoid further conversation, I communicated only with heavy sighs as if I were not in the mood to talk, hoping he would not see the fear and uncertainty my shrugs and grunts were covering up. When he pulled over and stopped in front of the schoolyard, I stepped out of the vehicle. Feeling a little safer, I told him in Russian, "Wait here!"

I went inside to confirm my appointment and returned to the cab. Reaching in through the open passenger window, I handed him a bill for the fare and said in Russian, "*Spassibo* (Thank you)."

He turned away suddenly, withdrawing from me as if it was a snake I was offering instead of cash. He put his hand on his chin and shook his head vigorously from side to side in a "no" gesture.

"I am not taking money from our people," he said in Russian.

Taken by complete surprise, I answered in Russian,

"Why not?"

"I recognized that you are Armenian. I'm Russian." He gave me as much information about himself as possible. I thought it was to convince me that he is not my enemy and one of us. "My mother is Armenian. My father is Russian. My family left already. I'm getting out of here in a couple of days myself. Too bad the Azeris have destroyed this wonderful city, Baku, but most important of all, is that Baku without pretty girls will not be the same."

"How did you know I am Armenian?" I asked.

"I knew because you do not speak Azeri. And you do not look Azeri."

So much for my attempt at subterfuge, I thought.

When I offered him the money again, he refused once more and asked me, "You want me to wait and help you to get back?"

"Oh no, thank you. It will take too much time."

He wished me good luck and drove off without taking payment. I stood there for a moment in shock, worried about how miserably my disguise had failed, having been recognized as an Armenian in my own city, now hostile to me and mine.

I had come this far, and I was not about to turn back. So I went into the old school building and entered a large room, which probably had been the principal's office. There were a number of tables behind which people were sitting and more chairs along the walls for visitors. I noticed right away that everybody was speaking Russian.

I told an attending official in Russian, "I want to get help to go to my apartment. I was here yesterday, and I was told to come back in the morning and fill out a document."

I was directed to another officer and asked to fill out a single-page form. It was simple; Name, address, date house broken into. I completed it and handed it back to him.

"Sorry," the officer said after looking it over, "but I do not have jurisdiction in your case!"

I asked in alarm, "Why not?"

"Our orders are to investigate the events from the 15th to 19th only. Those are the official dates of the pogrom. You have written down the 13th. We are here to investigate the pogrom in that time span, and to help Armenians to get out as soon as possible."

He conveyed this information to me with weariness on his face and in his voice, but it did nothing to alleviate the stress I felt after making this dangerous journey back to Baku by myself. I took the paper, crunched it noisily in my fist and threw it into the trash. "Okay, give me another form. I'll change the date and I will fit in the category of pogrom!" He looked at me with a combination of surprise and admiration.

I had heard about the Azeris ransacking our apartment from neighbors who still lived in the courtyard complex, and I estimated the date to be the thirteenth. It was such a letdown to have missed that cutoff date by only two days, but the intransigent bureaucracy had their orders to investigate those attacked only in this officially designated time span. In the military, orders were orders and there was no gray area. If someone was murdered before the fifteenth or after the nineteenth, it did not matter, it would be ignored. It's like the legalism of term life insurance; you have to die within the ten years for your family to collect. If you die one day later, the funds go to the insurance company. With the insurance, at least, it is your own decision, made ahead of time, but around the time of the pogrom in Baku you are an innocent Armenian victim. In both cases, the moral aspect is ignored and the letter of the law rules. It is as the French say, *Tant pis pour vous!* (Tough luck!).

"Go ahead! Fill out another form." The officer snapped his head back, looking startled at my persistence.

Taking another blank form, I filled it out. The official watched me, toying nervously with the pen behind his right ear. When I brought the document back for inspection a second time, the official read it, signed it summarily and thumped an official stamp near the bottom.

"Are you *actually* Armenian?" he asked as he added the paper to a pile off to the side.

"You actually have doubts?" I replied, incensed. I took umbrage of this question in large part because it was not the first time that I had heard it. When I was in Moscow, the same maddening insinuations revealed complete ignorance of the sophistication of my native city, Baku, of which I was so proud.

"Doubts, yes," his voice boomed emphatically, "and big ones!"

"Why, what kind?" I already knew what he was going to say.

"Well, you speak Russian too well. You speak Russian, but *not* the way the Armenians speak it."

"Obviously, you don't know this place." I said annoyed. "Here in Baku, with forty nationalities, you have to have one language to operate successfully. Here, the major language is Russian. In Armenia, they are almost 90 percent a one language country, one ethnic republic, so Russian is a second language there."

In the United States, I've frequently heard immigrants of all kinds make the comment, "How ignorant Americans are. They don't know geography, not Armenia, not Russia, not Guatemala."

Here, the Russians from Moscow regarded all the people in the Caucasus Region as the same, whether Armenian, Georgian, or Azerbaijani. They were guilty not only of being ignorant of the divergent nationalities but also of the religious and customary practices. It's ironic because the flight from Baku to Moscow takes no more than two and a half hours, the equivalent of flying from one coast of the United States to the American Midwest. In addition, all laws and regulations in the Soviet Union were exactly the same, standardized from region to region, unlike the United States which has federal and state laws, local certifications and education systems. Coming to Baku was not an excursion into darkest Africa, is my point, but some Russians seemed to think so.

Major Chernov was his name, and he was the chief investigator of the Baku pogrom. The Soviet military force was sent down from Moscow because there was no trust in the Azeri police of Baku.

After he had been taught his geography lesson, Major Chernov softly changed course, asking me personal questions. "Why did you leave Baku? Do you have family? Is everybody safe?" I told him what he wanted to know. Then, suddenly, clenching his fists and making a grimace, he opened up to me and confessed his personal frustrations.

"How could you possibly live in this wretched place?" he asked emotionally.

"It wasn't always like this," I sadly replied.

"I DON'T CARE!" he yelled, shaking his fist in the air. "It's a terrible place. I hate it. I want to go home. I'm sick of it. We have no reason to be here. We are not going to help anyone. We are not going to change anything, and nothing will improve!"

"Nothing will improve?" I asked, discouraged by these words coming from a respected official who should have been full of certainty and authority.

"What are you really doing here?" he asked in a confrontational tone.

"I just want to try to get my apartment back. I heard that the Soviet Army is here, and I was hoping that they might be able to help return the apartment that my neighbors took over."

He listened carefully to me as I naïvely spelled out my plan. After a long pause, he looked down at my face with an expression of pity, put his hands in his pockets and swayed his lean body back and forth.

"You're not going to get anything. Go home as soon as you can!"

Then he reached over and drew open a drawer that was overflowing with completed forms exactly like the one I had filled out, pointed to them, and said, "You see all these papers? They all are from people like you."

He was frowning with frustration and his voice was strained. "We catch them. We bring them in the front door. *They* let them out the back door!"

What he meant, I understood was *they* were the local Azeri police.

I scrutinized him, momentarily forgetting all my anxieties. It suddenly dawned on me that this honorable man, Major Chernov, had been thrust into an impossible situation and needed as much support as I did, more in fact.

"I'll give you a couple of people to escort you to your house," he sighed in resignation,

"You'll have twenty minutes, and then out you go!"

Three men came with me. I noticed that two of them referred to the third as "Major." None of them were in uniform. One was an Azeri whose arm was wrapped up in bandages. Chernov gave them the orders to escort me but instructed them that I was not to spend more than twenty minutes in the house.

It took ten minutes to get there. We all exited the vehicle and the men immediately surrounded me. In the time we maneuvered from the gate to the apartment, Azeri neighbors old and new started milling around us, staring as if they could not believe their own eyes. Even with my escorts shielding me from the Azeris, who very quickly became agitated and started screaming as we passed through the courtyard, I did not feel safe. My heart was beating wildly. We arrived at my door on the first floor, open to the courtyard, and could see everyone gathering there.

"How could she dare to come here?" they excoriated me. "She has gall to come back with her pals."

Listening to their comments was disconcerting. I felt like I was floating in inhospitable, airless, outer space.

"Do you have a key?" one of my military protectors asked.

"No. I had a key, but they changed the lock!"

Another military escort shouted, "Who is living here?"

"Me! Me!" Shafigah, the daughter of a former neighbor, shouted.

My escorts started to force the door open with shoes and shoulders. The Azeris, thinking these men were just friends or relatives of mine, rushed us. My escorts turned to face them, forming a circle around me, backing me into the now open doorway. We stomped across the broken blue-painted door, now lying flat on the ground, and faced the sullen crowd.

The escorts conspicuously flashed opened their jackets, and as soon as the Azeri neighbors caught sight of the pistols they pulled up, like startled animals in the wild before a searchlight. Realizing they were no match for guns and bullets, they vented their frustration instead by screaming and swearing. The outsiders had succeeded in igniting the Azeri squatters inside to ululated shrieking, like a flock of furious hawks.

"It's mine! It's mine!" the woman occupying my apartment began yelling.

She was standing behind us in the living room waving her arms in the air and holding onto a dirty rag in one hand.

"What do you want?"

By this time, more Azeris were milling around outside the open doorway. Most of them I did not know, though I instantly recognized them as peasant villagers from their actions and the way they were dressed. These were the typical *chooshka*.

Inside, the apartment was a mess. It looked like the interior of a gypsy caravan. Clothes were hanging on a line stretched across the kitchen. The front door and others had been painted what I came to regard as typical

Azeri blue. There was no furniture left. The floor was bare. Absent were the carpets laid down around the areas where Azeri villagers typically ate and slept.

I naively imagined that I could still smell the fresh paint that I had once applied to the balcony during a time when I believed that I could plan for the happy future. Then I walked to the corner of the living room where my grand piano used to be. There, I knelt down and sorted through a pile of rags which I recognized were part of the cloth wrappings I used to protect the new chandelier that I had plans to hang after the fresh painting was finished.

How many times under the pressure of emergencies have we heard of people reacting illogically under shock, carrying a table lamp out of the house that was on fire while leaving behind all their valuables and personal photos and documents. I had hidden my pair of sapphire earrings which I had purchased in Malta inside one of the pockets of my little boy's short pants. The shorts were green and shiny, but I could not find them now. Most of the other soft garments I had wrapped as padding around the crystal chandelier were also gone.

The thieves apparently carried their prize of cobalt blue gemstones away well-protected and concealed. Some Azeri might have become rich overnight, or maybe they just threw away a minor fortune with my son's short pants. Maybe one of their little boys found them in the pocket of the new pants he was wearing, played with the pretty blue stones, then got bored and dropped them in the gutter and watched them drain into the sewer.

Was my act of hiding valuables logical, well thought-out?

No. Probably not, but I dared not carry anything of value with me outside the house when we escaped. They were assaulting Armenians on the street, mugging them and gleefully seizing and destroying their passports and papers. It was either try to secret them away somewhere or willingly give them up to Azeri pirates who would not hesitate to take them from me.

Now, as I stood up without my sapphires, I thought in dismay how the same Azeri neighbors who had once begged me, "Let me hold and fondle your cute little baby Arthur!" and who shared a life with us for many years, who accepted help from us when someone in their family was critically ill, had now became my fierce enemies.

The apartment not only looked different, it smelled different. I began crying. My entire childhood had been spent there. I looked from the empty space where my grand piano had sat to the place where my father used to read in a stuffed chair listening to me practice and the room off the hallway where my brother slept. I reconstructed the whole apartment in my mind's eye exactly the way I remembered it.

I was jolted out of my reverie by the shouting of my protectors' voices. "Karina! Karina! Get out!"

One of them, who compulsively twirled a keychain all the time, approached me. "The Azeris are incensed at us and the atmosphere is heating up," he said. "We have to go now!"

All three escorts openly had their hands on their weapons just in case.

I felt someone tug at my hair roughly behind me, and I thought it was one of them, but when I turned around, I saw that it was Leila, the daughter of the woman squatting in our apartment.

My escort with the bandaged arm seized her hand and pulled it away from me. "Don't touch her!" he yelled. As he did this, his jacket fell open, exposing his black metallic pistol in a shoulder holster. Leila jumped back in great alarm while the others watched what was going on from outside in the courtyard.

"They have guns!" the mob screeched in Azeri to one another.

They not only comprehended that my accomplices were armed, but they almost certainly figured out that they were lawmen, not simply my pals, and not at all helpless to confront a mob of furious Azeris.

Falling far short of retreating, in their further frustration they yelled filthy phrases and tried to lay their hands on me, "Get out!" they screamed defiantly at me. "Get out or you will die! Do you know what we're going to do to you?"

"All of them are black sheep and all hard wired to kill," I thought.

It was not easy to get out of the apartment and courtyard. Two of the police escorts marched on either side of me, one in front in a vanguard position, as we backed out toward the gate, eyes on the mob following us. One of my escorts lowered his hand onto his sidearm. Behind me another stooped down, pretending to tie his shoe while evaluating the situation. From that position, he pulled out his weapon and brandished it in the air. When we reached the gate, he stood up, forcing his way through the screaming crowd and followed us.

We got in the car and they dropped me off, still in a state of shock, at a taxi stand not far away. One of the escorts stayed behind to protect me while the other two drove off. The Azeri Major Mamedov conversed with me while we waited for my taxi.

"My brother has an Armenian wife," he told me, "which I wouldn't trade for any Azeri sister-in-law, no matter what.

"I was injured in the war in Kirovabad, now we call it Ganja, between Azeris and Armenians, and spent eight days recovering in the hospital there. I was released early because of the shortage of military manpower here in Baku."

"When are you going back?" he asked.

"In two days," I replied.

"Get out as soon as you can," he advised me passionately.

The Major scrutinized two taxis and let them pass and then hailed the third, which finally met his approval. He spoke to the driver in Azeri, paid the fare in advance, then turned to me and announced loudly in Azeri, "O.K. See you later, *Bajim* (sister)."

Even knowing the tradition in Baku of hospitality of paying the cabby for your friend or guest, his kind gesture was to provide my address to the cabdriver and pay the fare without any need for a dangerous dialogue between me and the cabby which might reveal my nationality.

It was the last time I was in Baku. Looking back, I did not retrieve any personal belongings, but this disappointment was tempered by the sad condition in which I found Baku. I could honestly say, without any emotional attachment, that it was not the same Baku we worked to build. Not the same Baku we lived in and called home. It was a sad, dark, bloody, destroyed place.

I felt like the French king who said, *"Après moi, le déluge"* (After me, comes the flood).

At the airport, I stamped my feet to knock off the dust of Baku from my shoes. It was very much a symbolic gesture, like the Biblical Saints Paul and Barnabas departing from Antioch, erasing everything bad from my memory and leaving the dust behind.

Some people might misunderstand my motives for going back. I can tell you that I did not return only to retrieve my sapphire earrings. I really just wanted to sell the apartment, but you have to understand that it is not an easy thing to give up all hope on the country you loved and trusted. When we heard about the army intervening, I naïvely believed that at least some of our belongings could be salvaged. However, as it turned out, all the military could afford me was a safe escort in and out of the chaos, allowing me twenty minutes to grab what I could and no more.

There was never any real hope. It was open season in Baku on abandoned Armenian property. Nobody offered to help us sell any of our things. The military did not stop the theft. It was all they could do to keep you alive if you returned to try to claim what was rightfully yours. It was *sauve-qui-peut* (a stampede, run for your life). The shock of the collapse of a country that I always believed would protect us citizens left me feeling empty inside.

Now, more than twenty-five years later, I have my two grown children, I can state, *"Ea sunt mea ornamenta"* (These are my jewels) as pronounced by Cornelia, the Roman aristocrat, mother of the Gracchi, when a moneyed woman displayed and boasted of her luxurious gems.

Other known instances of violent ethnic conflict in the world since Baku often raise the same questions,

"How could you kill a neighbor and friend when you are such a part of one another's lives, when you have joined in mutual family celebrations of weddings and baptisms and other important life events?"

People will also ask refugees about the brutal and oppressive regimes they lived under; "How could you have trusted in your government when it was so obviously hopeless and meaningless?"

Some ask me still, "How could you have gone back to Baku when you knew they wanted to kill you?"

All these questions elicited the same answer, "I...DON'T...KNOW."

CHAPTER 13

Path to America

T HE FIRST TIME THAT I REALLY REFLECTED ON THE PATH THAT MY
family and I took to America was many years after the violent uprising
against Armenians in Azerbaijan reached the capital of Baku and forced
me to act. Maybe it was too painful to think about. Maybe I was simply too
concerned with beginning my new life to take the time.

It was July 2014. I was gathered with my relatives who came together to
greet the latest family members who had come over to the United States. My
last cousin on my mother's side arrived from Russia with her husband and
three children. They were from Baku but lived all the intervening years in
Russia since the Baku pogrom. They waited a long time for the visa because
of trouble with paperwork. Her brother, who had been in America a long
time, his wife, and their children were there. My mother's sisters, all six of
them, along with the rest of relatives, cousins, and their children filled my
aunt's apartment in North Hollywood.

The apartment was not that big, but for our family this was not unusual. There were often so many of us that even a large room felt small. There
was a welcoming toast to America, and of course, a lot of food: appetiz-
ers, Armenian lavash (bread), chicken salad, kidney beans with walnuts,
prunes, dolma (stuffed grape leaves), shish kebab, grapes and wine. There

was liquor, juice, dessert with fresh fruit and dried fruit, cakes, chocolate candy, champagne, and Armenian cognac.

People sat where they could. It reminded me ever-so-slightly of the "railroad" house my aunt had purchased in Yerevan. The newcomers were confused, being in a strange place, while we appeared to be comfortable in our own home. Over dessert and coffee, the newcomers told us about their journey and how they felt about being in America. There were many mixed voices and emotions. Those of us who had been here already gave them support and advice.

I held back until I found a way to say as succinctly as possible what the change in environment and culture would be like for them.

"America," I began, "first you hate it, then you are confused, and finally you are so much in love that you never look back."

I could tell that this statement put most of them instantly at ease, though it was not meant to be an emotional analgesic. It was something I found to be true.

Before any of them could respond, one of my aunts said,

"I never mentioned it before, but I want to say now that you are all here in California thanks to me. Did anybody ever say thank you to me?"

This statement befuddled and incensed me. It wasn't so much that she had no influence at all in the fate of some of the people in the room, but to be asking, practically demanding members of her family to express their gratitude to her was the height of arrogance.

I broke in and added curtly, "Nobody said thank you to me, either."

"Listen, Karina, I'm not talking about that," my aunt snapped.

"I *am* talking exactly about that," I retorted emphatically.

I guess it is very hard to admit the facts of owing a favor to someone. In real life when one must admit owing a favor, the situation is too-often twisted to a ridiculous inanity rather than the person facing the facts squarely.

"Karina, we are here because we filled out application forms," someone added.

"We came because everybody was coming," another pontificated.

Heads nodded.

When my Aunt Zulya's heavy body suddenly rose. Everyone took notice.

"You all have to listen to what I have to say," she shouted in a voice trembling with anger.

"You are disrespecting Karina. If she had not gone to the American Embassy in Moscow on numerous occasions during that troubling and dangerous time, risking losing her job just to find out if it was true about refugee status for Armenians, none of you would be here in America. And you never mention it. You should thank her. We all know that."

Nobody spoke. The silence was palpable after that cacophony of talking.

"None of you had the guts to go to Moscow," Aunt Zulya continued.

"We all know that thanks to her we are here. I remember, but you don't want to remember the song you all sang then. Remember, we said this was all an American trick. We thought that they just wanted to know how many people were leaving the USSR. We believed that they were playing with our minds, that it was all just agitation against the Soviet Union. All we did was talk, argue, make plans but do nothing. Karina was the one who actually took action and did something to ensure the safety of her family, including all of you."

She sat back down slowly, and there was an uneasy silence. While the sun was setting behind the San Gabriel Mountains that late fall afternoon in Southern California, I felt a shiver go up my spine. It was not because I felt cold; the chill I got was because I was reminded of so many early mornings before when the sun was rising over the Caspian Sea in Baku when like so many Armenians we would be huddled around the radio listening to the forbidden BBC and Voice of America. It consistently provided us with genuine information and knowledge about the violence in Baku that the local news simply did not. Despite the government's efforts to jam the radio signals, we still managed to make out most of the broadcasts and discover the most necessary facts. This is what helped me to decide that we could no longer safely stay in Baku and that it was time to leave.

It was while repeatedly listening to these broadcasts that the first step to America was taken. I remember the exact moment this fate was actualized.

It was hard to forget because a young female cousin had died in March, and the epiphany occurred at the end of the following month when my family was gathered together for a memorial dinner in Baku. It was the forty-day anniversary of her death, and such a memorial dinner at a hall, is a part of Armenian tradition.

After most of the people had left the restaurant, there remained a sizable number simply because we have a very large family. The conversations quickly turned to the topic of Armenians who were leaving Baku in droves because of the dangerous events taking place there and the incredibly wonderful American offer to accept Armenian refugees.

I broke the silence when I stood up suddenly.

"By the way," I announced, "I'm going to Moscow to check on the truth at the American Embassy."

It was not easy for me to say, "the American Embassy." In the Soviet Union, America was still considered the hated capitalist enemy, a threat to our nation, and our way of life. The political taboo was real but loud laughter suddenly broke out around the hall.

"Make sure we know where you are," chided one of my cousins.

"Don't get lost," another one mocked.

"Call me when you get there. I'll go, too."

The laughter and joking continued while I remained silent. When it was mostly quiet again, I said simply, "I'll be leaving tomorrow."

I didn't say anything else about it and just walked away. That quieted them down because they knew I was serious.

There was a lot of disorder, and the routine of simply getting a ticket proved difficult, but with a bribe to the right person you could get anything you wanted. And with the help of my friend, Maryam, who made plans to make the trip, as well, we had our tickets in hand the next day.

Despite this accomplishment, it did not happen without some conflict in my immediate family which needed to be resolved before the next step was taken.

"If you go to America," my husband threatened loudly and resolutely, "you're not taking the kids."

I rebuffed him, "Oh, yeah? Try to stop me."

But even my mother was against it. She was afraid.

"The KGB will find out," she said. "You're exposing yourself. You can lose your job and family."

While I understood this concern, I was focused on the bigger picture.

"In this miasma," I told her, "I don't care about a job."

I remained determined to see this through, but when I took a taxi to Maryam's house near the airport and when I saw her face, I knew something was wrong.

"You know what?" she said nonchalantly. "We don't have to go to Moscow. I heard that very soon they are going to open an American embassy in Baku, so there is no need to travel to Moscow."

She made it sound as if the embassy was going to open tomorrow, and we could just walk in and get taken care of without risking the trip to Moscow, even though it was only two or three hours away. I was shocked that she would make such a serious decision on her own for the both of us. With my family giving me such a hard time, this news effectively sabotaged all my plans.

"You should have told me in advance," I told her.

"I'll have you know that I'm going no matter what. I'll call Sveta, my husband's first cousin. She wanted to come with us, anyway."

Maryam recognized how serious I was, and she instantly took a softer tone.

"No, no, no," she said, "I'm coming. Okay. Okay."

Her suitcase was sitting open in the living room. It was empty, a sign that she had no plans to take off anytime soon. Now, however, she rushed and began filling it. Once she was packed, we were soon on our way to the airport.

It was a two-and-a-half-hour direct flight from Baku to Moscow. Maryam had a friend in Moscow who lived in an apartment on Prospekt Lenina. The apartment was what is called a typical "Moscow box." Her friend, Irina Samuelevna, was a heavy-set middle-aged woman. She seemed nice, though it appeared to me that she did not have a particularly difficult life. Near as I could tell, she spent much of her day sitting and reading with a fat orange cat in her lap. She had to lean over and lift the heavy cat that was too fat to jump up on its own.

The worst part for me was that the cat kept approaching me and rubbing against my legs to my utter horror. All my life I have been afraid of cats. I didn't know the exact reason, but I make every attempt to avoid them when they are in my vicinity. I had always thought that if you do not look at them or otherwise acknowledge them, they will pretty much leave you alone. Unfortunately, just the opposite is true. Cats seem to know if a person is afraid of them, and those are the people they always go to, the ones who turn their faces away.

That's just what this fat cat did. It was something I would have to endure for a short time.

As for Irina, she was not too knowledgeable about our situation, or my dislike for cats.

"Come and pet Murochka," she said to me. "She's a pearl!"

She was happy with her cat, but skeptical about our chances at the Embassy. I was afraid that I would have to sleep in her apartment in a not-so-tidy room that she was kind enough to offer us, and that's just what happened. The cat made me uneasy, and every swish I heard that night I was sure it was yellow Murochka. Even though I realized that this enormous animal was far too fat to jump onto my bed, I still didn't sleep.

The next day when I called Baku to announce that we had arrived safely, little had changed in the minds of my family members. Some openly scoffed; others were afraid for us or confused about what I was doing there. Nobody, I realized, even those in Moscow, could believe in the generosity of America. They said it was merely a propaganda show, a way for America to condemn the "big bad" Soviet Union for their refugee situation while at the same time glorify themselves as the savior of the "free world" for offering to accept the persecuted and oppressed citizenry.

To so many of us, the American political mentality of accepting refugees from all over the world was not a concept that was even remotely familiar. I knew that Jews, for example, were going to the United States and Israel, but this I had been led to believe was treason. Immigrants were going to America, but not from the USSR. The "perfect Soviet Union" could not have refugees—as I've mentioned before. They never had refugees. It simply wasn't a word in the government vocabulary.

What else were we, though, but refugees?

The next morning we went to Tchaikovsky Street, which was where the U. S. embassy was located: the happy target of so much effort and so much hope. I remember there being a long line outside a massive gate that enclosed the entire perimeter of the building. There was a guardhouse on each side of the gate where stocky men in KGB dress stood stiffly. Their winter uniforms that protected them against the cold of the Moscow early spring were bulky, making them look absurdly and frighteningly like gorillas carrying heavy weapons.

We joined the line, where despite all the gloom, I observed many people from Baku who surreptitiously all had a glimmer of hope showing through their otherwise guarded eyes. This was the first time that I was ever in an embassy of any country even though I had traveled abroad a lot.

It called to mind an old expression: *Your mood can switch suddenly like the Baku North Wind.*

Darkness dominated this tableau. The winter clothes silhouetted against the gray snow piles had a sad but familiar quality. People from the Soviet Union were used to standing long hours in lines, but here at the American Embassy in Moscow, there was a strange and unreal tone to the conversations. It was dreamlike, or nightmarish, depending on how you looked at it. The people around me all realized that we had something in common: we were Armenians from Baku, who were all concerned with the same thing.

I could hear the identical narrative thread to their lives, similar unfortunate experiences which bound us together. The questions asked most often were, "How did you hear about this American opportunity?" and "What happened to you and your relatives in Baku?"

Some of the people knew each other, while others got to know one another while we continued to wait. During the lunch break, when no one was allowed to enter the Embassy, the crowd broke up into small groups, where the conversations continued with a mixture of hope, fear, and doubt.

The conspiracy theories were unavoidable. Most believed that the KGB would keep track of people's names for betraying the country and that not only would they lose their jobs, but they would be watched or followed for the rest of their lives. The Cold War had been dragging on for three decades. There was as much distrust of the United States. The prevailing rumor was that America wanted statistics to show how many people wanted to leave the Soviet Union.

"We are just numbers in a game," bemoaned one white-haired stocky gentleman who had the look of a school teacher.

"We will be exposed by the KGB and all for naught," muttered an ancient granny to her young grandson. "Nothing at all will happen here in the embassy."

Similar thoughts were in the back of my mind, also, but like everyone else in line that day, I felt it was a risk worth taking. More so, it was a risk I could not afford *not* to take.

Still, the longer we were stalled in line, the more I found myself questioning the merits of the decision I had made. Here we were knocking on the doors of a country that had always been regarded as our enemy. In a moment of panic, I asked a man in charge if we were in the right line for people from Baku. He said yes. I asked someone else, a woman official, to be sure. She reassured me kindly. The negative conversations continued to spin all around us in a dizzying manner. I felt like I was on the edge of a cliff and my heart was beating faster and faster.

Was I doing the right thing, going to a foreign destination that was always painted in a negative light, a place that was so very different in culture, language, customs, and food, everything we were taught to hold dear?

After waiting awhile, a small group of people were allowed to go inside, including Maryam and me. We finally passed through the heavy embassy doors, while other people were shaking with nervous anxiety. Strangely I did not feel any fear in taking this irretrievable step. The officials greeting and welcoming us spoke Russian with a strange foreign accent, adding to the unreality of the experience.

We were then ushered into a rather small room where there was a man who was there to give us instructions and answer any questions we had. We each had to pull out a white plastic ticket with a large black number from a special apparatus. After we pulled on the ticket, it made a conspicuously loud click. It was not dissimilar to the machines that dispense numbered tickets at a deli, supermarket or Motor Vehicles Bureau there in America, which we have grown accustomed to here in the United States. But it was something strange and unknown to us in the Soviet Union.

On the floor was a green runner carpet and sets of chairs that were strangely connected together. There were three windows along one of the walls; each had an American consular employee seated behind the pane of glass. These interviewers were all women, but they were not dressed in any uniform or fancy outfits. There was a small metal perforated disk in the center of the windows to allow for communication between the interviewer and interviewee. It was all so strange. I regretted coming there again.

I was called to a window, the second from the left. My thoughts were that I would be rejected immediately because in the USSR, any visit to a government office was always difficult. I was asked to show documents, which meant my USSR passport and the birth certificates of my children. The Soviet passport included almost all personal information, including one's nationality on the notorious line number five. There it was in glaring black lettering; ARMENIAN. It was practically an open invitation for discrimination, or worse. It has always been that way.

I started shaking because I did not know the procedure. I believed that approval or rejection would come at the very next instant, one or the other, a swift judgment. I held my breath, not knowing which way things would go. She carefully checked my documents.

"How long have you lived in Baku?" the woman asked, "and where are you living now?"

I gave a simple, brief response and the woman promptly returned the documents along with a preliminary registration form to me with a smile.

That was it. All those hours in line only to receive this form! I could only wonder if all those concerns that people talked about in line were, in fact, true.

Was I now on a government watch list or blacklist?

Was I just a number in America's Cold War propaganda game with the Soviet Union? Whether it was nor wasn't, it was too late now. It was done.

The next day I dropped off the completed paperwork and pulled together the courage to ask about what I needed to do for other relatives, especially my brother and his family. I had already called him in Baku to get his military registration number and other details for the questionnaire. Knowing how close a family we are, I then thought about bringing the entire list of my mother's relatives. I was also shocked to learn that all I needed to do was make a photocopy of the document.

"Just go and make copies of the blank form and fill one out for each person."

"Really? Copies?"

"Of course. You can make a hundred copies if you like." To my further astonishment, she even kindly gave me the address of a copy center in Moscow.

I postponed my return home for another few days so that I could stay and fill out the forms for all the members of my large family. Why not? I was already there. I knew how they felt about my pursuing this action, but I was doing this for everyone I loved, and I thought they would be pleased.

However, when I called to inform them of my new plans their unenthusiastic reaction caught me by surprise.

"You're crazy to go to America," one of my aunts boldly exclaimed.

"Nobody wants to go with you."

I went ahead and made copies anyway. Xeroxing documents was not an easy thing to do in Moscow. I had to go to the special office that overcharged me for the service because they knew how desperate I was to have a large number run off quickly in a short period of time before departing from the city.

I carefully filled out the forms for my brother's family and one of my mother's sisters with trepidation. I truly believed that one slight mistake would result in immediate rejection, and then I would have to start all over again. It was the Soviet Union, after all, and not at all like in the USA where you can simply erase, white out, or cross it out, and rewrite it. I was even nervous about filling in my own name without making a mistake. I prepared six application forms for seven adults and five children.

When my friend Maryam saw my pile of applications, she looked at me incredulously.

"What are you doing?" she asked. "I thought none of them had the slightest intention to leave Soviet Union?"

"They will all have an opportunity now to say no. But later it might be too late to say yes"

"Are you crazy? Are you out of your mind?" She continued to scold me. And she is a talker, believe me.

"I must be," I answered, smiling, "and how about you? How many are you going to fill out?"

"None."

"What about your sister? How can you leave her behind?"

I should have kept my mouth shut because we ended up having an argument over her reluctance to fill out the form for her sister, Raya, who was also a good friend of mine. Although Raya was much older than me, we had worked together for years. Even knowing the corrosive nature of the relationship between the sisters, I just could not comprehend how one could deny the other an opportunity to escape the dangers that we Armenians were subjected to in Baku. It made no sense to me. We were already in Moscow and the blank application was right there in front of her.

"I don't want her to come to America," she insisted.

"Maryam, if you won't fill one out for Raya, I'm going to do it myself. She's my friend."

"Okay," Maryam unenthusiastically finally gave in.

So we stayed a couple of extra days in Moscow and took the time to make copies of completed forms as evidence of how we had filled them out before self-assuredly delivering my pile of paperwork to the embassy. I returned to Baku with more confidence than when I left the week before.

Now, although my family still believed it was a daydream, my recounting the details of the address on Tchaikovsky Street, the color of the carpet, the interview, the forms, I slowly began to convince them of the reality of this extraordinary opportunity in America. Soon, more of them wanted to fill out the forms.

When the news spread, others started coming in groups to see me and talk to me. I had to relate every tiny detail of my visit to the embassy over and over: the green carpet, the ticket with the number, the windows and female consular staff. At the end of the week, I lost my voice.

Before long, not only were family members coming to see me, but word quickly spread and when friends and neighbors realized how easy it was to add a relative to the application by simply photocopying the form, they all wanted an application. I cannot count the number of applications I filled out for people outside my family, maybe a hundred. They were afraid of making a mistake, but they trusted me to write the information correctly, so I did it for them.

You might think all this would put some of them a little bit more at ease, but infuriatingly it did not. The next level of suspicion began almost immediately. They simply could not believe that anything good could happen to them.

"Oh, these forms are just to find out how many people want to leave Baku," some said. "No one will go to America."

Now, this was 1988, and we still had to wait. I visited Moscow several times afterward to check on the progress of our applications. It was surreal. Since there are officially no refugees from the USSR, there had never been a need to issue exit visas to refugees before. But, since no republic in the USSR was willing to accept us Armenians, we finally obtained Soviet registration to be labeled "refugees," very probably because of pressure from the outside world, particularly from the United States. In the end it was no more than a piece of paper as far as the Soviet Union was concerned, but to me and my family and so many Armenians it was much more than that. It meant freedom and safety from pervasive violence and pogroms in and around Baku.

By 1990, with the situation escalating in Baku, I tried to see if we could settle in Moscow. It proved impossible. Everywhere we would go, our Soviet government officials shrugged their shoulders. "Your passport shows you live in Baku," was all we kept hearing, and the conversations never went any further than that.

"Go back to the Azerbaijan Republic," they would sneer.

Everything was based on the passport regimen. No chance to get help, work, or own property. We would not have been able to send the kids to school in Moscow or Leningrad, because we were not considered official residents.

We continued to wait and survived—the violence in Musabekovo, the Great Armenian Earthquake. While we continued to wait, my mother once again went to visit Armenia taking the children while the rest of us stayed behind. As feared, the pogrom ignited in Baku. At least my children were out of that harm's way. I was still working, still trying desperately to find a solution. This is when we discovered that selling our property was impossible because why would you pay for something you could later obtain for free? Amazingly, I was still able to go to work, but there were bad days when I would stay home. Many times my boss would call me from the office. "Don't come in today, Karina."

Some days they would send a car to transport me and other Armenians safely to work. On quiet days my boss would try to reassure me to get me to come in.

"Nothing will happen, Karina. Take as much time as you need."

I was called in one day to act as temporary payroll clerk because we were short-staffed. It happened to be payday, and there were Azeri workers waiting on both sides of the corridor for their wages. When I arrived at the office, I saw a primitively scribbled sign on a conspicuous torn piece of cardboard affixed to my door. It read, "ARMENIAN WOMAN, GET OUT BEFORE IT'S TOO LATE."

I was outraged, and I don't know where I got the nerve to challenge those who had been responsible for this threat, but I tore the sign down and held it high over my head. I made sure everyone in the corridor could see it.

"Who wrote this sign?" I yelled, demanding to know who it was.

They remained mute as I walked boldly between them. It reminded me of what you see in movies of the harsh punishment inflicted on a soldier in Tsarist times who had to "run the gauntlet" between soldiers who were commanded to beat their colleague from both sides. A description of the cruel process is in the short story "After the Ball" by Tolstoy and portrayed in movies about the French Foreign Legion and in pirate films.

I didn't expect anyone to strike me, but as I looked directly into their angry, hate-filled faces, I wanted to show them that I was not afraid. I still don't know how I found the courage to confront them.

I heard a car beeping in the parking lot, looked out the window and recognized our car. My husband was with my brother's wife, Natasha. There was anti-Armenian trouble at her workplace as well. She quit her job as an accountant on the spot and called my husband to fetch her because my brother-in-law did not have a car. My husband went to take her to safety and came to pick me up early. He dared not come up to the office and leave her alone among the Azeris milling around in the yard, so he kept sounding the horn for me to come out.

My boss eventually sent a vice president down to keep Natasha company in the car and another person to escort my husband upstairs into the main office. My husband was there to support me in announcing my final resignation. Anatoliy had decided. "That's it."

My boss, Samir Gadzhiv, who was Azeri, went back into his routine of trying to minimize the serious nature of all the turmoil. "This is temporary," he said. "There are just a few bad people. It's going to get better. I'll send a car for you."

But the more he talked the more his own words betrayed him, having the opposite effect to what he intended. He spelled out just how obvious the situation was dangerous. Then he suddenly changed his tone as he turned to Anatoliy. "It's not my fault," he confessed. "It's not your fault, either. It's getting bad."

He shook our hands and said to Anatoliy, "Now you just chopped off my right hand."

He sighed and picked up a cigarette and took a couple of puffs and then said. "I understand, I understand. I probably would do the same. But, please help me and stay a couple of days and finish the payroll process. I cannot rely on anybody else."

On our way out, we had to pass between smirking Azeris all around us.

It was the best of times. It was the worst of times. I thought these words by Charles Dickens about the French Revolution applied to this human drama that was playing out in front of my eyes as well. The best qualities of people were displayed in this time of chaos, as were some of humanity's worst qualities.

There were actually some Azeris who took chances to protect us, but most others clearly would have preferred to kill us. Talk about incongruous, I, an Armenian, actually took a very dangerous step in order to protect the payroll of an Azeri company whose employees hated me and wanted to see me and my family dead.

When my friends and relatives later heard the story of the payroll cash bonanza, they condemned me, calling me "an absolute fool" for being loyal to my company. After all, I had been my boss's "right hand," protecting the payroll funds. He knew how loyal I was from the payroll episode. They all thought I missed an opportunity to sabotage the company and take revenge on them and Azerbaijan for all the harm they brought onto us Armenians.

Because of the unstable political situation, I had actually been responsible for quite a large amount of unclaimed employee cash payroll. Payday was usually twice a month, but people were coming in only once a month because of the chaos and threats of violence. There were also many employees who avoided coming to work altogether, even to pick up their pay, so a considerable reserve of unclaimed money was just sitting there in the company safe. There was no such thing as a paycheck, so it was all cash, and I was responsible for all of it.

The whole time that I was acting as payroll clerk, I was fearful that someone else would steal the 62,000 rubles, mostly in fresh bills from the bank and wrapped in color coded paper bands, and it would be blamed on me, the hated "Armenian woman." So that entire last day, I was in a panic, and before leaving I went ahead and stuffed all the money into a large bag in my purse with the plan of handing it directly over to the big boss the next morning so that I would not be blamed if anything happened to it overnight. It was a huge risk, and if anyone at work knew I was carrying all that money with me when I left that afternoon, I'm sure I would not be here today.

When my husband picked me up, he did not have the slightest idea of this secret drama. He took me to my mother's house according to our routine and drove off to keep an eye on our house. I told my mother the story. She immediately flew into a panic and insisted that we leave her house right away.

"What if they followed you?" she asked hysterically.

We quickly called for a cab so we could be taken to my brother's house for safety. My mother could speak Azeri to the taxi driver, but we were both trembling as we made the trip, praying that we would be safe and not get caught with the bag full of money. If we were stopped and searched, it would be all over. The Azeri police would not be sympathetic to an Armenian for stealing money from an Azerbaijani state business.

We would never be allowed to leave the country and would be either jailed or killed, likely the latter. They could also harm my family as further retribution. But we safely made the trip to my brother's, then after dark we called for another cab to take us and the precious cache back to my mother's house. It was a nerve-wracking couple of hours. We arrived back home without incident but neither of us were able to sleep a wink all night.

My husband was still completely unaware of all this drama when the following morning he arrived to drive me back to work. Samir Gadzhiv, my boss, was going to be in early that morning because the "big shots" from the ministry were scheduled to arrive for a monthly consultation. Normally, he had a team of Armenians to help him. Most of his top employees were Armenian, including the carpenter, the electrician, the plumber, the floor installer, the masons, and the designers. He was going crazy trying to do it all by himself. I felt bad for him, and a couple weeks before I had promised to be there early on this important day to help him select the workers who were best qualified for the jobs in question.

I entered the room in tears. I couldn't help it; I was just so relieved that this crisis was coming to an end.

"What's wrong?" he asked me with genuine concern and guided me over to a chair. "Sit down, Karina."

He brought over some water and handed me the cup.

I took it and with trembling hands I brought the cup to my mouth and took a drink. After a few moments I was able to calm down and regain my composure.

"Now, tell me what's troubling you," Samir asked.

I stood up and dumped the plastic bag filled with money on the top of his desk and then emptied my purse. The bills spilled out and covered all the paperwork and employee files he had been poring over.

"There," I said. "I don't want this heavy responsibility anymore. It's all yours now."

Samir looked at me.

"What?" was all he managed to get out.

I told him what I did and why, doing my best not to get overly emotional or cry. I explained my fears that someone would sabotage me and use my Armenian status as an easy excuse to steal all the money and blame me.

"*Dali san?*" he asked in Azeri. Then in Russian, "Are you crazy?"

He seemed angry at me, but full of concern. He stood up and sat down several times, nervously pacing about. He put out the cigarette he had been smoking, clearly contemplating how tragically things could have ended up for him and for me.

"It's your job to do the payroll, Karina," he said, looking straight at me. "Can't you see that? There is nobody else I can trust to do the work."

The regular cashier was on vacation, an Armenian woman who was unwilling to come back, and Samir knew it. The only other person who could do the job was also an Armenian, and she had quit right after the pogrom in Sumgait. He needed me all right, but I knew that to every Azeri there I was the hated Armenian woman in charge of their money. In the current state of unrest, I was an easy target to be robbed or killed, even if when I wasn't at work. I had voiced these misgivings to Samir in the past and he offered to send a car to pick me up and take me back home. But this was not good enough anymore.

The exact moment I had decided to take the money home was when the assistant manager, who had been with me for the first couple of hours that last pay day, suddenly left me alone after the first wave of people came by to collect their salary. It crossed my mind that anyone there could hit me on the head, throw me into a corner, and steal all that money.

"I was up all night and couldn't sleep," I told Samir.

"My mother and I actually tried to sleep with the money packed underneath us in bed." I started to get choked up again.

Samir, a tall man, was calmly smoking another cigarette.

"Okay, okay," he said. "Calm down, Karina. Everything will be fine."

"No, no. I'm not doing it anymore! No way! This is it."

"All right, I'll find someone to do it."

To my relief, he seemed to accept, albeit unwillingly, my throwing off that burden from my shoulders once and for all. I remained for a while longer with the company, but I never again touched payroll. Shortly after that incident, my mother took my children to Armenia, this time for good.

More than twenty years later now, whenever I try to analyze how I acted in that particular time of crisis, I always wonder if I acted correctly.

"*Would I do it again,*" I ask myself, and I quickly conclude, yes.

Why take that risk? Fear of getting caught? Hope that the situation would get better?

I still felt myself an employee. Many people call me a fool. Many Azeris did not think twice about stealing Armenian goods, cars, or apartments. Why should I care about the money of the Azerbaijan Republic, a state which would not protect me and my family and was fomenting violence against me and my people? But I did it anyway.

In retrospect, the company lost three of their most reliable and highly placed administrative employees who happened to be Armenian. This occurred throughout the entire country in every field of endeavor to the great loss of Azerbaijan. Although the independent nation of Azerbaijan has built expensive and extravagant modern buildings in the style you can see today in Dubai, through the eyes of history it will be like the most powerful empire of Spain, which started its trade and industry decline when they expelled the Jews and Moors in 1492. The loss of the most talented and educated sector of its population will inevitably exact a heavy toll on the future of a country.

There was a common saying at the time: Azerbaijan was "trading golden hands for gold teeth." Educated, cultured people were expelled, and they were replaced by country Azeri peasants who filled their places in the big city and flashed their only proud possession; their gold-filled teeth.

After this crisis, the only thing that hit me was that I no longer had a job. My husband was also out of work. Our children were with my mother in Armenia. We were essentially homeless. Our beautiful ranch home with the fruit trees and gardens was occupied by an Azeri squatter. That's when we decided to flee Baku—and the rest, as the old saying goes, is history.

Finally, we received an invitation to go for the long-sought interview at the American Embassy in Moscow. It was almost three years of utter anxious, tortuous waiting.

As I stood in front of the American embassy on that gray April afternoon, I remember vividly the muscular Soviet guards and some people passing by casting us dirty looks, recognizing that we were Soviet Armenians trying to leave the country. A Finnish journalist standing among us tried to interview Armenians from Baku, but they quickly turned their faces away from the microphone and cameraman. Soviet citizens are not used to such interviews and are fearful of reprisals if they speak. I must confess that I also refused to cooperate.

When my name was called, my family and I were prepared for what awaited us, right down to the color of the carpet. We entered as a large group and passed through the entrance and sat in the waiting room.

A chubby woman, not too tall, with a friendly and smiling face, came over and invited us into a small room. She had a very upbeat attitude, which for us was unusual. It's sad when you distrust someone just for being nice to you, but after so much subjugation for so long, it's difficult to let your guard down. She took a seat at a desk that had a window behind her. Three rows of chairs faced her desk, and I sat in the front next to my aunt, my husband, and my brother occupying chairs against the wall. She checked our names and then asked, "How's everybody doing?" She spoke in Russian but had an accent.

"Okay, I guess." I answered for the group.

Before she started asking questions, we were instructed to raise our right hands and take an oath.

"How long ago did you leave Baku?" she began, "Why did you leave Baku?"

She wanted to know what kinds of things happened to us and why continuing to live in Baku was impossible. I am the only one who was responding, so she directed her questions to me:

"Where did you used to work? Are you working there at the present time? Do you live in your own house?"

"Our house doesn't belong to us anymore," I told her with sadness.

"Are you a member of the Communist Party?" she asked me.

"Because of my job, I had to be a member of Communist Party. I recruited people as members of the Communist Party with special paperwork. But I am no longer a member of that party and that's why I am here."

I was shocked at hearing myself openly expressing what I was now pronouncing.

She asked about the kids and how they were doing.

"Why don't you want to stay here in Moscow?" she queried.

"We cannot find a job. The kids cannot go to school."

"Why not?"

"According to the Russian system, everything is based on your passport and your residency."

She nodded her head in agreement and asked me to describe several disheartening experiences and unhappy incidents. I mentioned only a couple when she suddenly tossed out a question that hit me like a bombshell because I knew the serious implications my response would have on the outcome of these proceedings.

"Karina, have you ever gone overseas?"

My head was spinning. I wondered what I should tell her, then it occurred to me that it would be best to just tell the truth, which she may know already. I had been fortunate to have traveled frequently.

"Yes," I finally responded "Poland, Bulgaria, and Hungary..."

I listed only the Communist countries, hoping that would help to win favor.

"No, no, no. Any capitalist countries?" she insisted.

My mind was boiling now. I was trying to think from the American point of view.

"What did she want to hear?"

For that, you have to have money and connections working together to be able to travel outside the Communist East. We were so close, I didn't want to spoil it for everyone, and have my past actions be responsible for the fate of my entire family.

"Yes," I admitted it in a trembling voice.

"Name the countries."

"Egypt, France, Italy, Malta, England..."

"How about Japan and India?" she interrupted

"Yes," I answered with a sigh."

"She knows anyway," I thought.

After a short pause she said "All right. You have no negative comments."

She did not ask if I had negative comments. She knew all the countries I visited, and I understood immediately that she had access to a background check on my record where negative comments would show if I had engaged in any inappropriate activities abroad.

Since all visits to capitalist countries are in groups controlled by the Soviet government, each including secret KGB spies, the government knew if there were instances of shoplifting, prostitution, or black market activity in foreign countries involving police—anything at all. If so, a "negative comment" would be put on the report by the KGB agent who was embedded in the group.

"But, how does she know that? I suppose the capitalist countries have their own little lists."

My thoughts continued to race. "Why all these detailed questions?"

For a moment I panicked and thought, "Maybe all that talk about the United States merely gathering statistics for propaganda is true. Am I putting myself and my relatives in danger for nothing?"

The woman turned her attention to my aunt Mira. "How are you doing, Mira?" she asked.

Mira smiled at her. "Good, thank you."

The agent asks her about work, the house, and family. Then, "Are you a member of the Communist Party?"

Very proudly, Mira swaggered, "Yes!"

"Are you still a member of that Party?"

"Of course."

The chubby, round American face became long, and she asked, "Then, what are you doing here?"

Before my aunt could open her mouth to continue boasting about being a proud Communist, I contemplate kicking her to keep her from saying anything more. I spoke up instead.

"My aunt is under tremendous emotional stress," I explained. "Recently she lost a child. She meant that, like most of us, she was a member of the Party, but she left because of her belief. The country and the Communist Party made no effort to protect us citizens who are Armenian."

"Oh! I'm sorry to hear that. What happened?"

My aunt has never been able to communicate succinctly. She would go off on various tangents and never get to the point, so I took the initiative to address the question.

"Unfortunately," I began, "my aunt can't visit her child's grave and cry. She died of natural causes, but her biggest concern is to take the remains from Baku to Armenia. Under the present circumstances, the anti-Armenian craze makes it impossible."

My aunt held up a photo of her deceased daughter.

"I'm so sorry." The official is very sympathetic and asked only the names of the others. She asked my mother about her taking my children for protection to Armenia, what kind of work she had in Baku, and what made her make that radical decision.

"My grandchildren come first," my mother said

Then the woman looked at the paperwork and signed them before standing up suddenly.

"I'm sorry for what happened," she said. "Everyone is free to go."

As we all slowly rise to leave, my mother and I lingered behind.

"Hold on," the lady said to us. "Stay here a second."

My mother had a magnetic personality and whether she was in Azerbaijan, in Armenia, or in the United States, she made friends wherever she went and found herself welcomed and treated kindly, always with a smile on her face.

"Zhogefa, (the name on the passport), don't worry," she said to my mother. "Don't worry, everything will be fine."

The woman stroked my mother's shoulder. She walked over to the window which had multicolored knickknacks on the sill, something which appeared very alien to us. She removed some brightly colored packages of cookies and sweets that were sitting there and walked back to us, then placed them in my mother's hand along with a folded green paper bill.

Then, the woman turned her attention to me, "Karina, you're going to do very well in America," she says. "You will have many friends. You will look back and know you did the right thing."

Then, in a sudden change of subject and tone, she said to me, "Oh, how do I know? You dressed in the American style: a simple white blouse and black skirt."

Outside, my mother opened her fist and found a twenty-dollar bill folded into a little square mixed in with the candy. We had no idea why the embassy woman selected my mother out of the half dozen people in our group. Maybe she looked especially sad and worried.

Everybody joked "Give it to me!" they shouted excitedly. "Give it to me!"

"No!" she replied emphatically. To her dying day, my mother held on to that twenty-dollar bill for good luck.

"Wait outside the gate," we were told. We waited until closing time.

A man arrived and called out names. He came with a single piece of paper for our whole group. On the paper there were two little printed empty squares.

Next to the first box it stated, "You have shown enough evidence and have 'refugee' status."

Next to the second box it said, "Unfortunately you have not shown enough evidence."

To our absolute delight and surprise, the first box was filled with a large X.

My own glee was briefly put in check when I noticed the reaction of a woman who was not in our group and saw that the second box was marked on her piece of paper. She approached the closed gate and an embassy man on the other side and pleaded her case to him with tears in her eyes. She did not understand what he was saying, but I could clearly distinguish his American accent.

"I'm sorry," he said and walked away.

I know how easily I could have been that woman, but kind fate intervened on that day. I left the American Embassy in Moscow with my family, exultant. Finally, we could proudly, openly display the hope we held for our future.

CHAPTER 14

The Speech

IT WAS WITH MIXED FEELINGS THAT I LEFT ARMENIA FOR AMERICA WITH my family. It is what I had been dreaming of for so long, but all the propaganda perpetrated against America by the Soviet Russian government was hard to just give up. We settled in Rhode Island, and I have always loved that little state for welcoming us with open arms. We found jobs, our children grew up, and we established new friendships. But what happened to me and my family was never far from my mind.

Through the years various people have encouraged me to write the story of my family's coming to Rhode Island as Armenian refugees from Baku, USSR. However, there were others who did not think it was a good idea.

Who do you think you are? Professor? Poet Laureate? Ph D?

These are the kinds of remarks I would hear from people from the Soviet Union, and I cannot say I was surprised by the attitudes of people from the U.S.S.R., a country where you notoriously have to be born with these titles written on your forehead, unlike America.

Coming from the Soviet culture as I did, it was not easy to shake off the sense that you are born to a certain status and there is no changing that. That notion that you have control of your own destiny seemed so strange and impossible. It was uplifting to discover that in America it is not strange at all to say, "I am writing a book," and not get criticized or mocked for it. I am of a culture where you were discouraged from even talking about yourself and, in fact, encouraged not to talk at all.

In any manual or self-help book on writing, the typical advice given to burgeoning authors is:

"Don't be discouraged by family and friends. Ignore them. Keep working! Write, write, write!" There are numerous American books and magazines filling whole sections of the bookstore devoted solely to the craft of writing. To me, this was very liberating. It filled me with hope and helped change my Soviet mindset about what I could accomplish and overcome the barrier of negative energy from family and friends; *Keep your ideas to yourself, don't open up to your family, your friends and certainly not to the world.*

It was always my ambition that this book be more than a memoir, that it would not only chronicle what happened to me and my family but offer a historical perspective of what happened to Armenians as well as other people and why. I believe that societies should be challenged to argue, discuss, and learn from these events. And in some instances, they should become the source of academic case studies so that the same mistakes are never repeated.

The purpose of this book is not to merely present a personal account of the events I experienced leaving Baku, but to educate and entertain. There certainly are elements of danger and fear, but also some of humor. In the end, you, the reader, will be the judge. This book is written on behalf of all Armenian voices, survivors and non-survivors of the Armenian genocide, which began with the massacres in Sumgait, the horrors of which are forever on our minds.

In pursuit of finding my own voice in writing a book, I was inspired by an independently published Russian book about the events of Sumgait which documented the deaths with names and pictures. At the same time, I became acquainted with a new concept, "oral history," when it occurred to me to interview friends and fellow Armenians from Baku, using the techniques popular at that time to record their personal thoughts and experiences while the memories were still fresh. In this way, local history would be captured on tape and transcriptions written down word for word for posterity.

The Rhode Island Historical Society offered their insight and resources, including the storage and preservation of the material in their archives, even lending me the use of their reel-to-reel tape recorder, which maybe was not the size of a refrigerator, but certainly a medium-sized suitcase. They provided mentorship through a workshop on the techniques of working with and interviewing people who did not want to cooperate or perhaps had something to hide.

It involved much more than the technical problems of microphones, batteries and plugs, but real social interaction and how to get the history out of people when it could be like pulling teeth. The culture barrier in the Soviet Union made that aspect even more complex and challenging.

In the end, I decided that to sit down with a big machine on a kitchen table or on a coffee table in their living room was intrusive and would interfere with the comfort and trust level necessary to record people telling their most personal and intimate stories. Moreover, many had the Soviet mentality, asking me,

"Why do you want to record this?

"Are you making any money from this?

"Should you pay me for this?

"Who will see this?"

Others asked that I not use their real names and many simply did not want to cooperate.

I completely understood their reluctance. People were not trained to speak about themselves or others. It was not a concept for Soviet Armenians or any Soviets. I had to admit it to myself that *I was one of them*. Like these Soviet-Armenians, I was not particularly comfortable talking about myself, and it was something I struggled to overcome. With such a deeply instilled negative mentality, I had to sort things out, and for a long time I was not ready to open-up fully and answer these questions myself.

I also wondered if the opportunity had passed, taking into account all the years and the distinct possibility that a number of refugees who had gone through this horrific experience in Baku might now be resting in American cemeteries along with their memories that they likely never shared with anyone, even with their own families.

The rigid structure of the Soviet educational, political and belief systems make us like those captive elephants held by only a small rope tied to their front leg. No chains, no cages. While elephants could at any time break away from their bondage, they do not make any attempt to free themselves because when they were very young and much smaller the same size rope was used to tie them, which at that age was enough to hold them. As they grow up, they are conditioned to believe they cannot break away. They believe the rope can still hold them, so they never try to break free.

I decided to approach the Armenian churches and my concerns with the priests about oral history in general and the sad reaction of the Armenian refugees in Rhode Island.

"They still think like under the Communist system," they said. "They don't want to talk openly; they are still under the oppression of the dark past, scared with no sense of free speech, anxious about talking openly, and people don't want to look back to the darkness."

"Yes, we know and understand our flock," the priests counseled.

"Be patient. Inform people better. By prayer and petition, you eventually will reach them. Let us know if you need any help."

As time passed some people adapted. Sometimes it took five years; sometimes twenty.

It sadly seems that some people could never adapt.

I, myself, also needed a span of time to open up even to myself, just like the people I interviewed. I came across many hints of deep and perceptive tales, but with roadblocks. As time passed, I found that some people had changed and were ready and willing to trust me and cooperate to share the sad, painful experiences and still give enough details to make the story understandable to people in the United States and any other countries and other cultures.

Coming from the same region, for the same reason, at the same time, from the same culture, I myself found that I continued to be reluctant about speaking out, telling the world how it really was in Azerbaijan during that horrible time as the mighty USSR fell to pieces. What was a footnote to so many was the foundation for all that I had and had become.

I continued my project, often being discouraged, but I was following the priests' advice to persevere patiently. This is when I met Maya, the woman who told me the story of her father being pushed from a ladder by the Azeris and eventually dying from his injuries—all because he was an Armenian.

The book slowly took shape. Because I was starting to have success using oral history methods to document what happened to us Armenians in Baku, I had boldly set up a non-profit corporation under the name *Armenian Oral History Century 21*. I found very few to interview, and they were still reluctant to talk. Extremely disappointed, but not discouraged, I decided to try something different.

My idea was just to translate the pamphlet documenting the massacres in Sumgait, the earliest acts of violence against Armenians in Azerbaijan. It was not easy to obtain a copy. I tried to get my own in the United States, but research of U.S. libraries holding a print showed only the Library of Congress and the Huntington Library in California. Using connections of friends and family, I finally got my hands on a copy,

I found it to be horrifying and shocking, but in my lack of sophistication, clouded by my passion, I could not see that it could be boring, lacking in both appeal and presentation. The book, written in Russian, was arranged more like a spreadsheet, containing dates of birth, names, dates of death, manner of death, and short notes accompanied by grisly black and white photographs poorly printed that were almost undecipherable.

I was working for Japonica Partners, an entrepreneurial co-investment firm. The first person I shared my thoughts with about this project was the president, founder, and owner of the company, Paul Kazarian. He is a man devoted to philanthropic interests, especially Armenian causes. There are several generations of both victims and survivors of the Armenian genocide in his family. Knowing him to be a talented, successful businessman, I shared my idea with him to translate and publish this slim Sumgait pamphlet into English.

As documented, thirty-two Armenians were killed in Sumgait in the most brutal way. Although Paul Kazarian knew the history, he did not read Russian. He skimmed through the pages. Having worked closely for years with him, I recognized his business-like skepticism as he examined the pamphlet in his hands. Despite the obvious weaknesses in the material and its presentation, he kindly encouraged me to pursue the project, knowing how much passion I had for it.

He went further, suggesting a second opinion, and turned it over to another successful businessman, a friend and colleague, Robert Setrakian, founder and owner of Helios Group, a pro-active investment firm. To this fellow Armenian and supporter of Armenian causes, I gladly mailed the pamphlet. Robert Setrakian not only read it through but shared it with someone he trusted who was a specialist in documentary writing. However, when it was returned to me it was with a single negative critical comment:

"This book is not marketable and not publishable."

I was instantly deflated, but it was reassuring to me to have two prominent Armenian businessmen take the time to make a practical analysis of my nascent proposal. Maybe there was still more work I needed to do to improve my idea, but it was good to know that I had so much positive support from people. It made me want to continue to move forward to tell the sad story of Baku and its people, a process which I quickly learned had to be done patiently and assiduously.

As a result, I became more appreciative of the entire process of writing a book. I felt it was important to show evidence of what occurred in Sumgait because there are people who still do not know what happened. The Azeri government hid the terrible truth, but the pamphlet I wanted to translate was evidence of the killing of Armenians and the beginning of the modern genocide.

"To everything there is a season," the Bible states in Ecclesiastes. With my project, the important thing I came away with was not that certain experts deemed it as commercially deficient, but that my people, including my boss, encouraged me and found it to be important. It just wasn't ready, and I was grateful for the motivation and encouragement that these men had for my pursuit.

In my mind, I thought the project was dead. I remember one of my professors, Stephen Gross, who was my English teacher and tutor, now commentator on this text and a historian with some knowledge of Soviet history, asked me a common question several years ago:

"How is it possible, with all the highly educated Armenians who fled persecution in Baku, that there is not one book we know of telling the story in first person by an adult victim? Not in Russian, not in French, not in English. There are plenty of Armenian newspapers and magazines that would have highlighted such books. I searched and found nothing."

I thought to myself, this man may know history, but does not know the Soviet mindset.

I recognized that it all stemmed from the Soviet culture of not being honest and unable to talk about things negative.

Years back, Harriet Kazarian, a proud mother of five and wife of my boss Paul Kazarian, kindly invited me to a book signing. The author was Samantha Power and her book, *A Problem from Hell*, dealt with the inaction of the American government in several genocides starting with the Armenian. In the car with us was a woman, an Armenian-American professor and a close friend of Harriet Kazarian's. While driving, Harriet introduced us and told her friend a little bit about me, including my emigration from Baku.

The professor suddenly turned around to face me, sweeping her long, mostly gray hair over the back of her seat as she did so. With an expression of deep sympathy and sadness, she said firmly, "You have to write a book."

"Aw, who is going to publish?" was my Soviet-mentality reaction.

Later, while listening to Samantha Power's book presentation, I was very impressed but at the same time I was equally scared and intimidated by the overwhelming process and hard work that was required to promote a book after it has been written.

"You write, and I will publish," the professor boldly declared to me.

I remember the look of determination on her face and the firmness of her voice. Her strong offer to help me rang in my ears for years, but at that moment I was still not ready, not understanding, this unfamiliar, outlandish generous kindness. Sadly, not long after, I heard that she had passed away and the idea seemed to be put on hold indefinitely once again.

Unexpectedly, things changed at a special event that I attended, sponsored by the Da Vinci Center for Community Progress in Providence. I had been participating there as a board member the previous five years. My story of how I came to Providence as an Armenian refugee was known by other board members. In fact, the Da Vinci Center, as well as local Armenian churches, was instrumental in helping my family get settled in Rhode Island. They assisted in placing my children in private schools and arranged English as a Second Language classes for me as well as some college courses.

The Da Vinci Center for Community Progress presents an annual Humanitarian award, and this particular year it was being given to Giovanni Feroce, who at the time was CEO of Alex and Ani, a company that provided many jobs in Rhode Island and throughout the country which was mired in a period of recession. He successfully brought to bear his military skills as a U. S. Army Major to the remarkable success of this innovative jewelry company.

At one of the board meetings of the DaVinci Center, I was asked to talk at the Humanitarian Gala and present the Da Vinci Center and myself as one of the Center's success stories. Several other people were suggested, but it turned out that I was to be the sole speaker.

The founder and director, John DeLuca, whose organization welcomed my family when we arrived on Sept. 29, 1991, inquired about the text of my speech.

"Hey, Karina, are you getting ready?" he asked me. "Do you know what you're going to talk about?"

I pointed to my head, "It's here," I said. Then, I pointed to my heart, "And here."

"God bless you!" he said.

Sometime later, he asked me the same questions, and I responded in exactly the same way with a smile. He gestured, palms in the air, which I read as meaning, "I give up!" or "What are you going to do?"

Again, he simply said, "God bless!"

On the evening of the event, while setting up the registration tables with three other women, members of the Board, I was asked,

"So, how are you feeling, Karina?"

"Okay."

"Are you ready?"

"I think so."

"Do you have a script?"

"No."

"Did you make a video tape of yourself?"

"No."

"Do you have your written notes?"

"No," I said, suddenly feeling like I disappointed everyone.

They looked distressed. They stood speechless as they spread their arms in surprise and worry with widely opened eyes.

As a member of the Board one of my tasks was to work at one of the four tables that had been set up at the entrance to check off the names of guests from their letters of invitation and assign each of them to the numbered table. We were expecting upwards of four hundred guests, and while I was busy registering guests, I took particular notice of a tall woman who presented her invitation letter to me and said, "Hi, I'm Gina Russo."

"Hi, Gina," I said. "I'm glad you could come. Just go to Table #8. I'm Karina. I'm also at the same table Number 8 as you. I'll see you there."

About ten or fifteen minutes later, I noticed the arrival of the Reverends Mr. and Mrs. Russo. They thanked me for the invitation, and I told them,

"Gina, your daughter, is already here. She's at Table #8."

They both looked at each other astonished. The pastor's wife said,

"That's impossible! She was not ready when we left and she's already here?"

I could offer no explanation, and the pastor's wife just shrugged her shoulders.

The couple turned and walked through the entrance of the dining area as the light swing music of the orchestra boomed through the opened doors.

I took the pile of invitation cards and shuffled through them and there the name was clearly written: Gina Russo.

People continued to arrive, elegantly dressed. *Hors d'oeuvres* were being served. Several well-known faces from politics and television were being photographed in group portraits in front of sponsors' conspicuous display signs with the guests. It was a positively lovely evening.

The atmosphere was warm and cheerful, and the venue was second to none. Rhodes-on-the-Pawtuxet is a large, elegant banquet hall on the banks of the Pawtuxet River, in Cranston, just outside Providence. It has been the host of many important events in Rhode Island. We arranged for round tables adorned with white tablecloths, lavender napkins, and tasteful light flower centerpieces.

Impressive chandeliers reflected their brilliant luminescence in the polished oak wood flooring. The raised stage at the front of the room featured a fourteen-piece orchestra with a singer. On one side of the stage a large television screen was set up for the viewing of a short presentation about the event's sponsor, The DaVinci Center, and introduction for the guest of honor.

When they started serving dinner, I sat down at Table #8. I had no time to chat with the other guests at the table because in my mind I was preparing my speech. Conversation was difficult with the loud accompaniment of the orchestra, so most everyone concentrated on dinner and kept dialogue to a minimum.

When the time came for my speech, I rose from my seat and made my way over to the dais feeling a surge of pain that was not in my head.

A few mornings before my son had awakened me suddenly and I jumped out of bed, badly twisting my right foot in the process. The high heels I wore that night exacerbated the pain, which I bravely tried to hide as I stood before the microphone, which I pulled down to position closer to my mouth.

"Ladies and gentlemen," I began,

"*Dear friends. My name is Karina Yesayeva Khachaturian. Twenty years ago, my family and I came to this country as Armenian refugees.*

"*I remember coming to New York, a man in uniform came to us and said, 'This is your last choice, go in any direction you wish, or you're going* to Providence.' I didn't think twice. 'I think we're going to Providence and exercise our last choice for a piece of happiness,' I replied.

"I remember when we got our papers in Moscow from the American Embassy, I was asking, 'Where is Providence? Where is Rhode Island?' Nobody knew. I started searching in an encyclopedia and I came up with, Rhode Island is famous for three things: shoes, textiles, and jewelry. By the time we arrived in the state: No shoes, very few textiles, and a lot of jewelry.

"I never would believe I'd be standing here, and today as I speak, the difference is stark. The last time I spoke it was at a different event, and I was giving a presentation. A woman came up to me and asked, 'My dear, what is your nationality?'

And after many years, not being allowed to answer this question, I proudly proclaimed, 'I am Armenian.'

"She said, 'You don't know what I'm talking about. Someday you'll find out, but you have the accent of Zsa Zsa Gabor.'

"I took a pause and gave her time to be surprised at my reply.

"I told her the first thing that came to my mind, 'I may have her accent, but I am not as practical as Zsa Gabor.'

"Startled, she said, "You never know!"

"I did not tell her that I had read and appreciated Zsa Zsa's book One Life Is Not Enough.

"Little did she know that the satisfaction I had been reading the first entire book in English and it was by Zsa Zsa's Hungarian mother, Jolie Gabor. It was in very simple English and was about a mother making sacrifices for her daughters. It moved me very much.

"Coming to America wasn't easy. It didn't make any difference to us coming to Providence, coming to Chicago. No friends. No relatives. I remember staring the next two days and looking through the window and thinking, 'What now?'

"I never knew I would be accomplishing anything. I came with a good education, but I didn't believe I could do the same here. And that was when The DaVinci Center came into our lives. They listen. They support. They encourage and they help. I remember taking courses at The DaVinci Center when I didn't have a job. I remember having books to study, but I could not pay. And I remember they drove me to college because I did not have a car.

"I remember turkey. I remember toys. I remember taking the first English class at The DaVinci Center. I didn't follow. I didn't understand. I didn't believe. I had been living in a nightmare when my entire family's, but above all my children's, lives were in danger.

"And one event, it was when, still living in Baku, my children, son and daughter, being searched by people in school by their Armenian last names, having the brightest and most famous of Armenian names, Khachaturian. They were locked for two hours in the bathroom, and my daughter tried to calm down her little brother by telling him, 'Don't say anything. Don't cry because if they hear you, they will find us and kill us.'

"The only guilt they had was being Armenian.

"But we managed. We escaped, coming to this country thanks to people like you are. My children are so lucky, graduating from private school, thanks to The DaVinci Center. They've been helped in homework, in every matter. Every time when we knocked on the door of The DaVinci Center, we've been helped.

"Today, I want to take the opportunity one more time. I hope it's not too late after twenty years to say thank you, again. Thank you to this country. Thank you to people like you. Thank you to The DaVinci Center because without you—impossible!

"I am a proud member of Board of the DaVinci Center already for five years. It's my honor and duty to thank people like you, like me, like us. And I want to say thank you, again.

"Ladies and gentlemen, after all, I am The DaVinci Center."

I could never imagine after twenty years in this country I would receive such a reception. During my speech it was so quiet, my professor said, "If a dime dropped, you could hear it." At the end, the audience suddenly exploded in a rousing standing ovation. The first personal acknowledgment I received as I stepped down from the platform was from the guest of honor that evening.

Giovanni Feroce, smiling as he jumped to his feet, hugged me and said, "Congratulations, Karina. Good job! I am so impressed!"

Many people came over to my table to congratulate me and embrace me while expressing their support and admiration. Three very presentable ladies approached me expressing acknowledgment, support, and warmth towards my speech. One of them, the older woman, spoke to me in Armenian.

"I'm sorry what happened to you and your family," she said.

"Do you understand Armenian?"

I said, "*Ayó! An shush!*"

There was a kind look and tears in her eyes, full of understanding and a message.

"We know what you went through. We feel that we come from the same background."

Later on, I learned that she was the mother of the other two women next to her, one of which was Caroline Rafaelian, the owner and founder of the Alex and Ani Jewelry Company. It became well-known in Rhode Island and the entire country as one of the youngest, fastest growing and outstanding companies. It made me feel proud as an Armenian. We not only came from the same background, but we are Armenians, with the same dark eyes, dark hair. And Caroline Rafaelian and I each have a daughter with the same name, Ani.

The evolution of this book is directly connected with the events of that particular evening. Leaving the speaker's podium after the standing ovation, as I walked back to my assigned seat at table number eight, I observed the nice couple I had personally invited to this event after meeting them several days before, that being Reverend Russo and his wife, who is also a pastor. They were talking to a third person I did not recognize.

Their presence was the result of a chain of remarkable coincidences.

About a week prior, my car was filled front and back with packages of bread and pastry that I was on my way to donate to a church on my street. However, upon arrival I found that the door was locked tight and the building appeared deserted. It was near dark as I drove on, then I spotted one of my neighbors walking down on the same street. I pulled the car to the curb and stopped to ask him if he knew why the church was closed. He told me that it had recently moved about a quarter of a mile up the block, so he squeezed into the car and guided me to Oasis of Grace Church

"Let's see if the pastor is there now," he said to me.

"It isn't the time for services or the soup kitchen, but let's try. There's a sign with a telephone number on the door and address of their home nearby."

Luck or fate had it that the pastor and his wife pulled up in their car just then. They were very thankful to accept the donations and four of us worked together to carry the many loaves of bread and pastries into the chapel entrance.

When we finished, it occurred to me to invite them to the upcoming Humanitarian Recognition Event at Rhodes-on-the-Pawtuxet. I thought that the Russo family would be perfect guests. I decided that these two organizations, The DaVinci Center and Oasis of Grace Church, both in the city's North End, were relatively doing the same thing, which was serving people. It would be good for both to get to know each other, so I made arrangements with the reverend and his pastor wife to meet at the church the following day to deliver their tickets.

Upon my return to the church, I found Mrs. Russo waiting outside for me.

"Can I invite another abused woman?" she asked me.

The awkwardly phrased question threw me off a little.

I replied, "Of course!"

I handed her the two tickets I had, told her that I looked forward to seeing her there, and I would take care of the other ticket for the "abused woman" at the time of the event. When I called to confirm their attendance, Reverend Carl Russo strangely mentioned his daughter "Gina." In my mind, I now assumed four people were coming, the pastor and his wife, their daughter Gina, and the mysterious "abused woman."

The party was getting very noisy after I finished my speech. The orchestra stopped playing. The lights were turned up and the large screens went blank. Food was starting to be served, including the seafood specialties of Rhode Island. On my way back to my table #8, I received a lot of compliments about my speech. I returned to my table as the first course, the salad, was being served. The orchestra started playing show tunes with a singer of a certain age crooning Sinatra songs.

As we were all socializing, I became aware of an unusual air of excitement at our table and an animated conversation that developed between the tall Gina Russo I had sent to this table and a petite woman whom I did not know but to my complete surprise was introduced to me by the Reverend Mrs. Russo: "I want to introduce our daughter, Gina Russo," adding in a whisper to me, "that abused woman."

I was perplexed. She was not the same Gina Russo I had greeted and registered. I had assumed that this tall person was the pastors' daughter.

"Am I getting delusional?" I asked myself until the startling story of the two Gina Russos started to be revealed.

I did not say anything, but a moment later the petite woman rose and addressed everyone at the table who were all showing great excitement and interest.

"Listen, everyone. For years," the petite woman began, "people reached me by phone and email, asking, 'Are you Gina Russo?'

'Yes, I would reply.'

'Are you *the* Gina Russo, the survivor of the Station Nightclub fire?"

'No,' I'd tell them. People ask me on Facebook all the time the same question, but I always thought, *Some day* I know I'm going to meet that other Gina Russo of the Station Nightclub Fire.'

"Today is the day I finally met my namesake."

Unknowingly, I had brought these two Gina Russos together. The Gina Russo who survived the Station Nightclub Fire courageously wore a short-sleeved shirt that displayed her badly scarred arms and hands. I also recognized that she was wearing a wig, and I thought that maybe this was the "abused woman," that the reverend and his pastor wife had made reference to previously.

The other Gina Russo was petite with sharp features and long hair, and as I was looking at the two Gina Russos I soon realized that their names were not the only commonality between them. The biggest similarity I learned later was that they had *both* overcome great tragedies in their lives.

The Gina Russo, who was pastors' daughter, happened to be the mysterious "abused woman." She had been through two brutal marriages, suffering dreadful consequences, but found the strength to confront her sad history and has become a domestic abuse prevention activist. Today, she preaches in churches and other venues and is a leading advocate in raising awareness to this important social problem. Her organization is called, *Breaking the Chains.*

The Gina Russo who had sustained life-threatening burns in a horrific fire that killed one hundred people attending a rock concert at a Rhode Island nightclub in 2003, including her fiancé, published a personal memoir several years later. *From the Ashes* is the title of the book she wrote about her experiences recovering from the emotional and physical wounds she suffered that night. That night I saw a copy of her book on the table with the cover image of the phoenix rising from the ashes and found it to be not only inspiring but motivating.

We talked for a while, and I was amazed how much she had accomplished. Today she is president of the Station Fire Memorial Foundation, a charitable organization established to raise money to remember the victims and survivors with the construction of a permanent memorial park on the site of the fire. She is also very active politically, lobbying for changes in the law and building regulations to prevent other nightclub fire tragedies like this from happening again in this country and around the world.

I was overwhelmed by the level of success both Gina Russos had achieved, especially after they both admitted that public speaking was not easy for them. I was touched by the number of people, mostly women, who approached me after the event and offered their encouragement and support to continue speaking. Many expressed their admiration, admitting that they never could have done what I did, lacking the nerve to speak off-the-cuff in front of hundreds of people.

A week after that, I had lunch with Gina Russo, the chubby, tall woman, victim of the nightclub fire. We talked about the party and the amazing story of the coincidence that happened that night.

Gina then presented me with a copy of her book, *From the Ashes*, which was written by a local writer, Paul Lonardo, "who is a friend of my friend," she said. Talking about future plans, Gina told me, "I am going to have to give talks to promote my book, but I am terrified."

"Karina, how could you speak in public with no notes? Don't you panic? Aren't you nervous? Aren't you forgetting what you want to say?"

I shrugged my shoulders. "I really don't know. It's in me."

"It must be harder when you're not speaking in your own language."

"Yes, very much so, but, is there another way of doing? Now, look at you. You have your book already. I have been thinking about a book for many years, and I cannot even say aloud what I want to do!"

At that moment, sitting there with her, I had an epiphany. It suddenly occurred to me, "If she can do it, I can do it."

For weeks, I kept getting calls, letters, and comments from people at the DaVinci Center and people I did not know, congratulating me on my speech. It was a wonderful feeling and it strengthened my decision of writing a book.

I was unaccustomed to these accolades and such a raw display of emotions and feelings. It was all a new experience to me. Considering who I was and where I came from, it was shocking to me. Change is not in the Soviet mentality. People are attached even to their chair. After all these years, now, I looked at myself in an entirely different way as a result of all that I experienced since I came to America, and I realized that the change was not so much in this Russian mentality *per se.*

There might be some people who will not completely agree with me, perhaps, but that would only be because they do not have anything to compare it to. I have seen it from both sides, living in the Soviet culture and in a democratic society.

Believe it or not, I was still hesitant about including this speech in this book until sometime after this gala event when I became aware that one of the guests, without my knowledge, viewed the video and transcribed the speech and sent it to a venerable publication, *Vital Speeches of the Day* (published since 1924). I did not have the slightest knowledge about this monthly magazine until I received an email from the editor congratulating me for my "small, wonderful, timely speech." Though their guidelines specified that speeches had to be less than one year old to be printed, mine might be featured on-line on their website, instead.

For me, it was shocking to be praised directly by an editor who was an authority in the genre of speechmaking by having my words made available for readers all across the world to view.

The repeated encouragements that I had received over the years from family, friends, the Armenian Church, businessmen, and others had not moved me to complete the action that was my destiny. Now, however, the triumph of this public event became an epiphany, coalesced by the examples of two courageous women with the same name, the two Ginas and the two Russos, and sparked within me the driving force to produce this book.

CHAPTER 15

So That History Does Not Repeat

NOW, THE LONG JOURNEY HAS TAKEN ME AND MY FAMILY INTO A NEW country both geographically and spiritually from the Soviet world, where we had been constantly told that we were safe and taken care of by the State. The realization that our situation was in constant danger for ourselves, our family, our children, belied everything we had been taught.

Comfortably situated in Baku, Azerbaijan, where we had believed that ethnic strife would never happen, we were disillusioned and terrified that the horrors of hatred, division, violence, and chaos would touch our family. Our old family stories of persecution of Armenians fleeing from danger and oppression, mob violence, and wars were treated as stories from the distant past even though the signs were everywhere apparent.

Our multi-ethnic city of Baku seemed stable, but the conflicts were becoming more visible. We were smug in our position as an educated and modern minority in a backwoods land steeped in a non-European religion and culture that the rulers in Moscow did not trust—and rightly so. We lived among them but did not understand their deeply rooted beliefs and traditions.

Suddenly, as Armenians, our world view of beliefs and traditions in the news, information, music, and art media was thrust into a horrid picture from an antagonistic chorus of hateful epithets and accusations on the television, radio, and media that was reflected in public rallies of Azeris in the streets.

Our people looked on the rural area Azeris with pity and contempt, called them *Chooshkis* in ridicule. They voiced, when the time of conflict arose, their frustration and resentment against us Armenians and other nationalities who they considered to have seized jobs and positions away from the native population of Azeris. The protests were not against the Russian dominated Soviet government with the corruption, money grubbing, greed and inefficiency, influence buying, which were heavily mirrored in their own behavior, public and private.

I repeated what I have already written in this book for one very important reason. I want you to read what I've written but with a different viewpoint. What if what I was talking about what is happening right here in America?

It's not unfounded. For I see the same shadows of darkness eclipsing the sun of my newfound land.

Our moving to a small New England state, Rhode Island, introduced us to another multiethnic society. The neighborhood we moved into had been an industrial area populated by Italian immigrants arriving and working in textile factories at the beginning of the twentieth century. The northern town of Pawtucket first imported French Canadians to their mills one of which employed my husband as a maintenance mechanic supervising textile machines. Both places were rapidly changing as the older immigrants improved their economic and educational status and moved out into the suburbs. The French were displaced by Portuguese in the north. The Italians in our neighborhood were being displaced by Hispanics and Africans, both Nigerian and American.

Living in a milieu of many nationalities was a mirror of Baku. We accepted it as normal and were not puzzled by the multiple nationalities in place. Instead of Russian Jews, Ukrainians, Tartars and majority Azeris, we recognized immigrants of several ethnicities like us who kept their own language and culture active and spoke English as a second language if at all. Their children like ours were bilingual. Their grandchildren lost the language and spoke only English although outsiders noticed that the local

Italian American boys from the Italian neighborhood of Federal Hill had a noticeable singsong accent and syntax stemming from their background.

The difference is that the national language is English, and the original local language of the Narragansett American Indians had disappeared in the eighteenth century along with their population, devastated by wars and white men's children's diseases like smallpox, measles, mumps and chicken pox. Azeris are alive and well in Azerbaijan retaining their Islamic religion despite the Communist regime's long antipathy towards religion.

The national culture and language prevailed: Russian in Baku; English in Rhode Island.

Yet, I did not see any signs of ethnic strife. I became acquainted with nationalities new to us: Colombians, Puerto Ricans, Nigerians, Cambodians, and our Italian landlady and my husband's Portuguese employers.

I was curious to find out who were the earliest inhabitants of this region. My English teacher took me to a native-American Indian museum in the southern part of this small state in Arcadia, Rhode Island, where an old lady called Princess Red Wing, wearing a beaded headband shockingly read a true view of my past in the tea leaves in my cup.

"You have been involved in great violence," she read.

"There are guns and knives in the leaves, but, don't worry they are away from the ear of the cup, so it's all in the past." My future was rosy, much to my relief. It reminded me of the time a gypsy woman read the coffee grounds of my girlfriend's cup at a card party in Baku. It had been all in fun but turned out to be ominously true to life.

Another new nationality to me was Cuban. A few houses down the street an empty storefront was rented by Enrique, my teacher of salsa dancing. He is a black Cuban who has a degree in physical therapy and has made a career for himself in health and weight reduction through the dance. He is one of the Hispanics I have met who have adapted and changed their attitude positively. I learned the Caribbean dances in his classes so well that a Puerto Rican girl in one class assumed I was Spanish and started talking to me in the language. When I moved to Los Angeles, I regret that I did not learn Spanish since it would have been useful in this country.

But as time marches ever forward, I sadly see Providence, Rhode Island, has become a mirror of Baku. Both, formerly rich industrial cities, spiraling downwards in every way. The old textile company where my husband worked is selling its antique weaving equipment to a company in India. It will soon go the way so much industry has gone from this state. Costume jewelry, shoes, and textiles are no longer financially profitable here. All the nationalities attracted here in the last century are not going to find the jobs that will support their families anymore.

The contrasts between rich and poor are much like what I saw when I was a tourist in Cairo, Egypt, only there are no camels here. Nearby, the North Hollywood Congregational Church was the voting site of the Presidential election of 2016. The tension could be cut with a knife when I went to vote. I had participated as an official registrar at the Da Vinci Center in the election in Providence, Rhode Island and checked people's credentials and waved them over to the machines to vote.

The spirit was acrid that year. People seemed to be gritting their teeth. There was no greeting between residents in the voting district who meet only once a year or two at the polls in Rhode Island and said "hello." It was more like the tense crowded waiting room of a hospital with groaning and mutterings.

The mood in America has become divisive, and just like my old grandmothers who would yell, "I know what's coming, I've seen this before," when the violence in Baku was starting to break out, that is what I am now saying myself.

The refugees fleeing the crime and corruption of their thieving governments are called stealers of Americans' jobs. The President claims that they are full of Arab fanatic bombers, fakers calling themselves Spanish. The sad result is that children are separated from their parents. In Baku they just killed the children and raped the women. When the Ottomans attacked us a hundred years ago, they sold our children as slaves.

There is talk about caravans of illegal Mexicans coming into America. I honestly don't know what to believe about them. We had to wait so long to get our American visas as refugees. How can they gather in a "caravan" and march to the border? The President calls it an "invasion." It seems that they are running away from murderers and criminals but not because of their religion or nationality as we did but as victims of the kleptocracy of their corrupt governments.

My experience in Rhode Island as a small jewelry company owner, as neighbor and friend of the immigrant population, allowed me to meet very many different nationalities. My impression is that they contribute to the culture and prosperity of this country. Why would we keep them out? The world is getting small. It is essential now to get to know other cultures and habits to succeed in business. Living isolated in one's own unique culture is not sufficient experience any more to be a contributing citizen of this country in the twenty-first century. Anthropologists call it a negative term: being "ethnocentric."

We could escape only as far as next-door Armenia. The South and Central American families are running to a neighboring country, Mexico, with their same language, religion and customs. That country cannot support them, and they must march onward towards the USA border. I see the long view. I take the historical route that the very same people who disparage them as an "invasion" have histories of their own pioneer ancestors traveling in prairie schooners across the plains and deserts in the expansion of this country to the West and escape from privation.

Each of these families could write its own book. It is not written down, but in their memories and stories. Most will never be written down. What terrors and suffering their going through will not be recorded. Will the ten-minute interview at the border through an interpreter be a valid account? Is there time in their interview with ICE to relate the sleepless nights, the false rumors, the confusion, the courage it takes to face the unknown? Some of them cannot even speak Spanish and only Central American Indian dialects as we saw in some of our Providence neighbors.

The shattering of lives from political divisiveness is seeping into our modern fabric in America and my story of the Armenian-Azerbaijani conflict no longer seems foreign, far-fetched and abstract. It is also the story of the Palestinians and Israelis, of the Serbians and Croatians, the tribal conflicts in Africa, no matter where, no matter which religion. Some lessons could be learned of kindness, understanding and humanity from these chapters not just for here but everywhere.

No matter where and no matter when, unfairness and inequity starts quietly. But in time, the occasional storm turns into a major tempest. The inhumanity of some is allowed to take over and prevent others from defending themselves and their ideals. We see courage and tenacity in some. Inhumanity is so compelling. It is tribal mob mentality boiling up from cowardice to hate and dehumanization which allowed them to kill, kill, kill.

We must stand up and administer the antidote to the command to "kill" by allowing people's humanity to shine. It happened in Baku over and over.

I noticed that many things that I had admired have changed since I came to America. Today's America sometimes sounds and smells like the Soviet Union just before it collapsed. Bad service in chain retail stores, sloppy customer services, unreturned telephone messages, corruption in the justice system, long lines in stores because of untrained employees, contradictory information from offices, stores and government, interminable waiting on phone service numbers for information, the shootings in schools, opiate deaths and, most important, our government which is divided and which is more interested in battles of parties than in working in the interests of the American people. Democrats and Republicans do not want to sit together in the same room.

Will the same unholy outbreak of violence of one group against another be the downfall of this great nation? What my fellow countrymen and I experienced in Baku happened a scant three decades ago. Genocide is not something that happened "way back when." the propaganda that foments hate, the mindset that allows someone "not like you," to be "othered," and degraded, then "ethnic cleansing," is, sadly, inevitable.

I hope that this book will give a taste of what it means to face dangers and uncertainties in your own deteriorating country and society. To have to decide to give up *everything* in your life and flee to an uncertain future with small children and elderly kinfolk is not something I wish for anyone.

The details of what is happening here in America are different, but the result is the same. That this is the daily bread on the southern border of this great nation is stirring up the worst recesses of human nature seasoned with the sting of fear, the pepper of prejudice and the poison of ignorance. It looks all too familiar to me and my family. This is our story. Learn from it when something captures your attention or stimulates your imagination. If it rings a bell, just know that bell tolls for you.

I can imagine that some readers will take this with a sarcastic smile. Some will think she is so naïve, and some will ask "What does she know? "

I wondered how the system here controlled the interaction between peoples and not allowing labeling them by race, nationality, religion, color or ethnicity. Especially, this is the only country which has The Law of the Dirty Look. People seem now to be more divided by any differences, but in addition to that, they are sharply divided along political parties. Everywhere we see all these messy things are happening almost in every public place and more police protection necessary for politicians, judges, movie stars or anyone who expresses his political views as well as for regular people. The parties seem to be more interested in political ambitions than in the well-being of the average American man.

It starts like metastasis of cancer or like the behavior of a bad child. It starts with one small tattoo and ends with grotesque face like a New Zealand aborigine. It starts with one cigarette and ends with cartons. In Russia there was no news at all; here there is an avalanche of news. It was a dictatorship there and we had to accept what we were told. Here, there is now less freedom of speech because if your opponent does not like whom you voted for or whose name you have on your baseball cap, T-shirt or decal on your car, you can be harassed verbally or even physically. It is a not the America I fled to and fell in love with.

It is so sad to see that this country, a dream country as a destination, which has been a model for every country in every possible field in the entire world, is becoming what it is becoming. The history of this country passed through many trials but still retained the ideals of the founding fathers. This country passed to the present without the trials we suffered in the Soviet Union. I was impressed at how national or racial differences were not ending in violence here, where I was used to one ethnic group acting out violent acts against another. I suffered simply because of my nationality.

Nations should learn and act on the experience of other nations to avoid discrimination, unfairness, unkindness, injustice and heartlessness and lack of empathy and understanding of the other.

I don't keep a journal of these negative experiences. If you know and love your country, you can see it almost everywhere. It's just enough to look at social media. There is one case that shocked me out of my sense of expecting courteous and business-like responses in this country.

I wanted to ask about charges on my credit card bill which I did not recognize. My call to Customer Service was picked up by the branch in Florida. After having explained the situation and details of these unrecognizable charges, I got no satisfaction and realized that the representative was not making any sense, not willing to help and seemed to be wasting his time and my time. He appeared to be in a rush to pick up the next call.

In many cases we know if your data is correct, the problem will be solved right away. In this case, we were going nowhere and his attitude appeared more and more that I was bothering him. After a couple of attempts and failing to resolve the situation, acting reasonably, I asked to speak to a supervisor. Nothing unusual in this country. Instead of being transferred I was shocked to hear,

"Oh, you want to speak to my supervisor. Fuck you!" and he hung up the phone.

Am I delusional?

In the Soviet Union, there was no concept of customer service and nobody cared. The economic system did not depend on competition. There wasn't any.

In one of the classes I participated in, my professor told us a compelling story.

"Years back when I visited Romania," he said, "driving in the mountains with my cousin, I noticed that one village had all the houses the same color blue."

"Anything special about blue?" I asked him.

"No."

"Then why are they all blue?"

"The government," he answered with a smile, "delivered cans of only one color - blue. Take it or leave it! That's the way it is."

Here, the idea of capitalist competition is supposed to make everything better for the customer. If one store does not suit you, you go to another. Theoretically, when management finds out about the competition, they will try to make changes to attract the lost customer back. Down on the level of the service provider or the salesperson meeting and interacting with the customer, the policy of the store or government agency should be followed. But look around you. Where is the motivation to follow the guidelines? Is the customer still always right? Do we still believe in this?

Born, educated, and speaking Russian, I believed we had the best of everything. Then, one moment we were living in the Soviet Union and the next moment life was thrusting us to another nation and system. We had to leave our country, cross oceans, learn another language, and adopt an economic system we had been taught to hate.

We adapted to what we found, but we watch sadly as the good things we love—and never had in the USSR, are starting to evaporate. What caused us to pull up our roots and take a desperate gamble with our families in a new country are starting to corrupt what we were so happy to find here.

Now, I see American people, not having any comparison to another language and culture, viewing so many changes in their country and becoming perplexed and angry.

There are parallels to what I and my family and many people like us experienced. The divisiveness is very painful to see in politics, in public media, in internet comments, in conversations all around us. We lived in the Soviet Union in a society where ethnic groups could call each other hurtful names without being afraid of being criticized in school, work, neighborhoods, or the street even though we were always bombarded with the slogan, *BRATSVO NARODOV* (brotherhood of peoples).

Here, political norms mask the unhealthy mentality that was always there underneath against other races, religions, nationalities, and lifestyles, but the window shade has suddenly snapped up and exposed the dirty clutter inside the house for all to see. Some don't care just as what we experienced in the Soviet Union. Others make excuses. A few have the hope to improve it all.

Our experience was to need to flee for our lives because the government in charge used the hatred and divisiveness to hold on to power and divert attention away from the real problems of our society. It is starting to look all too familiar here. I hope that the insights of this book will sharpen the analytical powers of the reader to recognize what is beginning to wear away the great and wonderful qualities of this country like the constant crashing of the rising sea against the beaches and cliffs eroding the beautiful natural wonders into crumbling, colorless rubble.

Aware of the history of the survival of this country through many crises: civil war, depressions, world wars, social unrest, economic collapse, assassinations, racial oppression, bitter political conflicts, mob violence, and industrial conflicts, we know the people of this country can overcome its problems. We Americans always have. For what's happened before *will* happen again. America will come back and come back strong, but only if we have the fortitude to stand up for the goodness, the honesty, the fortitude that is in us all. If we don't, then I may find myself a refugee once again.

CHAPTER 16

Trust

"Love all, trust a few, do wrong to none."
—William Shakespeare, *All's Well That Ends Well*

NONE OF US, MYSELF INCLUDED, CAN EVER REALLY IMAGINE HOW MANY compelling or interesting stories we each possess in life: burning memories, heart-breaking, life threatening, and some happy. Stories are what give our lives meaning. You must decide what you want to do with yours Do you want to hide them? Do you want to burn them? Do you want to pretend they never happened? Or, recount them so that people can share and learn.

I chose the latter because even in the darkest hours of not knowing if we would live or die, I was always warmed by those who shouldn't have helped but did anyway and that is my most fervent wish for anyone who reads this book. Yes, the events are horrifying. But if it helps inspire you to keep your wits about you when your world is crashing around you, if you realize that even in the most trying of times, helping someone else can give meaning to your own life, then my efforts will not have been in vain.

I could have ended this book on a dark note, but that would be too easy. Instead, I want to leave you with three more stories, woven together by the fact that they all show the power that comes when someone decides to help someone else.

PART 1. THE RESORT

Our family used to go to Piatigorsk, a Caucasian resort, called a *kurort,* where people went to take the curative waters. This is a European tradition which we have in the United States with many elegant places popular in the nineteenth century: Saratoga Springs, Hot Sulphur Springs, etc. Going there two years in a row with us and the children, my mother became very close to a Jewish couple, Tanya and Mikhail from Donetsk, Ukraine, who had grandchildren of their own. They were lovely to us and especially to my children.

The children loved a special kind of treat, chocolate covered home-made fruit-flavored cottage cheese. And for that, twice a week the couple made an early morning special trip by bus to another town where the *syrok* was quickly sold out because of its uniqueness and popularity.

Tatyana was heavy and tall but had no typical female curves. She dressed the same with a flowery summer dress that did not show any real feminine shape. It is something typical I noticed in many Russian Jewish women: narrow hips and small bust, giving a straight silhouette. She was flat in the back and had contrasting wide shoulders. In spite of her height, she had a large belly, a worry of hers which she attributed to the results of surgery.

Tatyana and her husband both had big hearts. She and her husband would take our children for a walk every day which gabe my mother and me some respite. We first thought it would be for only a day or two, but without asking, it became a routine and they came every single day. If it happened that they arrived early and the children were taking a nap, they would wait until they would wake up, eat and get ready to go.

They became babysitters without our asking. If we protested from politeness because it was too much attention to the kids, they would not even listen and just wave their arms dismissing us. Later, we met them in the park and continued to spend time together.

They would buy the children little toys and showed them a lot of love. And the kids felt that love and attachment, too, and returned it to them.

Tatyana and Mikhail had their own grandchildren in Donetsk but they always came alone. The relationship grew for two years with a break for a year and a third meeting the next season. There were exchanges by telephone, gift exchanges for holidays and occasions and we looked forward to meeting again.

In the city of Donetsk my mother was paying a visit to Tatyana and Mikhail alone. She, Tatyana and Mikhail, one day were walking around the city, and as they passed by a furniture store window, they spied some furniture my mother liked.

My mother was gazing very appreciatively into the window display. It was noticed by Tatyana and Mikhail, and without asking her, they took my mother by the arms and led her into the store, saying, "Let's go inside."

After browsing some time, my mother really took a fancy to some pieces, but did not give any thought to purchasing it. Tatiana knew that my mother had talked about updating her furniture after remodeling the apartment, but she did not have any plans to do it now while she was traveling.

"Why don't you buy?" asked Tatiana encouragingly.

"No, I don't need it. Not now. Later. No, it's hard. It's all this distance."

"No, I don't want to," giving polite excuses.

But Tatiana was not even listening.

"But if you like it, what is the difference? I know you were not planning to buy furniture now, but you were planning any way and I'll lend you money and help you with everything."

It came to almost six thousand rubles.

After back and forth so many times "yes" and "no," it was impossible to resist Tatiana and Mikhail. My mother was shocked and almost melted from the kindness of those people. How much heart and trust in someone can you have whom you met on vacation for altogether only a total of sixty days?

"We'll come tomorrow and make the arrangements," Tatiana announced.

And when the two families continued their friendship communicating by telephone, Tatiana would not hear of any mention of the money, which would sound like she wanted to hurry up repayment of the loan.

"Why didn't you call last week, Tanya?" my mother complained.

"Because I don't want you to think about the money I lent you. You mention it every time I call."

Tatiana was very candid with my mother and she opened her heart and talked about trouble in her family. Unfortunately her son-in-law was lazy, loved to drink and never kept a single job too long. In the times of exchanging gifts, my mother also included presents for Tatiana's grandchildren and her daughter.

The relationship continued until a few years later. Knowing that Tatiana was not feeling well, and not hearing from her for a few weeks, my mother called. The daughter answered the telephone and my mother had a bad feeling that something was wrong.

"Oh, I'm living here now. I'm separated from my husband. Then she delivered the bad news. My mother died a month ago."

"Why didn't you call me immediately?" my mother asked, very upset.

My mother took it very hard, losing a good friend.

Perhaps, this relationship which I saw since I was young helped me to have a strong friendship and closeness with many friends, both in schools, work and neighbors. Kindness to people in trouble was part of our family *ethos* and mine as well. I maintained my friendship with my school chums of the past, and even those who emigrated here in the United States as well as new friends for many years.

PART 2. THE BETTER ANGELS OF OUR NATURE

I would drive to New York and Boston from Rhode Island at the drop of a hat. I did not fear the heavy Boston and New York traffic which my husband hated even though he had been a professional driver. My lack of fear and nonchalance about driving to the big city figures in my next Jewish encounter.

I met a Russian Jewish woman, Bella, for several of her doctor's visits at the Miriam Hospital where I interpreted Russian. She was a strong woman, so elegant. She thought always of others and accepted all negative news stoically. The heavy diagnosis was cancer, but worse still, the small state of

Rhode Island and even the biggest city in New England, Boston, did not have facilities to treat her rare form of the disease.

"She must go to a special clinic in New York. I will contact them and make an appointment." the doctor said.

"How can I go to New York?" Bella cried. "My daughter has small children. My sick husband can't drive. I can't drive," typically worrying more about others than worrying about herself.

"Don't worry. I'll take you," I said.

"Karinochka, no, no, no. It's too far. I will not allow you." she replied.

I turned to the doctor and told him in English, while he was waiting for her decision to make the paperwork arrangements,

"I will take her."

"No, I go there a lot. It's no big bother for me," I said to her.

I drove her to New York twice where they gave her the special examination. It was difficult for her to control her emotions on hearing the terrible news that there was not much they could do to help her.

I became friends with this family in several ways. My daughter, Ani, also worked as a part-time Russian medical interpreter at the same hospital while she had an office job and was a full-time college student. I am proud she has the same attitude of helping others plus a quick mind and ability to make quick decisions.

It turned out that the husband of my patient, Bella, was to be served as an interpreter by my daughter in the Emergency Room. The doctor reported the husband now was stabilized after a heart attack. Bella suddenly remembered, "Oh, I ran out to the ambulance and left the teapot boiling in the kitchen. There can be a fire! I have to run home!"

"I'll drive you," my daughter volunteered.

"No, I live close by. I'll walk." This lady was always unruffled and had an air of poise. "I'll be right back." All this was coming from an old lady with incurable cancer.

The Miriam Jewish Hospital was near her home.

"I feel I can leave my husband with you, Ani," she said as she left.

A few minutes later my daughter immediately recognized that something was not right with Boris. He was turning yellow and quivering strangely. She ran to yell for the nurses and the doctor and they went to work on him and stabilized him.

When Bella came back and heard what had occurred, she said,

"How could this happen, doctor? You said he was all right?"

"You never know what happens with the heart," he replied.

"Thank you, doctor," Bella said in her accented English.

"No, you have to thank this young lady," the physician said pointing to my daughter.

She felt so grateful that my daughter saved her husband's life after a marriage of more than fifty years. Then, I also became a welcome part of their lives, too. She felt so close and approached us by calling and asking for us to visit. She would call to say hello and continued the relationship with me. At the time of my and my daughter's relationship with them we probably knew more about their medical situation than their own daughter or son.

We met periodically, remembered holidays. I visited. I would take some holiday food I cooked, and they did not forget about us either. Enough time passed and Bella called me to meet them at their apartment. I have had calls from her but not to be invited to show up at a certain time, so I was a little curious. I went, not knowing what it was about. It was such a pleasure to be with them to see after all these years that their relationship did not lose its sweetness and love. Definitely many married couples could have learned from them. They used Russian precious names to each other. Boris was so solicitous to Bella. He would not let her even lift a teapot.

When I asked him, "How are you?" he replied, "Don't worry about me. Bella is the one who is sick." He left us alone in the kitchen.

"Karina, I want to tell you something which I decided with my husband, and both of us agreed to do it. I don't want you to feel uncomfortable or obligated. But you will do a big favor to us to accept it with kindness and grace."

I am sitting there thinking that this woman whose life is coming to an end very soon, I am thinking that she might want to give something to me as a memento gift. As she was preparing me to hear what it is, her husband walked into the room and he had two pieces of paper in his hands.

The purpose of calling me to visit was a surprise. No, she announced being cool, as she always was in spite of all her problems,

"My husband and I have decided; we want to do something for your kids. Even though I never saw your son, I am sure he is as nice a human being as you and your daughter."

As soon as I wanted to say something, she stopped me with a gesture.

"I want to give something for each of them."

"We are putting aside a thousand dollars for each kid for the day they are going to get married."

"I don't know what to say. Why? Why?" I even said in English, "What?" I was shocked. She had her own children and grandchildren.

"I am like your mother. What I say, you must listen."

The shock was on my face, but the conversation was about everything and anything as usual, but not about the remarkable gift she proposed.

The doctor gave her six months, but she survived three years beyond the prognosis. She rested her hand calmly on the table where my gift of stuffed grape leaves was displayed, tapping her fingers, preventing me from further questioning, Bella was dressed in a very bright dress, wore very bright lipstick as usual, and retaining, as always, her composure, she said,

"It was enough." Not only helping her and her husband at a critical time but becoming friends and following through with our support thereafter.

When I was in California taking care of my mother, I kept calling her in Providence to tell her of my daughter's wedding coming up. I wanted them to come to California for the wedding, but she said, "You know I am a sick woman and cannot travel."

A year passed and I had been phoning from California and calling her with no answer. The more often I called without answers, the more frequently I tried, but I did not know any contact person. When I was back in Rhode Island I went to a wedding. A bus was provided for many guests coming from Providence. I noticed a man with his wife on the bus for the guests going to the restaurant party kept staring at me.

In the banquet hall, I walked into a quiet lobby to make a phone call and get away from the music of the orchestra and dancing. When he approached me, he asked, "Are you, Karina? I am Bella's son."

I hung up the phone and said, "Oh, I keep calling without any answer."

"No, my parents died," he said, and I went into shock.

"When?"

"You know how ill they were, and they passed away within days of each other two months ago."

I nodded but it did not seem a great surprise.

"I have something to tell you. I know what my parents wanted, and I am in complete agreement with their decision. They liked you and your kids very much and always talked about you. Let me know when your son is getting married."

We continued talking about his parents.

"How did you know it was me?" I asked.

"I didn't know and didn't ask, but I had a feeling it must be you."

When I came back to the table, my friend noticed my sad mood, "Where did you go?"

"I was in the corridor and heard some bad news?"

"About your family?"

"No, someone else. I'll tell you later."

Coming from a multi-ethnic city in the Soviet Union, a rarity there, Baku had infused in us an attitude of cooperation and friendship with people of all nationalities. It was not just the architecture, the petroleum, the economy, the historic buildings of the city, but the benevolent culture of Baku instilled in us was what made us special, too.

We were living in an environment with an ever-present threat of danger, so we embraced the better angels of our nature as Abraham Lincoln said.

PART 3. THE MYSTERIOUS GUEST

Near the entrance to the Semashko Hospital in Baku is the site of my father's shoemaker shop, or cobbler's shop. We learnt the term "cobbler" in Rhode Island which still uses the old New England term.

I loved to go there and visit as a child. He had a big table with special rods that allowed my father to hold leather pressed onto the metal shape of a shoe upside-down, called a "last" while his free hand could tap in the nails and apply the glue brush. That smell of glue permeated the store. It was not offensive, but very strong.

The walls were white and the shelves were painted Rembrandt brown and matched the color of many of the shoes that were waiting to be picked up on the shelves that went all the way around the store. Shoes waiting to be repaired were on the right. Shoes finished and waiting to be picked up were on the left. The tools, brushes, nails, and dyes of different colors, and pieces of leather scraps were on one shelf. I watched him at work there and also at home.

Being so close to a major hospital on a busy street, the store attracted many people who would be killing time, waiting for an appointment, let out early before lunch or dinnertime, or staying to chat with my father. The conversations were mostly in the Russian language, although he spoke the local Azeri and, of course, Armenian. My father had a good clientele because he could manufacture or repair a custom-made pair of elegant shoes. This gave my father a nice source of income.

One day, a man came in and looked around without speaking. He was new to my father. Finally, when he spoke up, he asked in Armenian for a pair of new shoes to be made for him if it was possible within the week. He said he was from out of town. He was more than that. He was from out of town, from Kirovakan, in the neighboring Armenian Republic. It was the first of many visits.

The visitor talked at first very enthusiastically as people came in and out of the shop, about weather, the city, shoes, but eventually the topics were used up. There was very little in common to talk about for two people who did not know each other. In a moment of silence, my father concluded that this man was killing time in Baku and was tight-lipped about his business here.

"Is your family here?" my father asked.

"Yes, they are seeing the sights."

"Do you have family here in Baku?

"Do you have any relatives here? Where are you staying?"

The answers were "no" with a shrug of his shoulders and, "I don't know yet."

After some silence, my father was thinking, "He says he is with his family. It is almost evening and he does not know where he is staying."

This created the suspicion that something was going on in this man's life. After studying and observing him, his nice manners, his good Armenian language, his quick intelligence and quick grasp of the topic of conversation, my father came to a conclusion: "This man is laboring under some great pressure. No family here. No rushing off to go anywhere. No personal details except that he is from Armenia and no mention of his city of origin."

My father proposed an impulsive and unexpected invitation to this man, "It's almost closing time. Why don't you come home with me and stay with my family until you finish up your business here in Baku?" He silently accepted and continued to sit there without saying anything until closing.

He was a kind and pleasant houseguest. He sat in a chair while he talked to my father, but you could see that his mind was occupied with some problem and he went out on mysterious business every night. In the daytime my father went out very early. The guest left in the morning. Where he went and what he did we did not know, but he always stopped by my father's shop.

When he left the house about eight or nine o'clock, he would say, "I have to make some calls and I have a lot of things to do." Sometimes he came back in the evening with my father.

Then he would leave after supper, announcing he had to make a telephone call. My father thought he had to know the news of the day. We did not have a telephone at that time.

My mother, unnerved by this unexpected house guest, asked my father, "Who is he? Where does he go every night? How can you bring a man completely unknown to us into our house when we have two young kids here?"

"Oh, you and your wild imagination," my father waved her off with his arm in the air, dismissing her worries.

"He probably goes out to make phone calls to Armenia." My father said.

My mother never was convinced,

"If his family is here like he said, where is the family? Can't he stay in a hotel or guest house if he came to do business here in Baku? Couldn't he have made arrangements with family or the family of friends? He has to have money to travel around and do business here."

One day he came very happy and excited, saying, "Oh, I have to go home. It's time. I have nothing else to do," still not explaining anything.

Gagik, for that was his name, left, and he thanked us for our hospitality. My mother was so relieved. We little expected to hear from our mysterious guest. We forgot about him, but about two months later, we saw him again with a cortege of three automobiles showing up at the entrance of our apartment complex to the excitement of all our neighbors.

When we saw our mysterious guest with family, his male cousins, with about two people in each car, we were surprised all these people coming to see us from Kirovakan. We thought maybe he was here to thank us again.

"We came here to take you to our home. He introduced us to his relatives. You're coming with us," he said. "People are waiting for us." It sounded like he was just a trip across the street, not across the mountains into another republic.

"We are taking you back with us to Kirovakan in Armenia. No excuses."

"Don't take anything just your clothes. You don't need anything. I was your guest, now you are going to be mine."

We at first did not take it seriously, but when it was clear that all these people came just for us, we were overwhelmed with their respect and intentions toward us.

"I cannot leave just like that. We have things to do," my father said.

"No, no. You have to come. All my people, my relatives and family, are waiting for you. Just a couple of days."

This put even more obligation on us.

"No excuses," Gagik and his colleagues said.

The trip was direct over the mountains between Armenia and Azerbaijan at a time when there were no difficulties between the two republics which were both under the umbrella of the USSR.

On approaching the house, surrounded by fields of lumpy earth, it was obvious that some big activity was going on. Benches with chairs were set up near the house and people were busily preparing food. We realized that something big was going on.

Was it a birthday, an engagement, a wedding?

On entering the house, we met the wife of Gagik who gave us big hugs and invited us to freshen up.

"She asked us, "Do you want to rest?"

We entered a large cold room and she offered us coffee,

"Do you need anything?

My mother asked, "Could we have an iron to get our clothes ready?"

"Of course."

We passed through the kitchen where many women were preparing potatoes to be peeled and soaked in water. Eggplants were being cooked. Paklavah and Armenian lavash were laid out on a table in huge quantities.

As it started getting darker, people started arriving, nicely dressed up. Then, we saw the musicians arriving. But we still don't know the reason.

The tables were set up like the Greek letter *pi* and were covered with large white linen tablecloths which hung down over the sides. The top of the letter pi had chairs on both sides where we and our host were seated. The sides were set up with long benches. Our seating was central with Gagik, his parents and members of his family. Everyone there could see us and hear us and we could see everybody.

At the meal, the first toast was to my father, thanking him.

"Today you are here because I have here very important people close to me and my heart. I want to say to them 'thank you' for whatever they did for me," Gagik proclaimed.

When we sat down at the table, it was clear. The toasts were all in our name. We were the guests of honor. Then his father gave a toast. His father was crying and gave my father a hug. His brother followed in the same way.

My father returned the toast by simulating drinking a few drops of vodka because he was not a drinker. He said,

"What we did was nothing but human hospitality. It was not worth all this trouble you have gone to, but anyway thank you."

There were other toasts to my father with the same theme of "thank you."

They offered us anything we wanted. There was shish kebab, dolma, walnuts, fruit, Armenian brandy, Georgian wine, toasts left and right, music and dancing.

There were about one hundred people, eighty seated at the table, with about twenty preparing and serving food. They were informed in speeches about what my father did to help the mysterious guest in Baku. People seemed to be aware of the background of his trouble of which we had no knowledge yet.

Music and dancing just like at a wedding. There were live animals to be slaughtered for the next day's feast. Afterwards, my father was privately told by his thankful host of some details of the trouble that my father's instinct had perceived.

"But why?" we asked ourselves. We were hosts for a few days to Gagik, stranger though he was. We were polite not to ask too many questions. We did not lend him any money. The reception seemed out of bounds. It was a wonderful evening. Too much. The food kept arriving from the kitchen full of women working at preparations.

The table was cleared and now it became a dessert table. There was *paklavah* and *katah Badanburi*, another kind of pastry. Different cakes, tortes. Fruit, of all kinds. The same kinds in the form of dried fruits. Preserved cherries stuffed with walnuts. Apricots stuffed with almonds. Boxes of chocolate. Walnuts rolled in a sweet sauce. And, of course, with the best Armenian cognac and champagne.

Gagik privately shared with my father what his dilemma was. We finally heard it from my father later at home in Baku. It turns out that he is the director of a warehouse where, as usual, in the Soviet Union rarer merchandise disappears to purchasers with the right kickbacks. Not so unusual, but hard to prove. Unfortunately, someone died in an accident in the warehouse. It brought too much attention and brought investigators with better accounting and detective skills making an accidental death and illegal sales of merchandise possibly criminal activity.

Gagik was in boiling water. Not only could he lose his shirt, but also his skin.

"The shit hit the fan."

What to do? It meant finding the right connections to cover it all up. His friends who were the top officials in the city recommended,

"Gagik, take the next train out of town and disappear until this blows over."

By chance, the next train out of Kirovakan was headed our way - to Baku. That is where Gagik was holed up and my father gave him a comfortable, safe place to stay, to go out and make phone calls, and plan his defense.

They kept us for three days and were willing to keep us for more. My father insisted on our going back to Baku by train. They would not accept that.

"The same cars that brought you will take you back."

Not the same number of cars, but enough to carry us and the gifts we were given.

However, the greatest gifts were the examples of my father and Gagik; the one, offering kindness to a complete stranger, the other accepting hospitality from a stranger in an unfamiliar land.

There are so many stories, some violent, some sad. But the ones I remember best are those of great acts of unsolicited kindness. That is the only way to build trust between strangers—no matter when, no matter in what circumstance.

There was a bumper sticker that was popular a few years back: "practice random acts of kindness and senseless acts of beauty." While shadows were cast over Baku, the bright sunrise of hope for all mankind will always remain alive because I know the calm kindness and beauty can bring when everything around you is turning upside down. The worst of times brings out the best in a person. May you always find your best self in times when you need it most.

Appendix A

The Diaspora

The mass exodus of Armenians out of Armenia throughout its turbulent history has created the Armenian diaspora. It is a topic on which many have discussed. Because I am an Armenian refugee, I am part of this diaspora. I want to say a few words about it here.

In an Armenian Apostolic Church, the priest took this Greek word *diaspora* as the theme of his sermon. Here are some of the highlights.

The dictionary has two definitions.

- *Diaspora.* A dispersion of a people, language, or culture that was formerly concentrated in one place.
- The dispersion of the Jews from Palestine following the Babylonians' conquest of the Judean Kingdom in the 6th century BC and again following the Romans' destruction of the Second Temple in AD 70.

1. "We do not hear about the "diaspora" of Lithuanians or Albanians in this country even though there may be pockets of these nationalities in various places, but we know that Jews are scattered over all the continents as are the Armenians, both from persecutions in history, ancient and modern."

2. My collaborator on this book, Steve Gross, is my teacher and mentor, a son of Jewish immigrants, who is a part of the diaspora from Hungary. Steve was accepted at Brown University and granted a graduate fellowship. That is how fate brought him to Rhode Island in the same city to where I emigrated and where he became my first English teacher,

a man who knew Middle Eastern languages and history, worked with Armenians, and came from an immigrant family himself.

3.   Steve Gross also worked as a rare book dealer. With his understanding of many cultures, he came across an old business directory of fabric dealers in New York. Steve recognized its value as a fascinating mirror of how many nationalities in the big city cooperated back in 1923. There were Christian Lebanese, Muslims, Turks, Greeks, Syrian Jews and Armenians. He passed it on to his brother working as a manager in the fashion district of Manhattan.

4.   "That book was a sensation and you can't believe the number of hands it passed through all over New York," he told me once. The stereotype is that all these ethnic groups are rivals and competitors in business, but that remarkable collaborative directory puts a lie to that belief at least at that time and in New York.

5.   These nationalities worked together in New York. There are many children of Armenians and other nationalities that have become famous and successful.

Notable people of mixed Armenian-Jewish descent:

- Levon Aronian (Jewish father, Armenian mother), Armenian chess grandmaster
- Yelena Bonner (Armenian father, Jewish mother), Soviet and Russian human rights activist
- Sergei Dovlatov (half-Jewish father, Armenian mother), Soviet journalist and writer
- Garry Kasparov (Jewish father, Armenian mother), Soviet and Russian chess grandmaster, considered by many the greatest chess player
- Yevgeny Petrosyan (Armenian father, Jewish mother), Russian comedian
- Aram Saroyan (Armenian father, Jewish mother), American poet (son of William Saroyan and Carol Grace)

- Richard Shepard (Jewish father, Armenian mother), American film and television director
- Jackie Speier (Jewish father, Armenian mother), US Congresswoman from California
- Michael Vartan (Armenian, Bulgarian, and Hungarian father, Jewish mother), French-American film and television actor
- Zurab Zhvania (Georgian father, mixed Jewish-Armenian mother), Georgian politician

6. Also, inside the old business directory was a slip of paper of jokes. One of them was about Armenians which everybody thought was funny:

> *"French saying:*
> *Trust a snake before a Jew;*
> *Trust a Jew before a Greek;*
> *But never trust an Armenian."*

Nonetheless, trusting my mother, an Armenian, with her treasures, following her last wishes and for the care of her family, Manya, our Russian neighbor in the Courtyard, contradicts the stereotype. I have always referred to the story as "The Canisters of Aunt Manya."

"Aunt" Manya was our next-door neighbor in the courtyard for twenty-five years. She always called herself Russian, but my mother had a suspicion that there was a Jewish element in her background that she was covering up. Short and fat, she had the sagging jowls of old Russian women. She had no TV. Her passion was reading at home while sitting in an armchair or in the courtyard. She always was carrying books from the library under her arm when she arrived home.

Manya would take off for three days at a time and we wondered if she visited relatives, had a job, was a spy, or had a lover. The door had an old-fashioned latch and she took a long time to answer a knock on the door. She did not keep a clean house and when she got sick and could use some help, my mother and another neighbor talked about giving her small apartment a good cleaning.

"No way!" Manya was adamant. We could not fathom why. All that dust around was not good for a sick woman.

My mother was friendly with her, bringing her soup and food when she was sick in the last years. She offered to pay for the food and small snacks.

"No, no," my mother said. "I have to cook for the whole family, and there is always something to spare."

Sour cream was her favorite and my mother did some small shopping for her, buying her a farina-like cereal which Manya adored.

"God bless you!" she would say. She was religious and my mother would obtain some candles for her from the Armenian apostolic church downtown which Aunt Manya would place in a glass or small jar before an icon and say her prayers.

She often leaned her large belly over the fence next door and called to my mother, "Zhenoshka, can you come here?" She would entrust my mother with the keys while she went away to visit her niece and the children or on her mysterious journeys. Then she fell ill, recovered and then had a relapse.

The visits from the niece were always unpleasant altercations heard by the whole courtyard, full of unpleasant curse words and accusations by Manya to her niece that she was not a good daughter to her dead sister. Shura would arrive anywhere from slightly drunk to roaring drunk. The neighbors threatened to call the police with such dirty language for young children in the courtyard to hear. The niece Shura called her aunt a "bourgeois miser" and "You won't help me and my children before or after you croak."

Her husband was, according to Manya, "a nice man" but he could no longer stand what he called his "stupid blockhead" wife anymore. Nice or not, he did not pay the alimony to support four children.

As her health deteriorated, Aunt Manya, "*Tyotya* Manya," was more and more sick in bed, and my mother would visit with food and soup. As usual, Manya talked the same theme, "I have no husband, no children, and no sister. I am alone, just my niece and her children, but I have something very important to discuss with you. Please make time to come over and we can talk privately."

The day came when Manya and my mother arranged to talk the "very important topic." My mother thought maybe something about funeral arrangements for this sick lady but never had the slightest suspicion of the story of Ali Baba's cave of treasures.

Sitting in her chair barefoot in a thin cotton nightgown as she always was at home, near the windowsill covered with cactus plants and canisters, all covered in dust, she began:

"You know my drunken niece who comes here and bothers me. She even threw something right through the window from outdoors breaking the glass when I would not answer her knocking and shouting at my door. The neighbors always complain and ask her to leave. She doesn't care about me, but, even so, I want to leave her some money for her children, but I can't trust her with a lump sum."

"She knows somehow I have money but not how or where and that's when our fighting and swearing in public begins. What can I do?" she said.

"I want to help her four kids out. She won't even bring them anymore to me to visit no matter how much I beg her. My own dead sister's grand-children! Their father does not live with them and he stopped paying her alimony."

Breathing a deep sigh, she gestured toward the windowsill where the courtyard was barely visible through the dirty windows.

"You see all those bottles, urns, containers, storage tins on this window shelf? They are not to awaken me at night if a burglar opens the window. I don't use these for cooking. You see all the dust on the canisters even the ones marked FLOUR, RICE, SOUR CREAM, JAM, NOODLES?

Well, I have stuff hidden inside them. Bring me the big green canister marked FLOUR, she asked.

Manya pried off the lid and as she reached into the yellowed, mottled gluey flour a cloud of tiny insects rose up flying out at her face. She rubbed her two old hands together inside the discolored flour and came up with a small round object that shone a reddish yellow from the splotch of sunlight coming from the setting sun through the dirty window. It was what we called a "Nicolai" gold coin, from the time of the last of the Czars, Nicolai and before him, when Russia was still on the gold standard, as were most of European countries and the United States, before the Russian Revolution.

It was something we all knew was valuable from our grandmothers' tales of found treasure and often seeing the Azeri women in the marketplace displaying gold coins sewn into their colorful blouses or on chains around their necks. They are worth a fortune, not only because of their melted down value as gold, but as "numismatic collectibles." You could not refine the gold down for its precious metallic value like with a bracelet or ring. Collectors, museums, and historians valued them according to the year, which Czar's likeness was on the coin, and how crisp the portrait was of the emperor's profile.

Manya said, "I have a lot of them."

My mother was overwhelmed. She had not the slightest hint that this woman living next door so frugally, messily, and often away for days, had such a fantastic secret stash. No wonder she adamantly refused any help in cleaning the place.

"Zhenyoshka, I want to help my niece, a single mother, with her four children, but you know she comes here drunk and calls me a bitch. I can't trust her to spend money wisely. Here is a sheet of paper I wrote down the instructions to you after I die." The document was written in fine hand-writing and elegant, correct Russian grammar in a style the product of her constant reading of good books.

I remember the scrapbook album with the gray covers she maintained so elegantly about news events and a record of her reading. In particular, I remember how a Russian ballerina's life was portrayed with glued in news-paper articles and pictures, all labeled in a beautiful cursive hand, not with a ballpoint pen but probably with a pen with a steel point nib dipped into a bottle of ink like what was used in the past by our parents and grandparents.

The beautifully scripted instructions to my mother carefully stated how to dole out money slowly and steadily in specified amounts to her unreli-able niece after Manya's death, which was sadly to happen much too soon thereafter. Such a document cleared my mother of any fear of accusations or suspicions.

"I don't want to get involved," my mother had said. "I don't need a curse of your family on me!"

But Aunt Manya had insisted. "No, no. You have to. I have no one else to help me." This was an argument hard to refuse.

Neighbors in the courtyard began to wonder why my mother was spending so much time at Aunt Manya's. She and Manya decided that the best season to sift through the canisters of rice and flour and hunt all the hiding places would be in the winter when it was less likely for a neighbor or visitor to pop in unexpectedly and discover the precious metal "mining operation" in the house. No one exposed the secret in our courtyard where so few secrets could be kept undiscovered.

But in the Soviet Union you could not give your niece a Nicolai gold piece once a month which she would ill-advisedly take out into the public arena. Aunt Manya had suggested a jeweler in the marketplace who was Armenian who could offer cash for each Nicolai gold coin, and if he was not there, the partner who was his brother could be trusted. By being involved in business in the center of Baku, my mother happened to know both brothers. Also there was a Jewish jeweler on the outskirts of Baku who was trustworthy, Manya said, but my mother did not know him and it was a chore to travel there.

"Let one or both brothers come here to your apartment. I can be here with you," my mother suggested, but Manya was afraid. She did not want visitors.

"Take a sample coin to the jeweler," Manya insisted. "When I get all the money, I can arrange to be buried near my sister and help take care of her grandchildren. No, no. You have to take a few sample coins to their place in the marketplace in downtown Baku. No visits here!"

Manya got furious and very agitated about the low price the jeweler offered. My mother was upset that Manya might believe that she was in on a conspiracy to defraud the sick lady.

"Forgive me, Zhenya," she apologized.

"I know that they're worth a lot more than that. I know, but what can we do?" It was not a time in the Soviet Union as in the United States when a trust account could be opened in a bank in the children's names.

When the inevitable happened, my mother notified the niece. Her kids came with her and were crying because they remembered their Aunt Manya who loved them so much.

"You have to come back here sober, Shura. I want to talk to you alone." my mother told her.

When Shura arrived alone and somewhat more sober, my mother started the prologue very seriously and firmly. I remember the moment as she sat at the corner of our kitchen table. But as Manya had predicted, her niece was manipulative as many drunkards are, and asked for more money, but my mother insisted on following the written instructions of her dead aunt to the letter. Moreover, the aunt's stipulation was very strict that there would be no payments at all if news leaked back that Shura had been seen publicly drunk. With no job and no alimony this warning seemed to be a turning point.

After the Russian tradition of grieving for the dead after nine days, there were eight to ten people who visited and were served fresh pastry baked by my mother. The niece arrived weeping and apologizing, saying that she was wrong about her aunt. Her oldest daughter embarrassed us all by openly calling her mother an "alcoholic."

Strangely, the legacy seemed to have mended the niece's behavior and her drunken outbursts were less and less. Shura became a calmer mother and niece, voicing loving appreciation of her Aunt Manya and respecting the conditions of her last testament.

Only one ancient gold coin came into my mother's hands at Aunt Manya's insistence. Now that my mother is gone, I think it is somewhere hidden away among her belongings here in California, but certainly not in a canister of flour teeming with moth grubs.

It is a treasure I have not bothered to touch. The memories it would bring might in the end be too painful.

Stereotypes are unfortunate—and they can bring much pain.

As for Armenians, I would say that we are, above all, crafty. Here's a favorite anecdote to show you what I mean:

An old Armenian man was finally allowed to leave the Soviet Union, to emigrate to America. When his bag was searched at the Russian airport, the customs official found a bust of Lenin.

Customs: "What is that?"
Old man: "What is that? What is that?! Don't say '*What* is that?' say '*Who* is that?'

"That is Lenin, the genius who thought up this worker's paradise!" The official laughed and let the old man through.
The old man arrived at Kennedy airport, where an U. S. customs official found the bust of Lenin.
Customs: "What is that?"
Old man: "What is that? What is that?! Don't say '*What* is that?' say

'*Who* is that?' That is Lenin! The sonofabitch! I will put him on display in my toilet for all the years he prevented this old man from coming to this land of opportunity."

The official laughed and let him through. When he arrived at his family's house in California, his grandson saw him unpack the bust.
Grandson: "Who is that?"
Old man: "Who is that? Who is that?! Don't say '*Who* is that?' say '*What* is that?' *That*, my child, is eight pounds of gold!"

Armenians have often been compared to Jews. It is well-founded. In the special double session of the Swedish Collegium, the 39th World Congress of the International Institute of Sociology, Yerevan, Armenia, June 11-14, 2009, the topic was "Homeland and Host-land: Armenians and Jews compared."

Six similarities were discussed by Eliezer Ben-Rafael:

1. Dispersion. Citizens are out of their original homeland.
2. Diaspora. The dispersions occurred before the original homelands were created as independent states.
3. Religion as a binding factor.
4. The memory of genocide in the 20th century.

5. The diasporans are often living in affluent societies, but the homeland is peripheral.

6. The diasporans are living often in well-established strata, while the homelands are trying to keep up with Western standards.

In addition, *Quora,* the question and answer site, asked the question: "Are Armenians and Jews similar in culture, history?"

An answer by Andrew Michael Lenihan, retired, is as follows:

The similarities I can think of are:

- They are both non-Muslim nations in the predominantly Muslim Middle East.
- They were both victims of genocide during world wars.
- They both have a large diaspora scattered over the world.
- They both have a quarter in Jerusalem named after them.
- They both have a mercantile history. Of course that doesn't mean that most Jews and most Armenians are
- merchants/businessmen, but it is part of their history as nations.
- They are both ancient nations, older than many European nations.
- They both managed to reestablish an independent state in their national homeland, with the odds stacked against them.
- And of course: like everyone on the planet: they are human beings, which is something ALL national groups share

There is also a strong emphasis in both Armenian and Jewish ethnicities on writing and education.

The next question that comes to mind is where are the Armenian Jews? It has been asked of me and I could not answer the question. There are in the neighborhood of Armenia Kurdish Jews, Georgian Jews, Persian Jews, Greek Jews, but who ever heard of an Armenian Jew?

There is in the annals of ancient history a mention of fifty-thousand Jewish troops fighting as mercenaries of the Armenian Kingdom, Where are they?

All those family names ending in "-ian" or "-yan" with Jewish-sounding personal names: Mosessian, Davidian, Rafaelian, Abramian, and Israelian, to quote just a few, are thought-provoking. This was asked of me many times. Did those fifty-thousand soldiers intermarry and disappear into the population?

The possible answer has recently shown up in archeological circles in the article by Daphna Lewy, in *Ha'aretz*, sponsored by The Foundation for the Advancement of Sephardic Studies and Culture, "The lost Jews of Armenia"; Traces of a previously unknown Jewish community dating back to the Middle Ages have been discovered by chance":

> "The excitement stirred by the unusual letters engraved on the rounded stone pillars that were unearthed in boggy soil covered by thick vegetation in the area of Eghegis of southern Armenia was justified. A chance excavation there had exposed an ancient Jewish cemetery in a place where no one had imagined that a Jewish community had ever existed. A contingent of researchers from Hebrew University in Jerusalem, led by Prof. Michael Stone, the head of the Armenian studies program, set out for the site to carry out a preliminary survey. This spring, after the snows melt, he will return there to continue the research. Prof. Stone is a frequent visitor to Armenia for his research but, he says, it never occurred to him that evidence would be found of the existence of a Jewish community, and certainly not of a flourishing and wealthy community like the one whose traces have been unearthed."[5]

> "In Armenian sources, there is an account from the first century CE describing how King Tigranes II the Great brought thousands of Jews from the region into Armenia. There is a tradition about Jewish life [existing] there during the seventh decade of the first century, but no traces of it remained," says Stone.

> "The pillars uncovered turned out to be the elegant tombstones of about forty graves: They bore Hebrew inscriptions, quotations from the Bible and various Hebrew names, and constitute "a tremendous find," according to Stone. The researchers have

concluded from them that there had been a Jewish settlement in the area during the Middle Ages, which was associated with the rulers of the region. Presumably, it was not isolated, but part of a larger community settled in the surrounding region."

"All of the tombstones were erected over a period of only 20 years, but the researchers are convinced that this was not a wandering Jewish community that stopped in the region temporarily, but rather an established community that led a rich life and whose members held an important position in the life of the province."

"I [Stone] have already found in the historical literature and documents clues to the existence of Jewish communities in that area during that period. For us, this is a new page in the study of Jewish history. This is a diaspora no one had known about… When the Mongols invaded Georgia, Armenia and Persia in the 13th and 14th centuries, the rulers of this region wisely surrendered. They did not fight and they were not slaughtered, and it became the most flourishing and the wealthiest region of the period," says Stone.

"Very important things in the history of Armenian thought were determined there at the time, and into this a new element has now entered: the Jews.

This discovery is like getting hit on the head."

The following story about the renowned Jewish art dealer Duveen and Gulbenkian, the Armenian millionaire, and both of them businessmen, may lend support to another joke on that slip of paper in the rare book:

"*The Persian saying:*
If you can make a good bargain with an Armenian,
you can make a good bargain with the Devil."

In an elevator of the Ritz Hotel in Paris, the Armenian oil millionaire, called "Mr. Five Percent," Calouste Gulbenkian, came across the Jewish art dealer, Duveen, who had three galleries, one each in Paris, New York and London. The New York gallery had a building in 1911 that cost one million dollars.

Gulbenkian, the Armenian who negotiated the rich petroleum deals in Iraq at his 5 percent commission, the richest man in Europe, introduced himself and proposed a deal to Duveen. He would give him a tip about three fabulous English paintings coming up for sale from a private collection: a Reynolds, a Lawrence, and a Gainsborough.

The owner wanted to sell all three as one lot.

For giving the greatest art dealer in the world this tip, Gulbenkian wanted the privilege of purchasing any one of the three pictures at cost, at the same price that the Jewish dealer paid. Duveen was celebrated for his shrewdness in analyzing the psychology of his customers and proud of his success in his business transactions using this astute skill.

However, he mistakenly assumed that the "Oriental" Gulbenkian would choose the "most showy painting," not knowing that the Armenian was "a canny student of art as well as an Oriental."

(The present-day magnificent Gulbenkian Museum in Lisbon testifies to his impeccable taste.) To Duveen's shock, Gulbenkian chose "the finest, although the least dazzling of the three: Gainsborough's "Portrait of Mrs. Lowndes-Stone."

Duveen was not so much abashed at losing the profit he would make as by being outfoxed at his own game of trading in fine art treasures.

"It was one of the few times anyone acquired a Duveen without paying a Duveen price."[6]

Just as a side note, there is a marked similarity between Armenian and Jewish cuisines. Are we closely related? You be the judge.

Appendix B

BAKU TODAY

I HAVE NEVER RETURNED TO BAKU.

Some have asked, what happened? It is sadly a case of post-colonial violence and greed. The Baku I grew up in, the place I loved and called home, is gone forever.

Even as I write this, I recognize that even though I try my best to give an objective look at Azerbaijan today as an independent republic, it has been difficult.

Numerous sources from Azerbaijan, Russia, and international organizations will provide evidence to the conclusion that the country has declined in many aspects since its independence by having expelled its most educated and productive peoples and thus, has trod onto an irreversible downhill path.

If you look at "Baku" on the internet today, the media message gauged to attract tourists belies the bitter history of the cast out Armenian segments of this country who heavily contributed to the beauty of the architecture, the educational and cultural institutions, public parks, statues, and city planning.

A clear picture can be painted of the contrast of what life was like in Baku at the time I lived there with my family and what it has become since that time. This once vibrant cosmopolitan city of many nationalities is today a hollow shell of what it used to be, represented internally by one ethnic group and punctuated externally by gaudy buildings designed by American architects.

Baku had enjoyed a period of great and sudden prosperity due in large part to its petroleum reserves. However, the wealth was not reinvested in what economists call "human capital" (*i.e.*, education, teaching materials, school infrastructure). It was, instead, sucked out of the country by foreign investors and into the pockets of the corrupt government, which in turn invested the money abroad and squandered it on luxuries and indulgences. Arguably the greatest loss of "human capital" was our expulsion as Armenians along with the diaspora of the Jews and other nationalities. To balance that loss column of the bookkeeping page is not an easy task.

The Internet is rife with sites sponsored by the Azerbaijan government which paint a false picture of a tourist Mecca, even while oily pollutants float on the waves of its beaches along the Caspian Sea and leave lines of scum on the sands of its shores. Indeed, the pride in its architecture, its culture and its beauty—there is no mention of the contributions and legacy left by the Armenians who came to Baku in the early days of the oil boom, made fortunes and built the mansions, opera house, refineries, and oil derricks there.

Ashkenazi Jewish doctors, engineers, teachers and scientists took active part in the development of the Azerbaijan Soviet Republic. Eight of the ten professors who established the Baku Medical Institute were Jews. Prof. Levinson-Lessing (prominent geologist) was the Chairman of the Azerbaijan Academy of Sciences.

During World War II, Jewish evacuees from Russia, Ukraine and Belarus settled in Baku and many of them chose to stay in their country of refuge.[7]

For more than half a century, critics have been trying to find the answer to why the woman in Salvador Dali's picture "Geopoliticus Child Watching the Birth of the New Man" points at Baku. Maybe it's a coincidence but maybe Dali wanted to say something

The purpose of the baku.am website is to present and enlighten the prosperous past and inheritance of the Armenian community of Baku. The targets for the website are scientific organizations, achievers and in general all the people who are interested in the history of the Armenian communities and Baku.

It is important also for the citizens of Azerbaijan, and especially for the youth. The website has fundamental information about the Armenians' cultural and civilization contribution to the history of Baku city. For the young Azerbaijanis it will have the significance of the alternative source of information.

Unfortunately, there still exists an Azerbaijani government-enforced restriction on the freedom of the press, and the violation of human rights in general. Anti-Armenian propaganda is still alive and well, implemented on the state level and prohibiting any mentioning about the role of the Armenians in the history of Azerbaijan, and particularly in the history of Baku.

It is as absurd as if the Chinese government were boasting of the Victorian buildings of Hong Kong but neglected to mention that they were actually of British design, and as outrageous as the Egyptian government claiming that the pyramids were products of Arab science and engineering three thousand years before Muhammad.

The online history of Baku completely neglects any and all mention of the pogroms that killed many and drove my family from their home. When there is a mention of violence, it always describes reported ethnic violence *by Armenians* against Azerbaijanis.

The Azeris who had been killed by the invading Russian troops are regarded as innocent victims and honored as heroes. The Armenians are further accused of murdering innocent Azeris as collaborators of the Russians. When someone is guilty of something—especially something egregious—they will almost always accuse someone else of the very thing that they have done or are continuing to do. It's a clear case of the pot calling the kettle black.

Oil

The first modern oil well is drilled in Asia, on the Aspheron Peninsula north-east of Baku, by Russian engineer F. N. Semyenov.

Marco Polo wrote about the strange pools of black greasy liquids coming out of the ground in Baku when he visited the Persian city in 1264. On the shores of the Caspian Sea, what is now modern-day Azerbaijan, he saw oil being collected from seeps. He wrote that "on the confines toward Geirgine there is a fountain from which oil springs in great abundance, in as much as a hundred shiploads might be taken from it at one time." He reported to unbelieving medieval Europe that it burned like olive oil, though it was not good to eat. The locals used the goo to treat skin diseases of camels. We call it today, petroleum jelly, or Vaseline®. Centuries later, the first modern oil well in Asia was dug in Baku.

In addition to oil seeps, Marco Polo also saw spectacular mud volcanoes, sourced by natural gas seeping through ponds, and a flaming hillside, the "Eternal Fires of the Apsheron Peninsula," a spit of land that juts eastward from Azerbaijan into the Caspian Sea. This is where condensate and natural gas seeping through fractured shales has burned, and been worshipped, for centuries. The Temple of Fire Worshipers at Ateshkah has a gas seep that has burned since ancient times for example.

A string of huge onshore producers, beginning with the Tagiev spouter in the mid-1880s, elevated Bibi-Eibat to the largest field. Russian engineers, realizing that production extended offshore, began filling and draining the bay in 1909 to allow continued drilling. Over 300 hectares (741 acres) had been reclaimed by 1927, a project said to be second in magnitude only to construction of the Panama Canal.[8]

Because of the power of the oil lobby, Azerbaijan has attracted capital from Britain and the United States. After all, in 1917 the nation of Azerbaijan produced nearly half the world's petroleum. Contrary to most American histories, Titusville, Pennsylvania was not the first place in the world to discover and extract petroleum. They did not know spaghetti yet from China, or tomatoes from the Americas.

Very often a small country dependent on one commodity for export becomes a "banana republic" controlled by an outside international cartel whether it is cocoa, coffee, sugar, bananas, bauxite, or petroleum. In the case of Azerbaijan, the influence of the British BP cartel poured millions of pounds sterling in bribes into the families that controlled the Azerbaijan Republic.

Greg Palast, whom I will be referring to frequently, is a freelance investigative reporter for the BBC who has spent his career uncovering the connection between the world of energy and finance. He has been called by *The Guardian*, "the most important investigative reporter of our time – up there with Woodward and Bernstein." In his highly-acclaimed book, *Vultures' Picnic*, he spells out the corruption in Azerbaijan and the close relations with British Petroleum (BP) along with the repressive regime.[9]

"Baku," Palast wrote, "until recently was the largest oil equipment manufacturing center on Earth, supplying all of the Soviet Union. Now BP and Azerbaijan's own oil company have refused to buy virtually any of it. Contracts with BP require equipment be purchased from abroad, notably from British interests."

> *Oil revenues from the Baku–Tbilisi–Ceyhan pipeline made Azerbaijan the fastest growing economy in the world between 2005 and 2007. But production is dropping. In 2018, the Trans Adriatic Pipeline (TAP), set to deliver at least 10 billion cubic meters of natural gas annually from Azerbaijan's Shah Deniz field via Turkey to European states, is due to begin operations. By that year, Azerbaijan's oil exports are projected to be in decline—indeed, they have already dropped from their peak in 2010.*

—Thomas de Waal, Carnegie Endowment for International Peace, October 7, 2013

Lack of Education in Russian

In spite of all the oil wealth, Azerbaijan has one of the highest rates of child mortality. In 2018, the Gross Domestic Product per capita (GDP) was $10,100 per Azeri, yet the typical wage was $1,000 per year. GDP per capita is the value of the total production of the country divided by the population. A high GDP per capita could mean that wages are high and living standard of living is good, or on the contrary that there are a lot of poor people and a lot of oil production controlled by a multinational corporation who takes the profits out of the country if the average salary is low. Which element is clear: Azerbaijan President Ilham Aliyev, son of President Aliyev, in office since 2003, has a 2016 estimated personal wealth of $500,000,000.

This new independent government of Azerbaijan precipitously changed the alphabet from Russian Cyrillic to the Latin alphabet, mimicking the Turkish experience of a half century before when they changed from the Arabic script to the Latin or European alphabet. The Azeri language is related to the one spoken in Turkey, so some Turkish books and magazines became somewhat legible, but the result was "making most of the nation illiterate overnight," according to Palast.

Imagine someone reading their morning paper when they are abruptly confronted with gibberish in an illegible foreign alphabet. Consider the task faced by the writers and the typesetters. Envision the frustration of the school children presented with a new biology book that is written in some strange code, and the exasperation of parents as they try to help their sons and daughters with homework that is unfamiliar and foreign.

It may be easier to read newspapers and books imported from Istanbul in a sister language, but this massive kind of social experimentation requires profound and detailed planning. The State of Israel had a massive education program (Ulpan schools) to integrate the Eastern Europeans migrating from postwar Nazi territories to teach both a new language and a new alphabet.

Think how inaccessible the books on the shelves of the libraries and bookstores would be to children trained in the old system. It would be the equivalent to a national book burning. In an authoritarian state of George Orwell's *1984*, this would an effective method of brainwashing and rewriting history. There is no need to contact the *Great Soviet Encyclopedia* to have them remove pages and replace them according to the newest rewriting of history, as was done in the Stalin era. The illiterates in the countryside would not know the difference. All in the name of patriotism: to "throw out the baby with the bathwater."

The Russian language, which had been widely spoken as a first language in Baku, now is in danger. An article by the Russian Vera Ryklina that appeared in Русский Newsweek was later outlined in the linguistics journal *Languagehat* under the title "A Mighty Language Melts Away." Of Ryklina's article, they said it, "very accurately describes the rapid and probably irreversible decline in the use of the Russian language." It went on to say that, "Since the collapse of the USSR, it is studied and spoken less and less in the countries that have won their independence; even within the Russian Federation."[10]

Ryklina believes that the Russian language is needed by only half of those who now know it, and still less will it be needed by their children.

In Русский Newsweek, the author quoted a number of academics who compare it to the languages of other vanished empires. English, obviously, has been a tremendous success, French less so. I was particularly struck by the comparison to the decline of the Dutch language, which had been the widespread language of the enormous Holland Empire.

Historian Ivan Belenkii once said: "But Russia's situation is more or less like Holland's. A century later, there will remain not a trace of our presence over half the globe, just as happened with the many colonies of that great maritime empire. People without much education aren't even aware that Holland had those colonies; the language has remained only in Suriname. And yet only sixty years ago Holland ruled Indonesia, a country with a population greater than that of Russia. Today absolutely nobody there wants to study Dutch."

As in the Soviet times, today the use of Russian in Azerbaijan is concentrated among the intellectuals and "élite" of the nation, however, a survey conducted by the Eurasia Heritage Foundation ranked Azerbaijan among former Soviet republics with the worst level of knowledge of the Russian language. In 2002, President Heydar Aliyev issued a decree establishing Azerbaijani as the sole language of state operation. Shop signs, forms, and stamps in Russian were replaced with Azeri ones. At the same time compulsory teaching of Russian in schools, previously mandatory, was made optional.[11]

"A survey conducted by the Eurasia Heritage Foundation ranked Azerbaijan among former Soviet republics with the worst level of knowledge of Russian, along with Armenia, Georgia, Lithuania, and Tajikistan."

The mass of source materials in science, economics, technology as well as Russian literature and translations of world literature of Shakespeare and Balzac are in the libraries in the Russian language. This swing away from a world language without substituting another world language is devastating to Azerbaijani's cultural literacy. The small amount of literature in the Azeri language and now in the new alphabet cannot support a modern nation. The fundamental old material is now inaccessible, either in the Azeri language, which is illegible in the old Azeri alphabet to young people, or in Russian, which is less and less familiar to Azerbaijani youth.

Azerbaijan has been lowered to the situation of a third world country, where the colonial language is lost and there are no texts in algebra or calculus in dialect X of the Province of Y, where one tribe cannot understand the other just across the river. Who has the training and ability of writing a text in Wolof (West Africa) or Kaqchiqel (Guatemala) and what publisher would find it worthwhile to print the textbooks?

Spelling changes, language changes, underfunding of public schools all lead to a decline in the quality of education in preparing students for university or better jobs, even without the sudden jerking away of resources that still exist in libraries in the Russian language. It is shocking that 90 percent of Azeri youth who aspire to higher education are being tutored privately, according to Iveta Silova, Professor and Director of the Center for the Advanced Studies in Global Education at Arizona State University.[12]

This speaks convincingly of the inadequacy of the public-school systems.

"Furthermore," Professor Silova continues, "the capital infrastructure has rapidly deteriorated; pedagogical materials, equipment, and textbooks have fallen into short supply; there have been sharp conflicts over the language of instruction; and many qualified teachers and faculty have left the profession for more lucrative employment in the private sector or have simply emigrated. By 2000, for example, the percentage of GDP spent on education had fallen by approximately one-third in Uzbekistan and by one-half in Azerbaijan, Kazakhstan, and Kyrgyzstan compared with pre-independence levels. Educational corruption has economic as well as social consequences. Because of the mistrust in educational diplomas, employers in Central Asia now have to establish independent screening mechanisms to distinguish the competent from the incompetent, though both may show identical formal credentials."

In the United States this is called "grade inflation," "fake colleges" and "diploma mills."

The existence of fake diplomas in Baku is nothing new. "You have to bring a bag of money" was the old saying about getting your doctor's degree. The running joke was that a teacher asked the class, "Who is your Dad?" One child might respond, "A construction supervisor." Another might say, "Doctor." If one answered, "An engineer," the class would burst into guffaws.

254

The teacher would settle everyone down and with a smile on his face tell them, "How many times have I told you children not to laugh at people who are unfortunate."

The fact was that the title of "engineer" even in Soviet times was assumed by anyone who tinkered with his hands, such as a car repairman, who referred to himself by this professional title and earned very little for his efforts. With the exponential growth of corruption in Azerbaijan titles, certificates and diplomas have little meaning or believability today.

After the tragedy of the Sumgait massacre, which propelled many Armenians to leave the country, we lost so many friends who had been part of our get-togethers and entertainment. Also, the staff of the schools began evaporating while the Azerbaijani government was interfering more and more in the subject content of the curriculum and the administrative staff.

I remember the day in the center of Baku, after the Sumgait pogroms, when by chance I met my teacher of Russian literature, Elmira Sarkisovna. Her last name means "daughter of Sarkis," which is a rather typical male Armenian name. She was a straitlaced Communist, loyal to her School Number One, having started there a student monitor and working all the way up to teacher and administrator. She never married, and people have long said that she was "married to the school."

"Elmira Sarkisovna," I asked, "can you help get my two children enrolled in school Number One, your school and my school?" At the time I still believed that this was the most prestigious in the city.

She leaned her head, with its severe haircut, close to me, "DON'T! EVEN! THINK! OF! IT!" she whispered with staccato emphasis on each word.

I was stunned by this reaction, particularly because it came from her, someone who had been so loyal to her school.

Elmira pulled back, looked worriedly around and said, "It's not School Number One anymore. It's a *maktab!*"

Muslim Koranic schools are called *maktab* from the Arabic language where the rote memorization of the Koran is the highest and most honored achievement in countries such as Egypt, Yemen, etc. To call a school by this name is a derogatory slur implying no modernity, no European based culture or standards.

This was like slapping me in the face. That word was used for "school" in the Azeri language. The Russian word is *shkola*. The difference is like the difference between "house" and "hut." Both are residences in denotation. The connotation for a hut is a primitive dwelling made of wood, straw or adobe in third world countries. To our ears the *maktab* meant that you would never see the atmosphere we saw before. You would never see students coming early to do extra-curricular work. You would never see the intellectual demands made on the students. It sounded just "Azeri." Not any other nationality. You would never see the mixture of ethnic groups. The teachers often had a highly regarded designation issued in the Soviet Union of a "dedicated" (zasluzhenyi) teacher which we do not have in the U.S.A. Maybe it's like being named "Teacher of the Year."

To have Elmira Sarkisovna, the ultimate in a Communist "company man," scoff at her own school to which she had dedicated her whole life was beyond shocking. It was a turning point for me in coming to the realization that life in Baku, despite the ingrained belief I had in the Soviet system, was changing and it would never be the same again.

Later, I happened to run into the same Elmira Sarkisovna while in Moscow at an orientation meeting giving advice on emigration to America. She gave me a detailed account of how many other School Number One teachers had left for America, and then she said to me, "Karina, it is impossible for me because I am taking care of my old parents and I am staying with relatives here in Moscow."

However, I recognized by that time that her story of old parents seemed to me only an excuse. Many Armenians had already departed with their old parents. I, myself, had finally arrived at overcoming the barrier of the old way of thinking, but Elmira Sarkisovna, still rigid in her old beliefs, was not yet able or ready to cross the line.

Politics and Economics

"[For Azerbaijan] with stabilized or declining energy exports and the lack of any serious economic diversification into the non-energy sector, the current economic model is not sustainable. If the economic model is not sustainable, then the current political system—built as it is on corruption—will be stressed," stated Richard Kauzlarich, former U.S. ambassador to Azerbaijan

"I don't want to even remember that city anymore!" Adamov, poet laureate of Baku, once proclaimed. This was his observation of what was happening in Baku at the time of the pogroms. A websearch reveals horrible atrocities horrible atrocities and huge crowds chanting and waving their fists in the air parroting the phrase "Death to Armenians!" This picture is repeated again and again all over the Moslem world on our TV sets and computers. Just change the country and the enemy.

This country of Azerbaijan has been compared to the feudal system of Europe in the Middle Ages: "a handful of well-connected families control certain geographical areas, as well as certain sectors of the economy." We are back to the 17th century. It is like the fiefs which the great aristocrats of England controlled. Queen Elizabeth, the Virgin Queen, awarded monopolies on products to her court favorites. Sir Walter Raleigh, who chivalrously threw his cape over a mud puddle to allow her to cross, became her favorite and was granted the monopoly on all playing cards in England, a lucrative source of income when you consider that there were few other sources of entertainment at that time.

To find a more modern parallel, the images of Imelda Marcos or "Evita" Peron surface. The glamorous wife of the Azerbaijan dictator president, Mehriban Aliyeva, portrays herself as a champion of education and the poor with her nontransparent charity foundation.

According to a Wikileaks report, "Azerbaijan: Who Owns What? Part 1": "It is unclear where the money for the Heydar Aliyev Fund's activities comes from, though many assume that oil revenues fill the coffers. There are multiple anecdotal reports of employees of government ministries being strong-armed to make contributions to the Fund."[13]

The First Lady's Family is believed to own Pasha Construction, Pasha Insurance, Pasha Travel, Pasha Bank, a cosmetics line, as well as a Bentley dealership in the Old City. To attract tourism, the government has built casinos. This in a republic where trusting monies to chance is a theological affront to Allah and the Koran where gambling is absolutely forbidden.

As Shannon O'Lear, an associate professor of geography at the University of Kansas explains: "based on the experiences of countries in similar situations, with economies overly reliant on oil exports, an uneven distribution of oil rent benefits allows political elite to rule without having to do the work of statecraft to build a foundation for a flourishing society." She further cautions, "If Azerbaijan continues on what would appear to be a similar path, the expectations of its populace will continue to go unmet."[14]

In other words, what she is predicting in her diplomatic language of "unmet expectations" will lead to social unrest in Azerbaijan.

The international agency, Transparency International, which monitors government corruption, has concluded that Azerbaijan is "considered one of the most corrupt countries in the world."[15] Who could have dreamed that it would go from bad to worse?

Greg Palast observed, "Nearly half the adult men don't have full-time work."

This could have been excused when Azerbaijan was a part of the huge Soviet Empire, clumsily manipulated from afar. However, now there is no such excuse for Azerbaijan is an independent sovereign country.

"While the 1 percent rake in the loot, poverty resides close by," Palast writes. "It's Camelot meets Rodeo Drive just fifteen minutes from Calcutta on the Caspian."

The Effects of Brain Drain

That the cultural city I enjoyed has deteriorated is attested by an accomplished Azeri artist.

"There's a crisis going on in the arts; it has become very difficult for musicians to live in Azerbaijan. Many have abandoned their careers in opera, dance, and instrumental music even though it was like a second home to them," opera singer Khuraman Gasimova wrote in *Azerbaijan International*.[16] In the standard opera canon, her repertoire includes the roles of Mimi and Musetta (*La Bohème*), Desdemona (*Otello*), Aïda (*Aïda*), and Tatiana

(*Eugene Onegin*). In 1981, she was awarded first prize at the Maria Callas Grand Prix, an international opera competition held in Athens.

Khuraman Gasimova is not an Armenian or Jewish, but an Azeri.

"Nobody can really blame those who leave," she continues, "it's very difficult to survive. Musicians get such a pittance of a salary from the State and often payment is delayed for months. Many have left the country and signed contracts abroad. There has been an incredible brain drain."

Apart from the economy, the regime has become increasingly authoritarian as testified by Palast about the fate of the truth-tellers who disappeared and were arrested by the Azerbaijani police. When the luxuries of the court are so openly contrasted with the poverty of the people, the establishment knows that a *gendarmerie* (a civil militia, basically), is necessary. Substantial sums must be diverted from the purchase of Western luxuries to underwrite an oppressive, pervasive, and expensive secret police.

The effect of the "brain drain," or more elegantly, in the language of economists, "human capital migration," can be indirectly seen in such factors as: health, education, economy, music, infant mortality, and gender gap. The Organization for Economic Co-operation and Development (OECD), established in 1961 with headquarters in Paris, with a membership of 34 countries, published a 2011 study of the development of a group of countries in the post-Soviet era. The Human Capital Index: ranking in 2013 a country coverage of 122 countries.

Azerbaijan (#64)'s most miserable pillar (*i.e.*, column in the table of indexes) is "Health and Wellness," especially the Survival and the Health sub–pillars, and it has one of the world's lowest scores in the gender gap indicator.

This is the country we abandoned in fear for our lives, and where I was educated to the highest standards of Europe in school and then in music. This was where we Armenians looked around us at the splendid old architecture and proudly realized how much of this city was built by the efforts of our forebears, so innovative in industrial management, in architecture, in printing presses, in cultural institutions and international commerce.

Now, in the spirit of the State of Dubai, the Azerbaijan government has built its gaudy Flame Towers, three modern megaliths of glass and steel. At night, the facades of the high-rise towers are turned into gigantic display screens with the use of more than ten thousand high-power LED luminaries, a vulgar display of colored lights that would be the envy of Steve Wynn, (who oversaw the construction and operation of several notable Las Vegas and Atlantic City hotels). Construction on the buildings that would consist of residential apartments, offices and a shopping mall and hotel began in 2007 and was completed in 2012 before opening the following year at a cost of $350 million.

The design of these structures was intended to be symbolic, representing of the flames of the ancient Persian fire worshipers. They might also be suggestive of Baku itself, its name meaning "city of flames." However, in truth, these architectural oddities identify only with pre-Islamic pagans, and as such one would think that they should be anathema to a pious Muslim.

The towers appear like the giant talons of a bird of prey spattered with red blood or as if a triad of devilish horns have emerged from the soil of this once culturally diverse and cosmopolitan city with its elegant buildings and parks that I loved so much. Upon viewing scenes of Baku on the Internet today, I am often startled by the sight of these claws, or horns, casting long, dark shadows over the leafy trees of a park I used to walk through with my children.

These appalling skyscrapers are unavoidable, and they always jolt me out of my nostalgia. These towers represent to me the hideous transformation of my city. It is now a beautiful abandoned shell, an elegant but hollow spiral carapace of an animal long dead that a bottom-feeding sea creature might cozy up inside and take residence. It neither created this home with its own effort involving years of accretion of calcium nor appreciates its aesthetics. It simply lurks inside, ready to seize upon the unlucky prey that happens to swim too close for its own good.

The opposite effect of "brain drain" is called "brain gain." These emigres had important influences on their host countries. The French surnames of generals and scholars in the history of Germany and England testify to the historic importance of "human capital gain" which these countries enjoyed. One sign of this trend was manifested in the celebration of the alumni of my alma mater, the School Number One of Baku. The first alumni gathering was in New York in 2003. I saw so many people and was surprised at how many nations were represented: United States, Canada, Israel, New Zealand, even Spain. It included former students, faculty, and administrators. My teachers were there, including my English teacher, who came all the way from California.

There was no need at all to dwell on why we left. We all came from the same city. We all had the same reason to leave. We all spoke Russian. We were eating, drinking, and dancing. We exchanged with the teachers what we did not have the courage to say when we were students. There was no atmosphere of sadness or remonstrance. People were happy to be there. We all came from the same city Baku, and we had adapted to our new locations and lives.

All the participants seemed to be doing well, certainly well enough to travel distances and spend money on airfare and hotels, and moreover they felt the importance of participating in such a gathering. It was a happy occasion even though the circumstances that forced us to leave our country and settle elsewhere were not pleasant for any of us.

We had left a world where we once believed that the sun would always be shining on us, that any storm clouds would quickly pass, and when we saw the shadows that were being cast, we chose to ignore them for those very reasons. The "shadows over Baku" were not caused by clouds of water vapor being pushed around by mild breezes or atmospheric winds. Rather, it was like a meteor crashing into the earth and casting out clouds of debris. It was the poisonous vapors and particles of lava spewed forth from a volcano, it was the pyroclastic flows that cascaded down from mountainsides and massive earthquakes that were unleashed. Like the unsuspecting dinosaurs being blasted into extinction 65 million years ago, they did not see their demise coming either.

In Baku, all the destruction phenomena could have been predicted, but no one would believe. We are the victims of the unnoticed build-up of fumes and forces underfoot. They were always there, waiting to explode and destroy the beautiful landscape of flowers, trees and old mansions hovering over the blue of the beautiful Caspian Sea.

My heart will forever weep for my Baku.

Acknowledgements

I WOULD LIKE TO THANK THE FOLLOWING FOR ALL THAT YOU'VE DONE IN making sure the important story of the Armenian massacres in Azerbaijan was told correctly and as completely as I could in *Shadows Over Baku*. It has been a labor of love.

First and foremost I want to thank my beautiful late mom, who was always strong, who stood up for us always, found ways to protect us, and followed us to be with her children from Azerbaijan to the USA.

I also have not enough words to express my gratitude and appreciation to all of you because it would not be possible to complete this book without your help and support.

G. J. Libaridian, historian, diplomat. professor; Varoujan Karentz, retired executive; Paul Lonardo, local Rhode Island, author of *From the Ashes* and others; Foster Kinn, local Los Angeles author; James "Joe" Whiting, Acquisitions Editor. Middle Eastern, Islamic & Jewish Studies, Routledge, Taylor & Francis Group, UK; Georgi Derluguian, PhD in history and sociology and author of *Bourdieu's Secret Admirer in the Caucasus*; John DeLuca, Director of DaVinci Center and & members of the Board of Directors; Stephen P. Gross, professor, researcher, collaborator; Martha Jamgochian, Vice Chairman of Armenian Historical Association of Rhode Island; Oscar Barrera, IT consultant. ; And especially to Dr. Patricia Ross, Senior Editor and Publisher at Hugo House Publishers and the entire team who were responsible for the construction and design of this project. Thank you for your professionalism, creativity and personal involvement with feelings and sympathy for my narrative; and most of all to all my family and to my friends for their patience and support.

To each and every one who told, shared, and trusted me with their precious memories.

This is also for you my future readers—to each and every one of you who will read, learn, understand, appreciate, and feel entertained.

Thank you.

About the Author

KARINA YESAYEVA KHACHATORIAN WAS BORN, raised, and educated in the Soviet Union city of Baku, capital of the Azerbaijan Republic. After graduating from college, she worked as manager of human resources in a construction company. Even though travel was difficult in the USSR, she was able to travel abroad, even to non-communist countries.

She is married with two grown children. The crisis of anti-Armenian riots and massacres forced her family, like many other Armenians, to immigrate to the US. They lost everything, and no-one in her family spoke English. They settled in Providence, Rhode Island. Karina studied English and achieved an M.B.A. from J & W University in Providence. She became a small business owner, taking advantage of the thriving jewelry industry in her area.

She has since sat on numerous boards of non-profit organizations and co-founded a woman's investment club. Inspired by the tales of many other Armenian victims and refugees, Karina wanted to articulate their stories and the voices of the Armenian people as well as tell her own harrowing story of escape as well as her family's finding a new home in America.

Endnotes

1   Adam Jones. *Genocide: A Comprehensive Guide*. New York: Taylor & Francis, 2010.

2   Robert Kushen. *Conflict in the Soviet Union: Black January in Azerbaidzhan*. New York: Human Rights Watch, 1991.

3   Bertrand M. Patenade. *Stalin's Nemesis: The Exile and Murder of Leon Trotsky*. New York: Faber and Faber. 2009.

4   Vaserman, Arie; Ginat, Ram (1994). "National, territorial or religious conflict? The case of Nagorno-Karabakh". *Studies in Conflict & Terrorism*. 17 (4): 348.

5   Foundation for the Advancement of Sephardic Studies and Culture. http://www.sephardicstudies.org/entrance.html.

6   S.N. Behrman. *Duveen: The Story of the Most Spectacular Art Dealer of All Time*. New York: Little Bookroom, 2003, p. 17.

7   http://www.jpeopleworld.com/index. php?dir=site&page=articles&op=item&subj_ cs=3105&cs=3065&mode=print

8   http://www.sjvgeology.org/history/

9   For all references to *Vultures Picnic*, see Gregory Palast. *Vultures Picnic: In Pursuit of Petroleum Pigs, Power Pirates, and High-Finance Carnivores*. New York, Dalton, 2011.

10   Languagehat. "A Mighty Language Melts Away." Vera Ryklina in Русский Newsweek. Commented on September 22, 2006. http:// languagehat.com/a-mighty-language-melts-away/

11   Alexander Caravan. "Russian language and culture in the CIS countries (for example, Azerbaijan): A Study of Fund Eurasia Heritage Foundation. Information-Analytical Center, 2008.

12   Silova, I. (Ed.). Private supplementary tutoring in Central Asia: New opportunities and burdens. Paris, France: UNESCO Institute of International Educational Planning (IIEP)). 2009.

13   Robert Coalson. Azerbaijani President Aliyev Named Corruption's 'Person of the Year.' 30 Jan. 2013. https://www.rferl.org/a/azerbaijan-ilham-aliyev-corruption-person-of-the-year/24814209.html. 03 March, 2019.

14   *The Geographical Journal,* 173(3), 207-223. (O'Lear, S. (2007). Azerbaijan's Resource Wealth: Political Legitimacy and Public Opinion. DOI:10.1111/j.1475-4959.2007.00242

15   Azerbaijan Corruption Rank, 2018. https://tradingeconomics.com/azerbaijan/corruption-rank

16   Khuraman Gasimova. "Azerbaijan's Brain Drain in Music." Spring 1995. https://www.azer.com/aiweb/categories/magazine/31_folder/31_articles/31_braindrain.html

www.ingramcontent.com/pod-product-compliance
Lightning Source LLC
Chambersburg PA
CBHW021501090426
42739CB00007B/409